Terrorism and Counter Terrorism in South Asia and India

Terrorism and Counter Terrorism in South Asia and India

Brig V P Malhotra (Retd)

Vij Books India Pvt Ltd
Daryaganj, New Delhi (India)

Published   by

Vij Books India Pvt Ltd
(Publishers, Distributors & Importers)
2/19, Ansari Road, Darya Ganj
New Delhi - 110002
Phones: 91-11-43596460, 91-11- 65449971
Fax: 91-11-47340674
www.vijbooks.com
e-mail : vijbooks@rediffmail.com

ISBN: 978-93-80177-95-3

Dedicated

To

My Brother Rajesh and His Wife Pali

Contents

Maps

Preface

Terrorism is a kind of war, which is launched from hideouts by employing speed, surprise and indiscriminate violence. Assassinations, killing of innocent people including women and children, and invisibility, are at the heart of the strategy of the terrorists. Aim being to create fear, uncertainty and question the legitimacy and capacity of the established order. It is an organized system of intimidation and coercion by use of violence that does not obey the rules of war to achieve political or religious ends. One of its ingredients is that it is politically and emotionally charged. It is committed by highly trained and motivated people who have no value for human life, in some cases, including their own. It is a way of waging war by the weak and timid. A cause (real or assumed), political frustration, corruption and economic disparity, weak administration, foreign support, finance, drugs, arms availability and hungry media provide favourable conditions and environment for terrorism to take roots. Terrorist sees dividends out of proportion to the effort he puts in.

Indiscriminate violence or terrorism cannot claim roots in any religion, for religions teach and share core values of peace, tolerance and compassion. The terrorist, however, has succeeded in convincing the youth in the madrassa, mosque and the street that holy war has been sanctified in Islam and that the non believers are to be either brought on course or eliminated. The potential candidates are psychologically conditioned and graded for routine and high risk missions, including suicides.

Another school of thought is that the present scenario is continuation of the clash of civilizations with intricately interwoven roots in Palestine. As the situation stands, the militant Muslims, Christians and the Zionists are clashing with non state actors thrown in. Hindu India seems to be the latest addition to this list. The history cannot be undone, nor there can be a reconciliation in a foreseeable future. As the military measures are adopted and intensified, there is recoil in equal measure. Generally the terrorists exploit the rights and liberties provided in a democratic system to operate with comparative ease and then use the democratic laws to circumvent or evade the consequences. The prosecution, trial, award of punishment or acquittal draw their strength from hard evidence produced. The evidence either is not left or linked, or does not come forth due to fear of reprisals. In a democratic set up, the principle is that no one person, not proved guilty with evidence, be punished; let hundred guilty be let off for want of evidence or any other reasons.

International terrorism is facilitated by revolution in the communications, computer net working and portable sophisticated conventional and other weapons. Economic integration of the world further raises the stakes of the established order. The funding, training, safe haven, weapons and logistic support can be provided at a much wider canvas, encompassing varied systems of governance. Simultaneous bomb attacks on the US embassies in Kenya and Tanzania in 1998 followed by the 9/11 in 2001 marked the globalisation of terror in which a populist cause against the world order was communicated. State funding is the main source of its finance. The other sources to catapult terror are the net worked businesses, tax collections, extortions, hostage taking, smuggling, illicit drug trade, money laundering, gun running and availability of military hardware in the grey markets.

Traumatic in its impact, the crime of terrorism eludes exact composition, as such defies a definition and analysis. Generically, the act of terrorism is well understood globally, but does not stand the test of international law. It tends to overlap with the actions of freedom fighters, insurgents, separatists, guerrillas, insurrectionists, fundamentalists, rebels and law and order issues. The aim of the action and the act itself, become significant determinants. The aim could be ideological or political, but the act must not be indiscriminate, so as not to label it as an act of terror.

I am thankful to my wife Indu, who provided me the encouragement and environment to sift data and produce this book.

Jun 2011   V P Malhotra
Tel 011-26897022, 09818205817   D-11241
                                                      Vasant Kunj
                                                      NewDelhi 110070

South Asia: Political

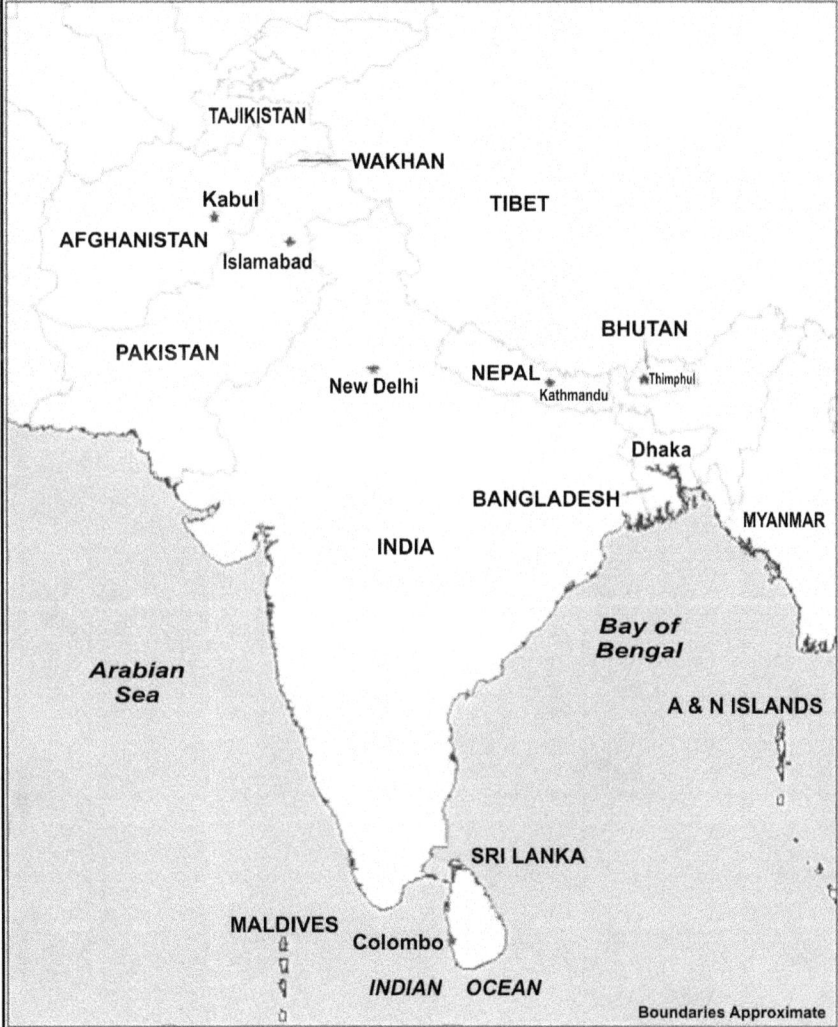

TAJIKISTAN

WAKHAN

Kabul

TIBET

AFGHANISTAN

Islamabad

BHUTAN

PAKISTAN

NEPAL

Thimphul

New Delhi

Kathmandu

Dhaka

BANGLADESH

MYANMAR

INDIA

Bay of Bengal

Arabian Sea

A & N ISLANDS

SRI LANKA

MALDIVES

Colombo

INDIAN OCEAN

Boundaries Approximate

Terrorism Not Defined

It is impossible to say any thing that is able to give a true idea of it to those who did not see it, other than this, that it was indeed very, very, very dreadful, and such as no tongue can express

Daniel Defoe, Journal of the Plague Year

The modern day acts of terrorism, as understood, include Bio-terrorism, Cyber-terrorism, Nuclear-terrorism, Narco-terrorism, Eco-terrorism, and other indiscriminate tools of destruction.

Bio-terrorism refers to the unauthorized release of toxic biological agents like Anthrax, Botulinum, Plague, Smallpox, Tularemia, Hemorrhagic fever etc, as an act of terror.

Cyber-terrorism refers to an attack on information technology in a way that would radically disrupt and degrade networked services.

Nuclear terrorism refers to attacking nuclear facilities, procuring nuclear weapons clandestinely or fabricating nuclear weapons or otherwise finding ways to disperse radioactive materials.

Narco-terrorism denotes violence used by drug traffickers to influence governments or prevent government efforts to stop the drug trade. It also includes terrorist groups using drug trafficking to fund terror operations.

Eco-terrorism refers to extremism to inflict economic damage on industries or people they see as harming animals or the natural environment. These include fur companies, logging companies and animal research laboratories.

It is well known that killing innocent people for political ends is terrorism, then why does an act of terrorism need to be defined precisely? Terrorism, more often, grows and operates globally (Terrorism anywhere is a threat to freedom everywhere - Don King). Absence of an agreed definition blocks the possibility of referring terrorist acts to another country's court. The players of the same act may well be tried simultaneously in different countries for the same or sympathetic acts or its abetment. The description of a terrorist act and consequent violation of law, as such, should precisely be the same internationally. Thus terrorism claims its exclusive niche.

The UN and nation states have been striving for decades to find an expression for terrorism, which narrows down to a specific profile of condemnable violence regardless of the cause which triggers it. The absence of an agreed definition leaves individual countries and international agencies to define terrorism as convenient, quite often subjectively. In 1992, UN Security Council Resolution 733 described the Somali situation as a threat to international peace and security; in 1996, UN resolution 1070 identified the failure of Sudan Government to extradite criminals who attempted to assassinate Egypt's President Mubarak, as threat to peace; Libya's failure to denounce terrorism was seen as threat to international peace and security. However the US invasion of Iraq and Afghanistan was not seen as a threat to international peace; on the other hand, Arab entry into Israel in the 1948 War was termed as a threat to international peace and security. There are numerous examples highlighting subjectivity that prevails in the world. Nations have their national interest supreme always and every time.

Fighting a war for independence has to meet certain set criteria. If freedom fighters meet standards of representativeness, rationality and responsibility then their resort to violence may be justified. Secessionists who turn to violence must answer some questions satisfactorily; will the use of violence be effective, does it have a chance of actually achieving its political objective, do the freedom fighters ensure that the violence is employed discriminately so as to avoid collateral damage, is the use of violence proportionate to achievement of aim? The famous cliché - one man's terrorist is another man's freedom fighter. The definition of terrorism is elusive because it is also difficult to state precisely the justifiable cause for struggle. A success will justify the cause; failure will label it as an act of terrorism.

History provides many examples of organisations and leaders who graduated from terrorism into respected governments and national leaders. This is so, particularly, in the case of national liberation movements employing multi prong engagements including violence, often as a last resort or out of frustration. Some of the movements that fall in the category are the Mau Mau in Kenya; IRA in Ireland; ANC in South Africa; Hezbollah in Lebanon, Hamas in Palestine, Palestinian Movement, Communist Party of Nepal (Maoist), separatist groups in Mindanao in the Philippines, the movements in Kurdish regions of Turkey and Iraq, and the movement in the Maoist Corridor across central and eastern India. There is a vide variety of views with regard to these movements, ranging from terror outfits to liberation movements. Some of these achieved outright success.

Indian leaders Bhagat Singh, Sukh Dev and Raj Guru were awarded death sentence by the British for lobbying bombs in the Legislative Assembly in 1930 and were hanged. They rose to become martyrs in independent India. Yasser Arafat was revered by many Arabs and the Palestinian people as a freedom fighter who symbolized their national aspirations. However, he was reviled by the Israelis and much of the West for orchestration of international terror activities. In 1994, Arafat received the Nobel Peace Prize, together with Yitzhak Rabin and Shimon Peres. Jomo Kenyatta of Kenya, Nelson Mandela of South Africa, Prachanda of Nepal rose to become heads of the states despite having been branded terrorists.

State sponsored terrorism refers to states practicing terrorism against its own people or in support of international terrorism. The rule of such states relies on projection of fear, threat and oppression. It could also be a country that uses surrogates as its weapon to attack other people. Without the state sponsors, international terrorists would find it difficult obtaining funds, weapons, materials, technology and secure areas they require to plan and conduct operations. Some of these states possess weapons of mass destruction as well. That is most worrisome.

As per State Department of the US notification 2007, Cuba, Iran, North Korea (removed in 2008), Sudan and Syria, have been described as the world's foremost state sponsors of terrorism. The United States has also been called terrorist, for its covert sponsorship of Nicaraguan Contras in the 1980s.

Pakistan has been accused by India, Bangladesh, Afghanistan, Iran and other nations (including US and UK) of its involvement in acts of terror in Kashmir and Afghanistan. Pakistan is a country which executes terrorism as a state policy. Here is what President Zardari has to say in this regard:

> *Militants and terrorists were willfully created by past Pakistani Governments and nurtured as part of a policy to achieve tactical objectives "Militants and extremists emerged on the national scene and challenged the state not because the civil bureaucracy was weakened and demoralised but because they were deliberately created and nurtured as a policy to achieve short-term tactical objectives. Let's be truthful and make a candid admission of the reality," he said at a gathering of civil servants in Islamabad on July 10, 2009.*

xxxxxxxxxxxxxx

> *India has long charged Pakistan with sponsoring terrorism in Kashmir by providing arms, ammunition and training to militants who have been engaged in a war of secession.*

Until Pakistan became an ally in the war on terrorism, the US Secretary of State included Pakistan on the 1993 list of countries which repeatedly provided support for acts of international terrorism.

State sponsored terrorism is a complex process which operates at many layers. Take the case of Pakistan, it provided nuclear know how to Iran, Libya and North Korea at the state level, Dr AQ Khan operated at another level and there was yet another level which was from terrorist to terrorist. All these levels were informally sanctified and linked. Like terrorism, 'state sponsored terrorism' also eludes exact description, as a large number of states can be labeled, states sponsoring terror in one form or the other. It is a very subjective label flowing from the national interests of the nations, particularly the powerful ones, who can impose sanctions or have international lobbies or can influence the UN.

League of Nations Convention Definition of Terrorism, 1937

Ethnic separatist violence in the 1930s prompted the League of Nations, formed after World War I, to define terrorism for the first time to encourage world stability and peace as:

> *All criminal acts directed against a State and intended or calculated to create a state of terror in the minds of particular persons or a group of persons or the general public.*

Definition of Terrorism under US Law

In 1975, the National Advisory Committee on Criminal Justice Standards and Goals of USA classified terrorism into six categories viz Civil disorder, Political terrorism, Non-political terrorism, Quasi-terrorism, Limited political terrorism and Official or state terrorism. Civil disorder is a form of collective violence interfering with the peace, security, and normal functioning of the community, Political terrorism aims at political goals through indiscriminate violence; Non-political terrorism implies indiscriminate violence for personal and collective gains but not for political purposes; Quasi-terrorism implies incidents of violence only as a means for a different purpose altogether, the aim being not to terrrorise the immediate victim; Limited political terrorism refers to acts of terrorism which are committed for ideological or political reasons but not for taking over the state, Official or state terrorism refers to nations whose rule is based upon fear and oppression similar to terrorism or such proportions. It may also be referred to as Structural terrorism defined broadly as terrorist acts carried out by governments in pursuit of political objectives, often as part of their foreign policy.

United States Law Code, the law that governs the country, contains a definition of terrorism which requires that Annual Country Reports on Terrorism be submitted by the Secretary of State to Congress every year.

Briefly:

> The term "international terrorism" means terrorism involving citizens or the territory of more than one country;

The term "terrorism" means premeditated, politically motivated violence perpetrated against noncombatant targets by sub-national groups or clandestine agents.

The US Department of Defense Dictionary of Military Terms defines terrorism as:

The calculated use of unlawful violence or threat of unlawful violence to inculcate fear; intended to coerce or to intimidate governments or societies in the pursuit of goals that are generally political, religious, or ideological.

FBI defines Terrorism as:

The unlawful use of force or violence against persons or property to intimidate or coerce a Government, the civilian population, or any segment thereof, in furtherance of political or social objectives.

*The USA PATRIOT Act defines terrorism activities as activities that (A) involve acts dangerous to human life that are a violation of the criminal laws of the US or of any state, (B) appear to be intended (i) to intimidate or coerce a civilian population, (ii) to influence the policy of a government by intimidation or coercion, or (iii) to affect the conduct of a government by mass destruction, assassination, or kidnapping, and (C) occur primarily within the territorial jurisdiction of the US.

The US National Counter Terrorism Centre (NCTC) described a terrorist act as one which was: "premeditated; perpetrated by a sub-national or clandestine agent; politically motivated, potentially including religious, philosophical, or culturally symbolic motivations; violent; and perpetrated against a noncombatant target.

The current US national security strategy defines terrorism as premeditated, politically motivated violence against innocents.

---

*Uniting and Strengthening America by: Providing Appropriate Tools Required to Intercept and Obstruct Terrorism, Act of 2001 (Public Law Pub.L.107-56).

United Kingdom

The United Kingdom's Terrorism Act 2000, in brief, interprets (defines) terrorism as actions involving serious violence against a person, damage to property, a serious risk to the health or safety of the public or is designed seriously to disrupt an electronic system.

The use or threat is designed to influence the government (including international governmental organisations) or to intimidate the public or a section of the public, and the use or threat of action is made for the purpose of advancing a political, religious or ideological cause.

Arabian Countries

The Arab Convention for the Suppression of Terrorism was adopted by the Council of Arab Ministers of the Interior and the Council of Arab Ministers of Justice in Cairo, in 1998. Terrorism was defined as:

> *Any act or threat of violence, whatever its motives or purposes, that occurs in the advancement of an individual or collective criminal agenda and seeking to sow panic among people, causing fear by harming them, or placing their lives, liberty or security in danger, or seeking to cause damage to the environment or to public or private installations or property or occupying or seizing them, or seeking to jeopardize a national resource.*

ASEAN

In Article II of the 'ASEAN Convention on Counter Terrorism, 2007', criminal acts of terrorism mean any of the offences within the scope of and as defined in any of the 'UN International Conventions on Counter-Terrorism' (in the box on the next page). The definition covers Brunei Darussalam, Cambodia, Indonesia, Laos, Malaysia, Myanmar, Philippines, Singapore, Thailand and Vietnam.

India

In India the first law which attempted a definition was the TADA 1987:

> *"Whoever with intent to overawe the Government as by law established or to strike terror in the people or any section of the people or to alienate*

any section of the people or to adversely affect the harmony amongst different sections of the people does any act or thing by using bombs, dynamite or other explosive substances or inflammable substances or lethal weapons or poisons or noxious gases or other chemicals or by any other substances (whether biological or otherwise) of a hazardous nature in such a manner as to cause, or as is likely to cause, death of, or injuries to, any person or persons or loss of, or damage to, or destruction of property or disruption of any supplies or services essential to the life of the community, or detains any person and threatens to kill or injure such person in order to compel the Government or any other person to do or abstain from doing any act, commits a terrorist act. "

In addition to the legislation mentioned above, the Supreme Court of India has defined terrorism in the case 'Madan Singh vs State of Bihar', 2004:

"In order to cut through the Gordian definitional knot, terrorism expert A. Schmid suggested in 1992 in a report for the then UN Crime Branch that it might be a good idea to take the existing consensus on what constitutes a "war crime" as a point of departure. If the core of war crimes - deliberate attacks on civilians, hostage-taking and the killing of prisoners - is extended to peacetime, we could simply define acts of terrorism veritably as "peacetime equivalents of war crimes".

Pakistan

The Anti-Terrorism Act (ATA) of 1997 defined terrorism as:

Whoever, to strike terror in the people, or any section of people, or to alienate any section of the people or to adversely affect harmony among different sections of the people, does any act or thing by using bombs, dynamite or other explosive or inflammable substance, or firearms, or other lethal weapons or poisons or noxious gases or chemical or other substances of a hazardous nature in such a manner as to cause the death of, or injury to, any person or persons, or damage to, or destruction of, property or disruption of any supplies or services essential to the life of the community or display firearms, or threaten with the use of force public servants in order to prevent them from discharging their lawful duties commits a terrorist act.

Darul Uloom Deoband

The All India Anti-Terrorism Conference (attended by 20,000 people) convened by Darul Uloom at Deoband on 25 February 2008 agreed on the definition:

Any action that targets innocents, whether by an individual or by any government and its agencies or by a private organisation anywhere in the world constitutes, according to Islam, an act of terrorism.

UN

Over the last 20-30 years the UN has approved 13 Conventions and three amendments which attempt to eliminate terrorist activity, culminating in a broad Global Counter Terrorism Strategy approved in 2006. The

International Conventions on Counter-Terrorism

1. 1963 Convention on Offences and Certain Other Acts Committed On Board Aircraft
2. 1970 Convention for the Suppression of Unlawful Seizure of Aircraft
3. 1971 Convention for the Suppression of Unlawful Acts against the Safety of Civil Aviation
4. 1973 Convention on the Prevention and Punishment of Crimes Against Internationally Protected Persons
5. 1979 International Convention against the Taking of Hostages
6. 1980 Convention on the Physical Protection of Nuclear Material
7. 1988 Protocol for the Suppression of Unlawful Acts of Violence at Airports Serving International Civil Aviation, supplementary to the Convention for the Suppression of Unlawful Acts against the Safety of Civil Aviation (Extends and supplements the Montreal Convention on Air Safety)
8. 1988 Convention for the Suppression of Unlawful Acts against the Safety of Maritime Navigation
9. 1988 Protocol for the Suppression of Unlawful Acts Against the Safety of Fixed Platforms Located on the Continental Shelf
10. 1991 Convention on the Marking of Plastic Explosives for the Purpose of Detection
11. 1997 International Convention for the Suppression of Terrorist Bombings
12. 1999 International Convention for the Suppression of the Financing of Terrorism
13. 2005 International Convention for the Suppression of Acts of Nuclear Terrorism

Global Counter Terrorism Strategy, as adopted, has a Resolution which covers generalities and a Plan of Action. The annexed Plan of Action enumerates measures to prevent terrorism and to build States' capacity to do so. It includes references to chemical terrorism and to the mission of the Organisation for the Prohibition of Chemical Weapons (OPCW).

The UN has resolved to "strongly condemn terrorism in all its forms and manifestations, committed by whomsoever, wherever and for whatever purposes. The Resolution is generic in nature and is far from making any impact on the ground situation in the present form. There seems no punch and hardly any compulsion imposed on the states to act on the advice of the UN. It is more an advisory than an implementation plan to reduce the menace of terrorism across the countries. It is also a reminder of the provisions like human rights, Millennium Development Goals, youth development, eradication of poverty, encourage UN system of cooperation, to consider damage control in the event of a terrorist act, United Nations counter-terrorism cooperation and so on. Nonetheless, it is a step in the right direction which has been taken collectively.

The UN is yet to find a wording which distinctly explains this resolve. Since 2002, the United Nations General Assembly has been negotiating a Comprehensive Convention on International Terrorism. The proposed definition reads as follows:

"Any person commits an offence within the meaning of this Convention if that person, by any means, unlawfully and intentionally, causes:

(a) Death or serious bodily injury to any person; or

(b) Serious damage to public or private property, including a place of public use, a State or government facility, a public transportation system, an infrastructure facility or the environment; or

(c) Damage to property, places, facilities, or systems referred to in paragraph (b) of this article, resulting or likely to result in major economic loss, when the purpose of the conduct, by its nature or context, is to intimidate a population, or to compel a government or an international organisation to do or abstain from doing any act".

The definition is not controversial in itself; the deadlock arises from the opposing views on whether such a definition would be applicable to the armed forces of a state and to self-determination movements. Also the basic issue continues to be what distinguishes a terrorist organisation from a liberation movement?

All the mentioned definitions and the ones not included have most common ingredients viz premeditated indiscriminate violence including threats of violence; the communication of fear to an audience beyond the immediate victim; serious damage to property, including a place of public use, a State or government facility, an infrastructure facility or the environment; and political, economic, or religious aims by the perpetrator (s).

The acts of terror can be dealt with, through the national laws as all its ingredients are covered, even though the punishment prescribed is not as severe as the act deserves. The holistic dealing with the act of terror is generally not covered in the national laws. Nonetheless, the national laws can be amended to deal with the acts of terror and will meet the requirement of the interim period as a large number of terror incidents occur locally due to local reasons.

While it is most desirable to agree on a definition in order to deal with this global menace in a coordinated manner, it appears not possible to cobble together a large number of issues involved in defining terrorism, some contradictory while others are overlapping. A nation must be firm on its security rather than please all the political parties of the state or to address the vote bank in democracies. To uphold the democracy, the means must be correct and firm. The terrorists exploit the porosity of the democratic systems and when cornered they exploit the open and sluggish laws of the state. The issue must be addressed boldly as no one comes forward to condemn the human rights violation by the terrorists. The UN has to continue its efforts and seems to be the only organization which could put in place an acceptable description to deal with the terror menace appropriately. The world at large, however, understands the issue well, and given the political will, is dealing with the issue. The international aspects can be dealt with through the established diplomatic channels. As it stands, internationally the terrorism can not be defined precisely but we can fight it.

Types of Terrorism

Extremism is a term used to describe the actions or ideologies of individuals or groups outside the perceived political centre of a society; or otherwise may violate common moral standards. In democratic societies, individuals or groups that advocate the replacement of democracy with an authoritarian regime are usually branded extremists.

Islamic terrorism is committed by Muslims, and aims at achieving varying political ends like ending American military presence in the Middle East and the Arabian Peninsula, over throwing infidel regimes, and stopping American support for Israel. Islamic terrorism also aims at propagating Islamic culture, society and values in contrast to the western values and culture. It also aims at creating an Islamic Caliphate.

Suicide attack is an attack intended to kill others and inflict widespread damage as part of terror, in which the attacker expects or intends to die in the process.

Narcotic traffickers attempt to influence the policies of a government or a society through violence and intimidation to hinder the enforcement of law and justice so as to continue the drug and narcotic activity. The term Narco-terrorism is used for terrorist organizations that engage in drug trafficking activity to fund their operations.

Nuclear terrorism implies the use or threat of the use of nuclear or radiological weapons in acts of terrorism, including attacks against nuclear facilities

Chemical terrorism implies use of poisonous gases, liquids or solids that have toxic effects on people, animals or plants. Chemical agents that might be used for terror purposes are:

- Blistering chemicals

- Blood chemicals

- Choking/lung/pulmonary damaging chemicals

- Incapacitating chemicals

- Riot control/tear chemicals

- Vomiting chemicals

- Industrial chemicals

Biological weapons spread disease causing agents, such as anthrax, plague, ebolla, salmonella, botulinum, typhoid, bacterial meningitis, dyptheria, dysentery, small pox and so on. Biological weapons have a limited shelf life and not easy to execute. The attacks in USA and Japan in 1984 and 1985 were only partially successful.

Nuclear, chemical and biological terrorism is difficult to execute because of their operational complexity and strict security. The threat, however, is within the realm of realties, particularly if it is state sponsored.

Hijacking includes aircraft hijacking, maritime hijacking or piracy, carjacking, truck-jacking and so on. In most cases, the pilot, captain or driver is commanded to the orders of the hijackers. Often hijacking targets the aviation industry where a large and important group of people are available to be traded for their demands which are made through the international media using the aviation communication network. The threat of hijacking has made the security of the aviation infrastructure rather costly and operations rather cumbersome.

Hostage taking means a person or an entity which is seized by a criminal act in order to compel another party such as a relative, employer, law enforcement agency to act, or refrain from acting in a particular manner, under threat of serious physical harm to the hostage (s). They snatch their targets in violent raids and then announce who they are and what they want.

*Cyber terrorism is the premeditated use of disruptive activities, or the threat thereof, against computers and/or networks, with the intention to cause harm or further social, ideological, religious, political or similar objectives. It aims to disrupt strategic networks like the ATC operations, power generation units and macro security networks. It differs from the cyber crimes like theft of identities, cyber intrusions, bogus business deals, viruses and so on.

Financial Terrorism may be defined as the employment of money to fan violence in a target territory or to address a group of people, religious or political, to achieve political, religious or other macro aims. It is like funding a state or a group of people to manipulate their behavior or actions or inactions. It is a wide term and could be used in other ways as well.

Eco terrorism refers to acts of violence or sabotage in support of ecological, environmental, or animal rights causes against persons or their property. The Earth Liberation Front in USA has been classified as the top domestic terror threat by the FBI since 2001, and is categorized as eco-terrorists.

The above descriptions are not exact and are overlapping. These descriptions can be fine tuned to definitions by legal experts so as to deal with them in the international courts. An attempt has been made above to describe the forms terrorism can adopt so as to take effective counter measures and prevent loss of life and property.

---

*Kevin G. Coleman

Global Terrorism

Jihad refers to striving for excellence at several levels. The first involves individual efforts, spiritual and intellectual, to become a better Muslim. The second addresses efforts to improve society. The third, 'holy war' involves self defense or fighting against oppression. The last level is the combat waged in defense of Allah, Islam and Muslims. Muslims, simultaneously, are commanded by Allah to lead peaceful lives and not transgress against anyone, but also to defend against oppression.

According to *Islamic Research Academy* (IRA) of *al Azhar*, the Islamic University in Cairo, jihad is referred to as 'defense of the nation against occupation and the plunder of its resources'. It, however, does not permit or condone the killing of innocent people, the elderly, women, and children, which is forbidden by Islam. The teachings of Islam also forbid the destruction of infrastructure not connected with a specific combat. Jihad has been profoundly misunderstood by a segment of Muslim population in today's world.

The situation as it is today, seems to have its beginning in the Cold War era when all kinds of methods were used to deal with the other super power. In recent times, it was triggered by Soviet invasion of Afghanistan and its reaction from USA, and Pakistan through proxy. The present scenario may also be described as a conflict between Capitalism and the Global Jihad. The capitalist world wants unfettered access to the world resources and the jihadis oppose these accesses in their own way, the low cost war with high dividends. The Jihad also aims at Caliphate along a swathe of territory.

An act of terror is deliberate, often has an international operational, logistical and leadership trail. Terror, as such, may be categorised trans-national or global and *per force* should be dealt with accordingly. Simultaneous bomb attacks on the US embassies in Kenya and Tanzania in 1998 followed by the

9/11 in 2001 were the fore-runners of the globalisation of terror. All attacks were traced to *al Qaeda*.

Global terrorism is facilitated by revolution in communications, computer net working, mobile phones and portable sophisticated conventional and other weapons. The methodology has become aggressive, like the suicide attacks, cycle, vehicle and aircraft bombs. The lethality has increased manifold. Economic integration of the world further raises the stakes of the established order. The funding, training, safe haven, weapons and logistic support can be provided at a much wider canvas. There are governments that sponsor terrorism by allowing terrorist groups to live with in their boundaries or by funding them to buy destruction tools to cause havoc any where. They also cover their movements. In October 2010, Pakistan's ex President Pervez Musharraf, in an interview to the magazine *Der Spiegal, stated* that Pakistan trained terrorists to operate in Kashmir to force India to discuss the issue.

The other sources to catapult terror are the net worked businesses, tax collections, extortions, hostage taking, smuggling, illicit drug trade, money laundering, gun running and availability of military hardware in the grey markets. Thus, the terrorists can strike any time and any where in the world. These are 'supported non state actors' with no fixed location or territorial boundaries. They do not stick around to see what happens when they blow up buildings or set traps for innocent people to die. They have no concern for collateral consequences of any magnitude. Hate is their driving force.

Nearly every country of the world is affected by the terror menace. Consideration of terror and its prevention or pre-emption is one new major factor while planning events of whatever hue. There is a massive additional expenditure and planning pre-requisite. Due to the uncertainty of terror, the general comfort level in society has come down. Terrorism draws its global character primarily from networking, which is facilitated by the internet and mobile phones. Internet is a powerful communication tool which is non-hierarchical and has inbuilt redundancy. Most physical and electronic measures against it will not be effective. Because of the all pervasive use of the internet across the world providing connectivity and knowledge, no blanket counter measures will be accepted by the states, scientific world, academic world and the financial institutions. Any effective general counter measures will lead to chaos and recoil. In fact any effective counter measures will be victory of the terrorists. In the transaction, the general public will suffer more than the terrorists. It does not imply that the situation should be accepted as such. In fact the terrorist is using the tool created by the educated and the sane world as a result of research over decades. The sane world holds the key to the inside knowledge, codes, communication frequencies and sensors. The terrorist is only a user or exploiter of one of the most powerful tools created by the developed world.

State funding is the main source of its finance to begin with. The concerned states provide terrorists the space to live in, train, plan, rest and refit. These states also fund the terrorists directly and indirectly. The indirect method is to allow the growing of poppy and coca, their processing in to drugs, movement of these drugs to the target areas and countries, and allow money laundering. These states also facilitate the employment of this money to procure the tools and facilities of destruction. Such states usually are sponsored by more powerful and affluent states to destabilize and settle scores with the rival countries. Once the game starts, it becomes difficult to extricate.

Narco-terrorism

Nearly every part of the globe is producing illicit drugs. Only the volume, variety and quality differ. Some are growing the crop, while others are providing support to convert the natural produce in to marketable commodity or are providing transit facilities or the markets.

Narco-terrorism refers to the nexus between narcotics and terrorism. Afghanistan and the NWFP of Pakistan are the biggest producers of opium in the world, which generates huge sums of money in the international market. The drug proceeds are used by the Pakistan Government and the non-government agencies to fan terrorism. Sponsoring terrorism is an expensive affair and money for killing, kidnapping and sabotage comes from laundering of money generated from drugs, besides many other sources.

The economy of narcotics producing countries is dependent on the illegal drug trade. Unless they have an alternate economy the illicit narcotic drug trade would continue irrespective of legislations. The answer is education and employment opportunities. Afghanistan is the biggest illicit opium producing country in the world. Poppy cultivation in Afghanistan is done in an organised manner under the shadow of drug mafia. Narcotic drugs are the most lucrative commodity that generate enormous money for illegal activities without leaving a trace to pursue legal action. Drug money also gives the criminal dons and smugglers an opportunity to collaborate with the political power in due course of time. The Pakistani drug syndicate operates in connivance with political and military establishment. In Pakistan, evidence exists in which a President, a Governor, a minister, a prominent political party, a bank and a large number of prominent citizens were found connected with drug trade and mafia.

The alliance of narcotic drugs, army and ISI goes back to 1978 when the US turned a blind eye to the drug trade which funded the jihadis operating against the Soviet forces, thus giving rise to narco-terrorism in this region. Landi Kotal in FATA and Peshawar in NWFP (Pakistan) are the main centres for business transactions of opium, heroin and weapons. This area is rather autonomous with its tribal laws; and drugs and guns being part and parcel of its socio-economic and political fabric. ISI and the army are the instruments that run the writ of the Federal Government in the region. Opium refining techniques have become more sophisticated with the army and ISI, and reportedly the Chinese chemists in this region.

The unorganised but systematic method of monetary transaction is popularly known as money laundering. It is the movement of money derived from illegal activity by concealing the identity of the originator and converting it to assets that appear to have come from a legitimate source. The large sum generated from narcotic drugs has become part of the international monetary system. This money can buy politicians, fund elections, contribute to toppling an elected government, take over business enterprises and destabilise an established politico-economic system. Such cash is also laundered into licit money through investments in foreign banks, real estate, hotels, entertainment business, 'gambling joints tax havens', hawala and so on. Switzerland, Hong Kong, India, Pakistan, Afghanistan and Thailand are among the important countries involved in money laundering. There are several other ways to launder drug proceeds through professional smugglers and gangsters. Many of these criminals deal only in narcotic drugs and run a parallel government to manage their global network. South Asia, especially Pakistan, Afghanistan and India offer vast opportunity for money laundering to drug smugglers, gun runners, criminals, builders, film producers and others. Finance of terror networking and execution of the terror acts is sourced from the drugs and laundering.

The Golden Crescent is the area of illicit opium production located at the crossroads of Central, South, and West Asia, which includes territory of three nations viz Afghanistan, Pakistan and Iran. While Afghanistan and

Some Common Illicit Drugs

Cannabis is the common hemp plant, which provides hallucinogens with some sedative properties, and includes hashish (hash), and hashish oil.

Cocaine is a stimulant derived from the leaves of the coca bush.

Depressants are drugs that reduce tension and anxiety

Hallucinogens are drugs that affect sensation, thinking, self-awareness, and emotion.

Hashish is the resinous exudate of the cannabis or hemp plant.

Heroin is a semi-synthetic derivative of morphine.

Mandrax is a trade name for methaqualone, a pharmaceutical depressant.

Marijuana is the dried leaf of the cannabis or hemp plant.

Methaqualone is a pharmaceutical depressant, referred to as mandrax in Southwest Asia and Africa.

Narcotics are drugs that relieve pain, often induce sleep, and refer to opium, opium derivatives, and synthetic substitutes. Natural narcotics include opium, codeine, Empirin.

Opium is the brown, gummy exudate of the incised, unripe seedpod of the opium poppy.

Opium poppy is the source for the natural and semi synthetic narcotics.

Poppy straw is the entire cut and dried opium poppy-plant material, other than the seeds. Opium is extracted from poppy straw in commercial operations that produce the drug for medical use.

Qat is a stimulant from the buds or leaves of *Catha edulis* that is chewed or drunk as tea.

Quaaludes is the North American slang term for methaqualone, a pharmaceutical depressant.

Stimulants are drugs that relieve mild depression, increase energy and activity.

---

*Contents extracted from article by Kshitij Prabha, Associated Fellow, IDSA, India

Pakistan produce opium, Iran is a consumer and provides trans-shipment route for smuggling. Pakistan has significantly curtailed poppy production. Its large addicted population, however, relies on Afghanistan's opiates. Afghanistan produced 6,900 tons of opium in 2009 and is the world's primary opium producer, supplying 92 per cent of the world's opiates. In 2008, wholesale prices of heroin (produced from opium) ranged from US$ 2,400 per kg in Afghanistan to US$ 10,300-11,800 per kg in Turkey and to US$ 44,300 per kg in Europe. In the Americas, prices range from US$ 10,000 per kg in Colombia to US$ 45,000-70,000 per kg (for heroin of South American origin) in the United States and US$ 119,000 per kg in Canada. Afghanistan alone produces around US$ 64 billion worth of opiates. A quarter of this is earned by opium farmers and the rest goes to government officials, warlords, insurgents and drug traffickers.

The Golden Triangle is Asia's other main illicit opium producing area. It is an area that overlaps the mountains of Myanmar, Laos, Vietnam and Thailand.

Drug Money

*An acre of poppy flowers produces approximately 7 kg of raw opium, which the farmers sell for around Rs 12,000 to 15,000.

The second phase is processing of opium. The raw opium is refined into heroin in a local factory. The heroin at this stage is sold for Rs 50,000 to 70,000 per kg.

In the third phase, heroin is smuggled out of the country by couriers. In the dealer network its value goes to approximately Rs 1350,000 per kg.

Finally, heroin is cut and packed into small bags for sale on the streets in the US. This now fetches Rs 4700,000 per kg. The price could vary with the purity and area in which the heroin is being marketed.

*Iqramul Haq, an eminent Pakistani scholar

Myanmar is the second highest producer of opium in the world after Afghanistan, and Laos third after Afghanistan and Myanmar.

Latin America is another area where drug production is a significant occupation. Major drug crops are coca bush, used to produce cocaine, poppy, and cannabis. Coca bush is grown in Colombia, Peru, and Bolivia; whereas poppy is cultivated in Mexico and Colombia. Colombia remains the leading producer of coca with approximately 90 per cent of the cocaine processing industry in the world. Cannabis is cultivated virtually in all countries in the region, mainly for local consumption. Notable cannabis exporters include Mexico and Jamaica. Drug processing and refining takes place in the cultivation areas as well as along the transit routes.

*According to an estimate from the US State Department Office for International Narcotics Matters, the production of 1 kilo of cocaine costs about $3,000. The wholesale price of that kilo is about $20,000. Cocaine production takes place as long as the leaves grow, and in Colombia, Peru, and especially Bolivia, they grow fast.

The 2009 United Nations World Drug report indicates that the illicit drug market worldwide has now become a $320 billion per year industry.

Zakat

According to the Koran, possessions are sanctified by setting aside a proportion (Zakat) for those in need. This principle is an obligation for every Muslim. Over the time, this religious obligation has been abused by terrorists and their supporters. The *al Qaeda* network extensively utilizes these funds by diversion from the Zakat and other charities and donations through Islamic banks. Osama bin Laden made regular calls to Muslims to donate liberally through the Zakat system to his organization. In September 2001, in an interview with Pakistani newspaper Ummat, he declared that:

> *Al Qaeda was set up to wage a jihad against infidelity, particularly to counter the onslaught of the infidel countries against the Islamic states. Jihad is the sixth undeclared pillar of Islam. [The first five being the basic holy words of Islam - there is no god but God and Muhammad is the messenger of God; prayer; fasting (in Ramadan);pilgrimage to Mecca; and giving alms (Zakat)].*

Saudi Arabia is the richest in the region and it has been the backbone of the logistics and operations of *al Qaeda*. For years, individuals and charities in Saudi Arabia have contributed to jihad; *to which* Saudi authorities have turned

---

*Rachel Ehrenfeld, Funding Terrorism: Sources and Methods

a blind eye. Other contributors are the Arab world, the Persian Gulf states, Egypt, South Asia, Europe, the Americas (including the United States), Africa and Asia. *Al Qaeda* is also expanding its fund raising activities in Southeast Asia, which would be a cause of significant concern. *Al Qaeda* is also focusing on Laskhar Jihad and Jemaah Islamiyah in Southeast Asia with independent financial support networks.

*Zakat is levied pursuant to a Royal Decree on Saudi nationals, both corporate (wholly Saudi-owned companies) and individuals, and on the Saudi share of profits of companies jointly owned with foreigners. It is levied at 2.5 per cent of all zakatable wealth. The Zakat funds are controlled by the Department of Zakat and Income Taxes of the Saudi Ministry of Finance and National Economy. These funds are estimated annually around US$10 billion in Saudi Arabia alone.

Most of Gulf countries do not have effective rules of transparency ie accounting and auditing, thus facilitating a part of religious philanthropy into money laundering. In November 2002, Adel Al Jubeir, spokesman for the Saudi Kingdom acknowledged that "People have taken advantage of our charity, generosity, our naivety, if you wish to call it that way and of our innocence", and calling for a global audit of every charity in the Kingdom.

The International Zakat Organisation (IZO), an important new charitable body of the Organisation of the Islamic Conference (OIC), in 2009, announced its selection of the **BMB Group to lead a new global charitable initiative which promises to be the largest in the Islamic world. The proposed Global Zakat & Charity Fund would be over US$ 3 billion to address the cause of the poor and needy in the Muslim world.

It is assessed that within a 10-year period, the financial support to *al*

---

*Jean-Charles Brisard, JCB Consulting, TERRORISM FINANCING, Roots and trends of Saudi terrorism financing, Report prepared for the President of the Security Council United Nations December 19, 2002, New-York

** The BMB Group is one of the most exclusive investment and advisory firms in the world with clients that extend to prominent individuals, ruling families and sovereign investors from the Middle East and Asia.

Qaeda or its associates, received through direct donations, Zakat funds or through various schemes range between $300 and $500 million for an annual income of around $50 million. According to estimates, less than 10 per cent of this amount goes for operational planning, while 90 per cent goes to infrastructure, mainly facilities and organization.

Money Laundering

Money laundering is the generation of an asset or a value as a result of an illegal act, involving actions such as tax evasion or false accounting. It facilitates turning dirty money to clean. At some point in the process there is a switch between the two. The art is to keep that switch hidden and the process diffused. It is committed by private individuals, drug dealers, businesses, corrupt officials, members of criminal mafia, fundamentalists and even states. Money laundering always hides a crime behind it. Movement of the asset created is a subsequent act which is also illegal.

US$1.3 trillion worth worldwide is laundered every year, providing a huge resource for criminal activity. Gangs have become sophisticated at hiding their ill gotten gains. Billions of transactions the world over, make conventional surveillance a rather difficult task. The bouncing of money, however, can be detected, but is an expensive process.

The Cause

Above we have discussed the global terror network and its prosecution. Why sudden spurt in the global terror? Is it that the cause was always there and the global realization has come because the world has shrunk in to a global village and the terror is the effect of a cause which occurred in the Middle East centuries ago? The origin of Judaism, Christianity and Islam in Middle East are inexplicably tied to one another. Judaism is the base around which Christianity and Muslim faiths have been structured. Despite common origin, there have been fundamental differences which have led to conflicts.

The Jews were driven out of their homes by the Romans. They scattered all over the globe and converged in Israel in the heart of the Arab world in the twentieth century. The conflict was a foregone conclusion. Then there was all round progress in the west, amongst the Christians leaving the Muslims in

Middle East way back in time. Is it a war between the enlightened and those who are still clinging to the age old beliefs and tradition, despite the oil wealth? Is it jealousy of the under/undeveloped world with the developed world. These events have also been called part of a modern "clash of civilizations" between the radical Arab-Islam and the western world. The causes seem to be so deep rooted among the masses that a clean solution seems most unlikely.

Another cause would be the western overbearing attitude towards the third word countries, Middle East in particular. Americans bombed Japan resulting in 150,000 killed. The on going Arab-Israel conflict, Iran-Iraq war, Iraq-Kuwait war, the Afghan situation and many more have led to gravitation of western forces in the region. Millions have perished. Economic exploitation is another reason for the west to be in this region.

It is the west that is researching and mass producing tools of destruction and creating markets and needs in the third world countries. The reasons may be foundational or recent man made, the world has a situation. There could be many more causes, big, small and local for the terror to go on. Terror has become a new tool of irregular warfare and is recoiling. A direct action or sanctions, most likely, will not work as the dissidents have very little to lose. Reconciliation or compromise may work, but what about the ego of the west and their economic greed.

Hijacking at Sea and Air

Hijacking includes maritime hijacking, aircraft hijacking, or piracy, carjacking, truck-jacking and so on.

Maritime Terrorism*

With the pressure on land the terrorists may be shifting their actions to the sea. The maritime targets are easy to exploit since the land targets are often under tight security. These could include suicide attacks, ship hijacking for further utilisation in the terror acts on land or on sea as bombs to attack another ship or an infrastructure. Indian Ocean with Red Sea, Gulf, Arabian Sea and Bay of Bengal containing well defined choke points as Straits of Hormuz, Cape of Good Hope, Bab-el- Mandeb, Sunda, Lambak and Straits of Malacca are some of the choke points. To quote an example, roughly 40 per cent of the sea trade passes through the Straits of Malacca. The Persian Gulf and adjoining areas accounts for 50 per cent of the world containers and 30 per cent of the bulk cargo. Should these be choked by the terrorists, there will be devastating effect on the countries on both sides during the time of interdiction. There have been instances but not many as yet. The terror outfits with maritime terror capabilities are Abu Nidal Oerganisation, Palestine Liberation Front, Aum Shinrikyo, LTTE (since defeated), HUM, South Molluccan Terrorists, IRA, Continuing IRA, GIA, PIRA and Sikh Terrorists. Maritime capabilities also facilitate operations on land. Most of these outfits have been described in the relevant Chapter. These may grow with the passage of time. The world has to watch out and create effective countering mechanisms to secure the seas.

---

* Alok Bansal, Maritime Threat Perceptions: Non-State Actors in the Indian Ocean Region, National Maritime Foundation India

* Mihir Roy, Maritime Security and Regional Cooperation in the Indian Ocean, Journal of Indian Ocean Studies, Vol 18 No. 1 April 2010

International Laws

International Maritime Organization (IMO) was established by UN in 1958 and became effective in 1974. IMO is responsible for drafting conventions concerning maritime safety.

Against piracy, merchant vessels transiting through Gulf of Aden, Southern Red Sea and Bab-el-Mandeb straits are advised self protection.

Aircraft Hijacking

Aircraft hijacking, also known as skyjacking and sky controlling, is the unlawful seizure of an aircraft by an individual or a group. Hijacking in the air involves the lives of high profile passengers in a compressed space. In most cases, the pilot is forced to fly according to the orders of the hijackers. Occasionally, the hijackers have flown the aircraft themselves. It all started in 1931. Since then 300-320 hijack incidents have been reported. 138 of the incidents originated from Middle East. 124 had their destination Cuba. Around 80 of all incidents resulted in violence and employment of force.

In recent years the airport security has been tightened to obviate any hijacks. Some air lines have also employed sky marshals, who are always there in the aircraft during the flight.

Most aircraft hijackers intend to use the passengers as hostages, either for ransom or for some political or administrative concession by authorities. Motives vary from demanding the release of certain inmates to highlight the grievances of a particular community. Hijackers also have used aircraft as a missile as in 9/11.

There is a need to communicate with the ATC at the earliest before the terrorists deploy themselves. Squawk 7500 or Squawk 7600 are systems available to the pilots to inform the ATC about the hijack. Each situation will suggest the response from the passengers and the crew members, even though they are not trained to handle such situations. The response could be passive altogether or sudden action. More reliance should be placed on trained negotiators who operate from outside the aircraft with sophisticated gadgetry including communication with the hijackers, which makes the interior of the aircraft transparent.

Hijackings for hostages commonly produce an armed standoff during a period of negotiation between hijackers and authorities, followed by some form of settlement. Settlements do not always meet the hijackers' original demands. If the hijackers' demands are deemed too great and the perpetrators show no inclination to surrender, authorities sometimes employ Special Forces for rescue. There are sophisticated tools to storm the aircraft on the runway even if the doors are closed from inside. But the timing and surprise is of paramount importance. Major decisions are left to the negotiator and the authorities on ground.

International Laws

Tokyo Convention is a multilateral convention, which came into force in 1963, and is applicable to offences against penal law and to any acts jeopardising the safety of persons or property on board civilian aircraft while in-flight and engaged in international air navigation.

The convention, for the first time in the history of international aviation law, recognises certain powers and immunities of the aircraft commander who on international flights may restrain any person(s) he has reasonable cause to believe is committing or is about to commit an offence liable to interfere with the safety of persons or property on board or who is jeopardising good order and discipline.

Hague Convention signed in 1970, is the Convention for the Suppression of Unlawful Seizure of Aircraft contains 14 articles relating to what constitutes hijacking as well as guidelines for what is expected of governments when dealing with hijackings. The convention does not apply to customs, law enforcement or military aircraft, thus its scope appears to exclusively encompass civilian aircraft. The convention is applicable only if the aircraft takes off or lands in a place different than the country of its registration.

Cyber Terrorism

The definition of Cyber Terrorism is debatable. There is the aspect of intention, targets, methods and centrality of computer use in the act. An act of generic terrorism is indiscriminate violence, destruction of property, infrastructure and generation of fear. In the act of Cyber Terrorism, the result is disruption or chaos due to disruption in cyber space, space application, air line traffic, railway traffic, stock exchanges, telephone exchanges, hospitals etc and is not leading to any direct or indiscriminate violence or destruction of property or infrastructure or fear, it is yet an act of terrorism or Cyber Terrorism because the disruption has far reaching unacceptable consequences. As the Internet continues to expand, and computer systems continue to be assigned more vital usage, sabotage or terrorism via cyberspace may become a very serious threat. But acts of such magnitude are rare, difficult to execute and difficult to define. The disruption in cyber space, more often, is more akin to Cyber Crime than Cyber Terrorism.

Cyber terrorism, as such, is defined as the premeditated use of extreme disruptive activities, or the threat thereof, in cyber space, with the intention to further social, ideological, religious, political or similar objectives, or to intimidate any person or a group in furtherance of such objectives. The definition cannot be made exhaustive as crime needs to be inclusive.

Cyber terrorist has many advantages over such other methods:

- It is cheaper than traditional methods.

- The action is very difficult to track.

- There are no physical barriers to cross.

- It can be executed remotely.

- A number of targets can be addressed simultaneously.

Some of the incidents of cyber terrorism have been:

- Bombardment of Sri Lankan embassies in 1998 by LTTE with 800 e-mails a day over a two-week period.

- NATO computers were blasted with e-mail bombs and hit with denial-of-service (DOS) attacks during the Kosovo conflict in 1999. Businesses, public organizations, and academic institutes were attacked with highly politicized virus-laden e-mails from a number of countries. Web defacements were also reported.

- Crackers in Romania gained access to the computers controlling the life support systems at an Antarctic research station, endangering the life of 58 scientists.

- In 2007 Estonia was subjected to a mass cyber-attack by hackers inside the Russian Federation.

Cyber terrorism can be reduced by adopting some of the following measures:

- All accounts should have passwords, which should be changed often.

- Change the network configuration in case of a doubt.

- Check with venders for upgrades and patches.

- Audit systems and check logs to help in detecting and tracing an intruder.

- If you are ever unsure about the safety of a site, or receive suspicious email from an unknown address, don't access it.

Terror Affected Areas of the World

Terror affected areas of the world in order of intensity are Middle East/ Gulf countries, South Asia, Western Europe, Latin America and Caribbean, East Europe, South East Asia and Oceania, Africa, East and Central Asia and North America. The priority of tactics seems to be bombing, armed attacks, assassinations, kidnapping, arson, hijacking, hostages and unconventional attacks in that order. More acts of terror are domestic and marginally less are of global nature. Both the domestic and global acts are interlinked at some point. Militants more often attack business facilities, diplomatic establishments, government and military establishments recorded generally in that order of priority. The group classification appears to be nationalists/separatists, communists/socialists and religious radicals in that order of incidents.

Israel/Palestine

The conflict between Israeli Jews and Palestinian Arabs is fundamentally a struggle over land. Without going in to the historical background, it is evident that the identity and homes of both, Zionists and Palestinians are at stake. There is a legitimate cause. It is a war for survival which has led to perpetual extreme violence. Both sides inflict casualties on civilians, women and children, receive international funds from diverse sources, are state sponsored, do not believe in use of minimum force and violate human rights. Israel has outright support of USA. It is reported that Israel has developed a large number of weapons of mass destruction including nuclear weapons. Since there is requirement of funds to purchase and sustain inventory of diverse tools of destruction, the conflict has serious international ramifications.

---

* Here the author wishes to mention that Judaism and Zionism need to be understood. Judaism is a religion and tradition, while Zionism is a political ideology. Zionism believes in the idea that the Jews must relocate from the diaspora to their ancestral homeland.

Iraq

Saddam Hussein provided support bases to terrorist groups fighting the governments of neighboring Turkey and Iran, as well as to hard-line Palestinian groups. Iraq has aided the Iranian dissident group Mujahadeen-e-Khalq and the Kurd separatists fighting the Turkish Government. It has sheltered several Palestinian splinter groups that oppose peace with Israel, including the mercenary Abu Nidal Organization. Abu Nidal was found dead in Baghdad in 2002. Iraq also supported Hamas and reportedly channeled money to the families of Palestinian suicide bombers.

Iraq has remained in turmoil since early eighties. There was the Iran-Iraq war for eight years. Iraqi troops used

Al Qaeda

Al Qaeda, an international terrorist network, was established around 1988 by Osama bin Laden, to be part of an Afghan resistance to defeat the Soviet Union. The al Qaeda's current goal is to establish a pan-Islamic Caliphate throughout the world by working with allied Islamic extremist groups to overthrow regimes considered non-Islamic and expelling westerners and non-Muslims from Muslim countries. In February 1998, al-Qaeda issued a statement under banner of "The World Islamic Front for Jihad Against the Jews and Crusaders" stating that it was the duty of all Muslims to kill US citizens—civilian or military—and their allies everywhere.

Tactics include assassination, bombing, hijacking, kidnapping, suicide attack, including use of biological, chemical and nuclear weapons. It has operatives located around the world through an intricate network in Europe, Yemen, Pakistan, Afghanistan, Lebanon, North Africa, Palestine, Central Asia and elsewhere. As such it has a multi-national network with global reach and has supported through financing, training and logistics, Islamic militants in Afghanistan, Algeria, Bosnia, Chechnya, Eritrea, Kosovo, the Philippines, Somalia, Tajikistan and Yemen. Al Qaeda has also been linked to attacks in Africa, Asia, Europe, the former Soviet Republics, the Middle East, as well as North and South America.

Bin Laden, member of a billionaire family that owns the Bin Laden Group construction empire, is said to have inherited tens of millions of dollars that he used to help finance the group. Al Qaeda also maintains businesses and collects donations licitly and illicitly. Drug money is a major contributor.

chemical agents (mustard gas and the nerve agent sarin) against Iranian soldiers. Iraq invaded Kuwait in 1990 and was evicted by the US and Allies in January 1991 resulting in its occupation and execution of President Saddam in 2006. Violence against coalition forces and among various sectarian groups soon led to the Iraqi insurgency, strife between Sunni and Shia groups, and possibly the emergence of a faction of *al Qaeda* in Iraq. There are 4.7 million refugees (2.7 million IDPs and 2 million refugees outside

---

Osama bin Laden

Bin Laden, born in Jeddah, is the 12th child of construction magnate Mohammad bin Aaud Bin Laden, whose assets were once worth $5 billion. His father served the Saudi royal family as a Cabinet minister and was a close friend of the late King Faisal.

He joined the US backed jihad against the Soviet occupation of Afghanistan during the 1980s. He went on collecting money and going in short trips once or twice a year until 1982. He took with him construction machinery and put them at the disposal of the Mujahedeen. In 1986 Osama decided to have his own camps inside Afghanistan and within two years he built more than six camps. During the period 1984-1989 he was staying more in Afghanistan than Saudi Arabia. According to the Central Intelligence Agency, which helped arm the anti-Soviet Mujahedeen, bin Laden had between 12,000 and 20,000 supporters trained in arms, explosives and the use of U.S. Stinger missiles. In 1989, after the Soviet withdrawal from Afghanistan, he returned to the Kingdom.

In the wake of US invasion of Iraq in 2003, he succeeded in extracting a fatwah from one of the senior scholars that training and readiness is a religious duty. He immediately circulated that fatwah and convinced people to have their training in Afghanistan. Around 4000 went to Afghanistan in response to the fatwah. During his stay, it is alleged that the Saudis tried more than once to kidnap or kill him in collaboration with the Pakistani intelligence. After his failure in sorting the Afghani dispute, he decided to leave Afghanistan. In Sudan he had again escaped an assassination attempt which turned out later to be the plan of Saudi intelligence. The Saudis decided to announce their hostility in 1994 when they withdrew his citizenship. He fled Sudan with many of his followers straight to Jalalabad in Eastern Afghanistan. As of now he operates from Afghanistan/Pakistan.@

@ While this book goes to press Osama bin Laden is killed on 02 May 2011 in a military operation by US special forces at Abbottabad inside Pakistan. While Osama is dead, Osamiat is likely to continue.

Iraq).

There are 5 million orphans in Iraq. Despite elections, Iraq is in turmoil. Terror in Iraq is in sync with terror elsewhere in the region and has objectives in the developed world. Iraq has about *55 per cent insurgents from Saudi Arabia, 13 per cent from Syria, 9 per cent from North Africa and 3 per cent from Europe.

Saudi Arabia

Saudi Arabia sponsored a US backed holy war against the Soviets in Afghanistan in 1980s. A large cadre of the jihadis was created under Osama bin Laden, who lost their relevance after the Soviets were driven out of Afghanistan in 1989. The Saudis had created a monster inside the Kingdom. Osama bin Laden, who was earlier considered a Saudi asset and hero became inconvenient to the Kingdom.

There is home grown terror, particularly against the US and western civilians affiliated with its oil-based economy, as well as Saudi civilians and security forces. Western oil derricks and rigs make attractive targets for the terrorists. *Saudis make up 55 per cent of foreign fighters in Iraq. Half the foreign fighters held by the US at Camp Cropper near Baghdad are Saudis.

After 9/11, there was sustained world pressure for the Saudi Government to crack down on terror cells and the radical imams preaching against the Americans in mosques. These calls grew stronger as it turned out that 15 of the 19 hijackers were from Saudi Arabia. Saudi officials pledged to crack down on these imams, yet preaching continues. Also the Saudis' ambivalence towards terrorism persists.

Charitable organisations such as the International Islamic Relief Organisation and the al-Haramain Foundation, accused in American courts of having links with extremist groups, flourished; sometimes with patronage from senior Saudi royals. The Centre of the Islamic World, Saudi Arabia also propounds global terrorism. State and the wealthy Saudis remain the chief

---

* Nick Fielding and Sarah Baxter, 'Saudi Arabia is hub of world terror', Sunday Times, November 4, 2007

financiers of the terror worldwide, particularly *al Qaeda*, LeT, Taliban and Hamas.

Wahabism, a particularly austere and rigid form of Islam in Saudi Arabia, is the most aggressive proponent of Islam and it portrays as if it represents all Muslims. Many terrorist groupings, such as Hamas, the Egyptian Islamic Jihad, *al Qaeda*, Abu Sayyaf and so on are followers of Wahabism.

*It is estimated that since 1973, the Saudi Government has spent some $87 billion to promote Wahabism in the US and the Western Hemisphere. It is further estimated that some $500 billion is floating around the world to fund terrorist activities. The bulk of this funding goes towards the construction and operating expenses of mosques, madrassas, and other religious institutions that preach Wahabism. It also supports the training of imams, domination of mass media and publishing outlets, distribution of Wahabi text books and other literature, and endowments to universities (in exchange for influence over the appointment of Islamic scholars).

Saudi wealth and charities contributed to the madrassas during the Afghan jihad against the Soviets. In these madrassas, there have been students from Central Asia, Philippines, Indonesia, Nigeria and Arab region with funds from Persian Gulf, in addition to Saudi Arabia. Richard Holbrooke observed that the Saudis have exported their problems through these madrassas to the Muslim world. This may well be the by product.

Algeria

Algeria has gone through civil war since the early 90's when the military backed government scrapped a parliamentary election that an Islamist political party (Islamic Salvation Front) was set to dominate. Since then, the bloody campaign between the militants and the army claimed over 200,000 dead.

"The GIA *(Group Islamique armé)* decided in 1994 to enlarge the focus to waging global jihad against western culture and its encroachment on Islamic society. The struggle would not only be confined to Algeria but will be carried abroad to establish worldwide Caliphate.

---

* Oppose Terrorism- Islamic Fundamentalism- The Epitome of Evil - Wikipedia

The hijacking of Air France flight with over 200 passengers on board on Christmas Eve in 1994 marked the GIA's most dramatic and audacious attack since its launch. The flight was diverted to Marseilles where French Special Forces mounted a rescue operation, killing the hijackers and rescuing the passengers and the crew. Six months later, the GIA took savage revenge making its external jihad a reality by bombing the Paris Metro in June 1995. Ten people were killed and hundreds wounded. The situation in Algeria continues to be volatile through the activities of GIA and GSPC (Groupe salafiste pour la prédication et le combat), a regional franchise of *al Qaeda.*

Italy

While not having had many cases of terrorism as some other countries, it could be affected by Slafist Jihadis, who seem to be gaining a foothold in Southern Europe.

Turkey

Turkey is a democratic, secular and constitutional republic, with an ancient cultural heritage. 99.8 per cent are Sunni Muslims and 0.2 per cent are Christians, Jews and others. Located at the cross roads, Turkey has become increasingly integrated with the west through membership in organizations such as the *Council of Europe, NATO, OECD, OSCE and the G-20. It is the only Islamic nation in NATO.

Kurds are non Turkic people who comprise 18 per cent of the population and are concentrated in the southeast. The main threat remains the Kurdistan Workers Party (PKK), which aims at gaining independence for the Kurdish people. Although dominant, the Kurdish insurgency is only one among many other related problems. Turkey is also home to several left-wing militant groups such as the Revolutionary Left and its successor organisation, the Revolutionary People's Liberation Party-Front, which have weakened but have remained active in Turkey and among the Turkish diaspora in Europe.

---

* Council of Europe (47 members, to achieve European unity and facilitate economic and social progress), NATO (North Atlantic Treaty Organisation, a military alliance), OECD (Organisation for European Economic Cooperation), OSCE (Organization for Security and Cooperation in Europe) and the G-20 (major and emerging economies)

The Turkish Hizbullah and the Great East Islamic Raiders' Front are the most prominent Islamist groups, who aim to establish an Islamic state in Turkey. Some individuals took part in the wars in Bosnia and Chechnya in the 1990s, others travelled to Pakistan and Afghanistan to receive terrorist trainings in the camps of *al Qaeda*. Ever since, a distinct Turkish Jihadist scene has developed. Turkey is also an important logistics hub for *al Qaeda* and Jihadists travelling to Pakistan and Afghanistan.

From 1987, the Turkish Hizbullah posed as a rival to the PKK and tried to win the loyalty of those who opposed the PKK's Marxist ideology. A violent struggle between the two groups developed which escalated in the early 1990s. The Hizbullah also entertained close links with Iran, inspired by the Islamic Revolution there. In recent years, it has reorganised and has emerged as a non-violent group. However, it has not explicitly broken with its violent past.

The Great Eastern Islamic Raiders' Front was founded in 1984. In contrast to the Hizbullah, its members are mostly Turks rather than Kurds. It is a small organisation with limited resources.

The US war against Iraq in 2003 became an important turning point for the Turkish Jihadists. A first consequence was the Istanbul bombings of November 2003. In the course of the investigation, it became clear that the plotters in the Istanbul bombing were not only linked to *al Qaeda* but also to terrorist organisations in Syria, Lebanon and Iraq.

In the 1980s and 1990s, Jihadist terrorism in Turkey was an isolated phenomenon represented by the Hizbullah and the Great East Islamic Raiders' Front. Both were nationalist in outlook and strategy. From 2001, however, many Turkish Jihadists have integrated into larger transnational networks. They are increasingly attacking western targets like the Israeli cruise ships in August 2005 and the US Consulate in Istanbul in July 2008. They have developed a new interest in Jihadist cooperation with Uzbek, Afghan, Pakistan and Arabs. The Turkish diaspora in Europe plays an important role. If this trend continues, the terrorist threat in Turkey and in countries with sizable Turkish diaspora communities may grow.

Pakistan

In the recent times, terrorism in and around Pakistan started with Soviet invasion of Afghanistan in 1978-1979. In the war between anti-communist forces and the Soviet-backed Afghan Government, anti-communist guerrillas, jointly called the mujahideen emerged. These guerillas were supported by the USA through Pakistan. By 1983, the CIA supplied intelligence, military expertise and advanced weapons to the rebel forces. American-trained Pakistani officers were sent to Afghanistan to set up a secret mujahideen Stinger training facility. USA maintained its oversight on the war in Afghanistan by entrusting Pakistan's ISI to handle direct contact, which included training of the mujahideen and operations.

Terrorism in Pakistan is mainly a result of Pakistan's support of terrorist activities in its neighbouring countries, India and Afghanistan through state funding of Islamic terrorists. ISI of Pakistan is an autonomous body as part of the army, exporting terror in the name of jihad. It is widely believed that in the incidents of 9/11; attack on the Indian Parliament; London bombing; Bombay, Hydrabad, Bangalore, Ahmedabad and Jaipur bombings; ISI had an active hand. Pakistan has become the epicentre of Muslim jihad and has been training jihadis for Chechneya, Xinjiang, Phillipines, Indonesia, Sudan, Uzbekistan, Iraq, Lebanon, Palestine, Morocco, Libya, Egypt and other Muslim and Arab countries. The ISI also supports Taliban and mujahideen to fight in Afghanistan and Kashmir. Pakistan also provides bankrolling operations, diplomatic support, planning and directing terror offensives, providing logistics and so on.

Along its western borders and along Indo-POK border, and inside Pakistan, Pakistan has a large number of madrassas and jihadi training camps. In recent times, although the madrassas came in to being to fill a void in the education spectrum of Pakistan and Afghanistan, during the Soviet invasion of Afghanistan, a new kind of madrassa emerged in the Pakistan-Afghanistan region, which was not so much concerned about scholarship as making war on the infidels. Many madrassas in Pakistan are funded by Saudi Arabia, particularly the ones that teach Wahabism.

Subsequent to 9/11, Pakistan had to do a *volte face* under extreme US pressure and had to fight the very own Islamic militants who had long been harboured and nurtured by them. There is violence and terrorism by its own creations in side Pakistan. Pakistan is on the brink and may remain so for quite some time. South Asia will also bear the consequences.

More details are given in a separate chapter on Terrorism in Pakistan.

Afghanistan

Opposing the Soviet invasion of Afghanistan in 1978-79, the mujahideen, found support from a variety of countries including the United States, Pakistan, Saudi Arabia and other Muslim nations. On withdrawal of the Soviet forces in 1988-89, the state was left in turmoil and taken over by the Taliban in 1996.

In 2001, post 9/11, war on terror was mandated by the United Nations Security Council. 'International Security Assistance Force (ISAF)' was raised to help maintain security and assist the Afghanistan administration.

ISAF was initially charged with securing Kabul and surrounding areas from the Taliban, *al Qaeda* and factional warlords, so as to allow for the establishment of the Afghan Transitional Administration headed by Hamid Karzai. In October 2003, the UN Security Council authorized the expansion of the ISAF. As of January 2011, there are 132,000 international troops in Afghanistan from 43 countries. Troop contributors include the United States, the United Kingdom, Canada, France, Germany, the Netherlands, Denmark, Belgium, Spain, Italy, Turkey, Poland and most members of the European Union and NATO, also including Australia, New Zealand, Azerbaijan and Singapore. The intensity of the combat faced by contributing nations varies greatly, with the United States, United Kingdom and Canada sustaining substantial casualties in intensive combat operations.

There are *al Qaeda*, Taliban, mujahideen, splinter terror groups and the foreign state sponsors. Assassinations, suicide bombing, crashing of vehicle loads of explosives resulting in frequent casualties has become a routine matter in Afghanistan. *The coalition forces have lost around 2000 soldiers; estimates of the Afghan deaths vary from 100,000 to 1 million. 5 million Afghans fled to Pakistan and Iran. Another 2 million Afghans were displaced within the country. Along with fatalities were 1.2 million Afghan disabled and 3 million maimed or wounded.

Afghanistan is the centre of terrorism of the world along with Pakistan with intense ramifications for all the countries of the word, Pakistan, India, other South Asian countries, Europe and USA in particular.

More details are given in a separate chapter on Terrorism in Afghanistan.

India

Terrorism in India is primarily attributable to multiplicity of religions, historical baggage, soft handling, illiteracy, poverty, disparity, unemployment and political injustice. The regions with long term terrorist activities today are Jammu and Kashmir, Naxalite areas in Central and Eastern India, the Northeastern states and metropolitan cities. Nearly 40 per cent of India is affected by terrorism or insurgency movements. According to the World Markets Research Center, which ranked 186 countries by the degree of risk of terrorism, India stands at No 9.

Northeastern India

Northeastern states - Assam, Meghalaya, Tripura, Arunachal Pradesh, Mizoram, Manipur, and Nagaland, as a region, share porous borders with China in the north, Myanmar in the east, Bangladesh in the southwest and Bhutan to the northwest. The region is connected to the Indian mainland by a tenuous 22 km wide corridor at Siliguri.

These states accuse the Central Government of ignoring their development, as such, demand - ranging from secession to autonomy, self determination and special rights for their distinct identity. There are also ethnic and territorial disputes between Manipur and Nagaland.

Nagaland

There are about twenty tribes, who are commonly known as Nagas. Till their Christianisation in early 20th century, they preserved their faith of animism amongst the tribes. All of them have their distinct cultural tradition, dialect, custom and system of governance. Under the influence of Christian missionaries the Naga National Council (NNC) unilaterally declared Independent

---

*Soviet war in Afghanistan, Wikipedia

Naga Hills on August 14, 1947. This was the beginning of the Naga insurgency.

The representatives of Insurgents signed Shillong Accord in 1975 by accepting Indian Constitution and a sizeable section of insurgents surrendered. Some rejected this Accord. Their leaders formed a new underground party namely Nationalist Socialist Council of Nagalim (NSCN) in late 1970s. They maintained the old stand of sovereignty and merger of the adjoining Naga ethnic areas, and revived hostilities.

A Cease-Fire Agreement was signed between the Government of India and the insurgents in 1997. The cease fire has been extended on yearly basis and is still in force in 2011 on the conditionality of no sovereignty. There has been decline in violence during 2009-2010 due to decrease in inter-factional violence, the success of the cease-fire mechanisms, talks with the Government of India and the civil society efforts.

Manipur

Manipur became a Union Territory in 1956 and in 1972, a full-fledged state of India. The People's Liberation Army (PLA), the United National Liberation Front (UNLF) and the People's Revolutionary Party of Kangleipak (PREPAK), all demand independence. Entire Manipur is affected by varying degree of militancy. Since 2008, however, there is improvement in the situation.

Assam

The people of Assam demand that the illegal emigrants from Bangladesh should be deported. Bodos, an ethnic and linguistic community, demand a separate state. There are also other organizations which advocate the independence of Assam. The most prominent of them is the United Liberation Front of Assam (ULFA) with two main goals, the independence of Assam and the establishment of a socialist government. The ULFA, a terrorist group, has strong links with Maoists and Kachin Independence Army in Myanmar.

The ULFA leaders have expressed willingness to enter into talks with the Government in 2010-2011. Its founder-chairman, Arabinda Rajkhowa was released from jail paving the way for the start of a peace process again. There are other leaders as well who have been released to strengthen the peace process. The talks will be unconditional and with in the frame work of the Indian Constitution.

Naxalites

The Naxal insurgency started as a peasant movement in Naxalbari in eastern India in 1967. They are fighting oppression and exploitation in order to create a classless society, a Maoist Indian state. They seek more employment for the poor and land reforms in order to reduce disparity. The movement has spread to a large swathe in the central and eastern parts of the country referred to as the Red Corridor, covering 83 districts, mainly in the states of Bihar, Jharkhand, Chhattisgarh, West Bengal, Orissa, Madhya Pradesh, Maharashtra and Andhra Pradesh.

Most notable of India's Maoist groups are the People's War Group (PWG), mainly active in the southern Andhra Pradesh and the Maoist Communist Centre (MCC) in West Bengal and Bihar. In 2004, the two merged to form the Communist Party of India - Maoist (CPI-Maoist). CPI-Maoist maintains dialogue with the Communist Party of Nepal-Maoist, Lashkar-e-Tayyiba (LeT), LTTE, Communist Party of the Philippines and China. PWG, MCC and CPI– Maoist have been proscribed by the Government of India.

Naxals are ruthless when dealing with rivals. 10,875 personnel have been killed between 2001 and 2010. Militarily well equipped, in 2006, Prime Minister Manmohan Singh referred to them as "the single biggest internal security challenge ever faced by the country".

Jammu and Kashmir

Jammu and Kashmir was invaded by Pakistan trained tribals backed up by the Pakistani Army in 1947. A part of the province was annexed and is still with Pakistan. As a result of legal Instrument of Accession, the state acceded to India in 1947. 78,114 sq km area of the state is under occupation of Pakistan, 101,387 sq km is with India, 37,555 sq km is in adverse possession of China, and an area of 5180 sq km has been illegally ceded to China by Pakistan. The parties to dispute are India; the people of the Valley, Jammu region and Ladakh; Pakistan and China.

Jammu and Kashmir is a Muslim majority state with the Valley being overwhelmingly Muslim, Jammu region with Hindu majority and Ladakh with Buddhist majority. A large part of the demography is non committal. The insurgency/terrorism in the state is Pakistan sponsored with funds diverted from the US aid and from the Muslim countries. According to estimates 85,000 personnel have been killed as a result of insurgency in the state.

Major Cities

On 13 December 2001 the Parliament of India was attacked in which 9 policemen and a staffer were killed, and all the five terrorists, identified as Pakistani nationals, were also killed. Delhi was again targeted on 29 October 2005 and 13 September 2008 killing more than 60 and injuring at least 200.

Mumbai has been the most preferred target of the Muslim terrorists. Since 1993, a series of attacks have led to over 700 killings. The unprecedented attacks of 26 November 2008, where two of the prime hotels, a landmark train station and a Jewish Chabad house, were brutally sieged killing 160-170. There have been major terror incidents in other major cities to include Srinagar, Gandhinagar, Hydrabad, Lucknow, Faizabad, Ahmedabad, Pune and so on.

Religious Violence

Ram Janam Bhumi/Babri Masjid structure, believed by the Hindus to have been built over the birthplace of the Hindu deity Ram, was demolished by Hindu *kar sevaks* on 6 December 1992. The resulting riots caused 1200 deaths.

In 2002, a train burning incident took place in Gujrat. The coach, which was occupied by Hindu *kar sevaks*, returning from Ayodhya caught fire resulting in death of 58 Hindu pilgrims. The fire was alleged to have been started by a Muslim mob. In retaliation, the toll was around 1,500.

In 2005 elements of, Lashkar-e-Tayyiba attacked the disputed structure at Ayodhya but were gunned down. A series of blasts took place across the holy city of Varanasi in 2006.

In recent years, there has been an increase in violent attacks on Christians, often perpetrated by Hindu fundamentalists. In Orissa, starting 2007 through 2008, there have been attacks on Christians, resulting in deaths and destruction of property including churches. The violence has also spread to Chhattisgarh, Andhra Pradesh, Tamil Nadu and Kerala.

There have been more attacks on Hindu temples and Hindus by Muslim militants. Prominent among them are the Chamba massacre in 1998, the attacks on Raghunath temple Jammu in 2002 and attack on Akshardham temple in Gujrat in 2002 resulting in many deaths and injuries.

Ethnic Cleansing of Kashmiri Pandits

In Kashmir, approximately 300 Kashmiri Pandits were killed between 1989 and 1990. Between 250,000 and 300,000 Kashmiri Pandits, have migrated from Kashmir Valley. The proportion of Kashmiri Pandits has declined from about 15 per cent in 1947 to less than 0.1 per cent.

Nepal

Nepal is a landlocked country with China in the north and India to the south, east, and west. The mountainous north has eight of the world's ten tallest mountains, including Mount Everest. The fertile and humid south is heavily urbanized. Hinduism is practised by a larger majority of people. Many Nepalis do not distinguish between Hinduism and Buddhism and follow both religious traditions. Nepal was a monarchy since 1768 till 2008.

The CPN-Maoist resorted to an armed struggle in 1996, thereby declaring a People's War. They strongly believe in the Mao's philosophy, "political power grows out of the barrel of gun" and won the largest number of seats in the Constituent Assembly election held in April 2008, and formed a coalition government. Nepal, thus, became a secular and inclusive democratic republic. Nonetheless, political tensions and consequent power-sharing battles continued. In May 2009, the Prime Minister resigned in the wake of the Army Chief's refusal to integrate PLA members into the Army and for general insubordination. The Maoist led government was replaced by another coalition government with all major political parties barring the Maoists. CPN-Maoist, now Unified Communist Party of Nepal – Maoist, has warned that the Maoist agitation will be intensified. While the new Constitution drafting body is at work, an uneasy peace prevails in Nepal. The outlook for Nepal is uncertain.

The terrorism in Nepal stems from a completely domestic conflict between the Government and the Maoist rebels. However, there will be telling effect in the region, particularly Bhutan, India, Myanmar, Bangladesh and Pakistan, as the Nepal's territory and systems are being used by terrorists.

Bangladesh

Formeraly a part of Pakistan, Bangladesh came in to being in 1971. A nation of 160 million; 89.7 per cent are Muslims, 9.2 per cent are Hindus and the remaining include Buddhists, Christians and others.

Terrorist organizations, Jagrata Muslim Janata Bangladesh (JMJB), Jamaat-ul-Mujahideen Bangladesh (JMB) and Harkat-ul-Jihad-al-Islami Bangladesh (HuJI-B) were banned in 2005. Hizb-ut-Tahrir was banned in 2009. Hizb-e-Abu Omar is another militant organization that broke away from HuJI-B and maintains links with *al Qaeda.* The cadres of the Islamist outfits are estimated to be around 40,000. Despite the Government's efforts there is evidence that Islamist organizations are regrouping.

JMB is moving cautiously toward its goal of an Islamic state. Its inclusion in the government has encouraged other fundamentalist groups like the Bangladeshi Taliban and HuJI-B. In addition, 69,000 madrassas, which have mushroomed in the past decade or so, provide a safe place to plan and train. Madrassas, poorly equip students to enter mainstream life and thus, a ready material for anti-social activities.

The Left Wing Extremist (LWE) movement, in its history of over three decades, is a highly dispersed, low-scale and criminalised movement. There were 72 fatalities by LWE in 2009 as against none by the Islamist outfits.

Bangladesh territory provides a transit haven for Pakistani terrorist groups. LeT and HuJI have used its territory to launch terrorist attacks against India. For the time being Bangladesh's secular roots are holding. India and Myanmar in the neighbouhood, with Muslim minorities, hold stakes in Bangladesh's stability and secular governance.

Sri Lanka

37 militant groups operated in Sri Lanka at one time or the other, but the

Liberation Tigers of Tamil Eelam (LTTE) was the most active separatist organization based in northern Sri Lanka. It waged a secessionist campaign to create Tamil Eelam, a separate country for the Tamils, in the north and east of Sri Lanka. It possessed a well-developed militia and executed many high profile attacks including the assassinations of former Indian Prime Minister Rajiv Gandhi in 1991 and Sri Lankan President Ranasinghe Premadasa in 1993.

Indian Peace Keeping Force (IPKF) performed the peace keeping operation in Sri Lanka between 1987 and 1990. The task of the IPKF was to disarm different militant groups. It was to be quickly followed by the formation of an Interim Administrative Council. The force was not expected to be involved in any significant combat, but got embroiled in battle with the LTTE for enforcement of peace. The IPKF withdrew from Sri Lanka in 1989-90.

Indonesia

Most populous Muslim nation with 90 per cent Muslims, Indonesia's Muslims are generally moderates. The constitution guarantees religious freedom. Terrorism in Indonesia intensified in 2000 with the Jakarta Stock Exchange bombing, followed by four more major blasts. The deadliest killed 202 people (including 164 international tourists) in the Bali resort town in 2002. The group responsible for the attack was Jemaah Islamiyah, a militant Islamist group with alleged links to a*l Qaeda*. Three members of the group, who aim to create a unified Islamic state encompassing Indonesia, Malaysia, the southern Philippines, Singapore and Brunei, were executed for their part in the 2002 plot.

In 2005, a bomb was detonated outside a stall selling pork in Palu in Sulawesi province. Eight people were killed and 45 injured. Tourist areas on the island were targeted again in 2005 when 20 people were killed in a series of bombings. In the same year there were attacks on Ahmadiyahs, forced closure of some Christian places of worship, attacks on bars and night clubs, threats to the liberal Islamic network, and issuance of *fatwas* against pluralism, secularism and liberal Islam.

Thailand

An Islamist separatist insurgency is beginning in the south of Thailand, predominantly in the Malay Pattani region, made up of the three southern most provinces. These areas are in close vicinity of Malaysia, Cambodia and Indonesia. South Thailand, which is predominantly Muslim, as such, has the potential to become a hospitable unsuspecting ground for terrorists of the region to plan and spread terror, particularly on the tourist resorts. Leaders of Jemaah Islamiyah have been spotted in the region

Philippines

Since 2000, radical Islamist groups and Islamist separatist forces in the Philippines have carried out over 40 major terrorist incidents against civilians and civilian property, mostly in the southern regions of the country around Mindanao, Basilan, Jolo and other nearby islands. Terrorist incidents have also occurred in and around Manila, several hundred km north of the conflict regions. During the period 2000-2010, around 450 civilians were killed and over two thousand injured.

Abu Sayyaf is a militant organization based in the southern Philippines, seeks a separate Islamic state for the country's Muslim minority. It claims ties with *al Qaeda* network, as well as the Indonesian network of Jemaah Islamiyah. Jemaah Islamiyah is a Southeast Asian militant Islamic organization dedicated to the establishment of an Islamic state incorporating Indonesia, Malaysia, the southern Philippines, Singapore and Brunei. The entire region, as such, is a suitable ground for terror planning and execution.

United States

Terror in the context of United States of America may be dealt as domestic terror, global terror and terror as state policy. According to the FBI, between the years 1980 and 2000, 250 of the 335 incidents were confirmed or suspected to be terrorist acts which were carried out by the American citizens. The organisations indulging in domestic terror are Animal Liberation Front, Army of God, Black Liberation Army, Earth Liberation Front, Jewish Defense League, Ku Klux Klan, Symbionese Liberation Army and Weathermen. The Earth Liberation Front has been classified as the top domestic terror threat by the FBI since 2001, and is categorized as eco-terrorists. The FBI has credited to eco-terrorism $ 200 million in property damage from 2003 to 2008 and a majority of states have introduced laws to deal with them.

USA has suffered approximately 3,600 dead and over 14,000 injured during terror attacks on its facilities in and out side USA since 1983. This is despite all possible precautions that the country takes to secure its people and facilities, both in and out of USA. There is a fair degree of animosity against the Americans by the world at large barring the Europeans. In fact the Americans have lost the freedom and ease with which they lived both in and out of America. Its overbearing attitude is the main reason behind its positioning among the peoples of the world. When I say overbearing attitude, it is not the ego or feeling of superiority, it is part of the state policy of the United States of America which is amply clear from some of the international happenings.

A top Secret declassified document of US State Department's Policy Planning Staff, headed at the time (February 1948) by George Kennan says it all:

"We have about 50 per cent of the world's wealth, but only 6.3 per cent of its population... Our real task in the coming period is to devise a pattern of relationships which will permit us to maintain this position of disparity without positive detriment to our national security. To do so we will have to dispense with all sentimentality and day-dreaming... We need not deceive ourselves that we can afford the luxury of altruism and world-benefaction... We should cease to talk about vague and unreal objectives such as human rights, the raising of living standards, and democratization. The day is not far off when we will have to deal in straight power concepts."

Such policies do not change fundamentally, they move in a groove with little scope for manoeuvre. Since then USA has operated in Vietnam, Nicaragua, Dominican Republic, Cuba, Chile, Columbia, Egypt, Aden, Jordan, Oman, Iran, Iraq, Kuwait, Afghanistan and Yugoslavia with clear state terror footprint directly and indirectly.

When required, USA has supported the overthrow of democracy in favor of friendly regimes, like Brazil in 1964, Philippines in 1972, Chile in 1973, and military aid and financial support to the military and the generals in Pakistan.

There are many more examples like the Mujahideens in Afghanistan, Taliban and so on. It has often shifted policy from the support of friendly fascists like the Somozas in Nicaragua and Ubico in Guatemala to hostility and active subversion of successor reformist or radical democrats like the Sandinistas in Nicaragua and Arevalo and Arbenz in Guatemala. To suit its future policies, USA plans in great details and goes proactive to effect desired macro scenario changes including regime changes and destabilizing undeveloped countries to maintain their dependency. Between 1900 and 1945, the U.S. had 5,000 marines in Nicaragua, invaded the Dominican Republic four times, occupied Haiti for twelve years, deployed troops into Cuba four times, into Panama six times, into Guatemala once, into Honduras seven times, Iran, Iraq, Kuwait, Afghanistan and so on. According to Amnesty International, in Guatemala alone, the government supported by the US had killed around 80,000 people by 1987.

Notwithstanding the 1948 top secret document and other facts mentioned above, all nations have their national interests first and foremost. The document of 1948 reveals nothing new except the hard geographical and demographic facts, and what any country would do. Here the capabilities are enormous - financial, technical and military, which has led it to be all over and overbearing. It is also a complicated mixture of feelings of envy, admiration, cultural misunderstanding and love/hate. USA, however, must review its hegimonistic policies to change the world order, which is well nigh not feasible. The uni-polarity may not be sustainable indefinitely.

Colombia

Republic of Colombia is a democracy, but its society is beset with violence and corruption fueled by the drug trade. Colombia is the world leading producer of coca and exporter of cocaine for many years. Columbia is also a major producer of heroin. 46 per cent of Colombians live below poverty line and 17 per cent in extreme poverty. Eighty per cent of the cocaine entering the United States either originates or passes through Colombia. Illegal profits have permeated the vital instruments of the state including armed forces. While the country has no known ties to global terrorism, it suffers from weak government, drug trafficking, drug economy and civil strife.

Europe

Casablanca Bombings, Istanbul bombings, Madrid Train bombings, the Van Gogh murder in Amsterdam, London train bombings, uncovering of a bomb factory in Grenoble and a large number of terrorist actions in and around Spain and France between 2003 and 2009, are a clear indicator of the spread of terror in Europe. *Great Britain and the Netherlands seem to be at the greatest risk with 12 of the networks operating in Great Britain, seven in the Netherlands, four in France and three each in Spain and Belgium. Homegrown terrorism seems to be the new trend among Europe's jihadis.

The United Kingdom stands at number 14 on the list of countries affected by terrorism. Its terrorism threat is largely home grown with a large disenfranchised immigrant population and a controversial foreign policy.

Spain has a rather loose immigration from Northern Africa making it a polarized society. In addition, Spain still has a serious problem, the Basque separatist movement known as ETA.

Russia

Russian Empire has history of terror since the beginning of twentieth century. Terror tactics, such as hostage-taking, were widely used by the Soviet secret agencies during the Red Terror campaigns of 1918-1922 for extermination of social groups or former ruling classes. The year 1999 witnessed significant terrorist activity, 'apartment bombings in the cities of Buynaksk, Moscow, and Volgodonsk, killing 293 and injuring 651 and the 'Moscow theater hostage crisis in 2002' by 40 to 50 armed Chechens taking 850 hostages who demanded the withdrawal of Russian forces from Chechnya. In 2010, Chechen women suicide bombers bombed two Moscow underground trains killing 39 and injuring many more. The counter terror operation by employing chemical agents led to a large number of casualties. Many more acts of terrorism have been committed in Chechnya and Dagestan, and other parts of the country. Russia has become a prime terror target since its entry in Chechnya in 1999. The Russian government has banned seventeen terrorist organizations.

---

* Yassin Musharbash, *Terrorism in Europe, Bin Laden's Euro-fighters*

Significant World Terror Organisations

Al Qaeda

Al Qaeda is an international Sunni Islamist movement founded in 1988. Though on the run and sick, its leader, Osama bin Laden, killed in May 2011, still remains a motivating strength for radical pan Islamic movements and creation of a Muslim Caliphate. It has a well developed world wide militant network which was responsible for 9/11, resulting in war on terror world wide by the US. *Al Qaeda* has been labeled a terrorist organization by the UNSC, NATO, European Union, UK, US, Austria, India, Canada, Israel, Japan, South Korea, the Dutch, Sweden and the Swiss. Also see pages 32 and 33.

Taliban

It is a Sunni Pashtun movement, primarily operating in Pakistan and Afghanistan. Its rank and file comprise of Afghan refugees who were educated in madrassas along the Afghan-Pakistan border. Its strength is estimated at 7,000-11,000 and ideology - Islamist fundamentalism and Pashtun nationalism. Taliban are intolerant to other religions. In 1994 they took control of 12 provinces in Afghanistan and by 1996 they had captured Kabul. Taliban governance was rather primitive, ancient Islamist and harsh. The allied forces inflicted massive casualties on Taliban and drove them out of power in 2001. In Pakistan they run their writ in Swat, North and South Waziristan and are capable of striking anywhere.

Harkat-ul-Mujahideen (HUM)

HUM was formed in 1985 by a group that separated out from Harkat-ul-Jihad-al-Islami (HuJI), a militant group based in Pakistan, comprising several thousand armed personnel. Most of its cadres are from *Tablighi Jamaat (TJ)*. It is based in Pakistan and Afghanistan. It is financed by Saudi Arabia and other Gulf and Islamic states including Pakistan. With the Soviet withdrawal from Afghanistan in 1989, the outfit turned against Jammu and Kashmir in 1990 at the behest of Pakistan. On proscription by the US, HUM re-merged with HuJI to form Harakat ul-Ansar (HUA), which has links with the Kashmiri militant group, Al-Faran. It has considerably weakened because of capture of its prominent leaders by the Indian security forces.

Al-Faran

Exact aim of this group remains murky. It is believed that it comprises of members from HUA and JeM, and operates in Kashmir.

Hizb-ul-Mujahideen (HM)

HM was formed in 1989 as the militant wing of the Jamaat-e-Islami (JeI) at the behest of the Inter Services Intelligence of Pakistan. HM is one of the largest terrorist groups operating in Jammu and Kashmir and stands for the integration of Jammu and Kashmir with Pakistan. HM also aims at the Islamization of Kashmir. It has approximately 1500 cadres, mostly indigenous.

Harkat-ul-Jihad-al-Islami (HuJI)

The movement of Islamic holy war aims to wrest control of Jammu and Kashmir and merge it with Pakistan. HuJI members are mostly Sunni Pakistanis who fought the Russians in Afghanistan and lost relevance after the Russians pulled out. The organization has been banned by the US in August 2010.

Harkat-ul-Jihad-al-Islami Bangladesh (HuJI-B)

It aims to turn Bangladesh in to an Islamic state and has support from HuJI, HUM and *al Qaeda.*

Jaishe-e-Mohammed (JEM)

JEM was formed in early 2000 by Maulana Masood Azhar after the IC-814 hijack to Kandhar and his release. It comprises of several hundred armed personnel and supporters. Supporters are mostly Pakistanis and Kashmiris, and also Afghan and Arab. Based in Peshawar and Muzaffarabad, it is funded by *al Qaeda* and primarily operates in Kashmir with the aim of merging Kashmir with Pakistan. JEM maintains training camps in Afghanistan.

Lashkar-e-Tayyiba (LET)

LET is a Sunni organization formed in 1989, which is responsible for a string of attacks, including on Indian Parliament and the Mumbai blasts. Its goal is to unite Kashmir with Pakistan, and also to destroy the Indian republic and annihilate Hinduism. Banned, but operates through the front organization, the *Jamaat-ud-Dawa*, which was operating Taliban-supported training camps in Afghanistan before 9/11. *Jamaat-ud-Dawa* has also been banned post Mumbai terror attacks in 2008. Its cadres are from Pakistan and Afghanistan, who are armed with sophisticated weapons and are well trained. It is the armed wing of the Pakistan-based religious organization, Markaz-ud-Dawa-wal-Irshad (MDI) and is anti US and anti India.

Lashkar-e-Jhangvi (LeJ)

A Sunni Deobandi Islamic organization, post 9/11, it provided safe houses to *al Qaeda* men on the run. The LeJ aims to transform Pakistan into a Sunni state, primarily through violent means. The LeJ was proscribed in 2001 by Pakistan.

Sipah-i-Sahaba

It is a Sunni party in Pakistan which emerged in the wake of Shia Islamic revolution in Iran. It is anti Shia and calls for killing Shia clerics and declaring Shias as non Muslims.

Communist Party of Nepal-Maoist (CPN-Moist)

CPN-Maoist strongly believe in the philosophy of Mao Tsetung, "Political power grows out of the barrel of gun" and won the largest number of seats in the Constituent Assembly election held in April 2008, and formed a coalition government. Political tensions and consequent power-sharing battles continued. In May 2009, the Maoist-led government was toppled and another coalition government with all major political parties barring the Maoists was formed. CPN-Maoist leader has warned that the Maoist agitation that his party had launched will be intensified. The terrorism in Nepal stems from a completely domestic conflict between the Government and the Marxist rebels.

Liberation Tigers of Tamil Eelam (LTTE)

LTTE waged a secessionist campaign to create Tamil Eelam, a separate country for the Tamils, in the north and east of Sri Lanka. It possessed a well developed militia and executed many high profile attacks including the assassinations of former Indian Prime Minister Rajiv Gandhi in 1991 and Sri Lankan President Ranasinghe Premadasa in 1993. The LTTE pioneered the use of suicide belts, and used light aircraft in some of their attacks. The sourcing of LTTE has been the smuggling of weapons, explosives, and dual-use technologies. It had a clandestine logistics KP Branch dealing with the arms shipments in its own fleet of ocean-going vessels. It operated a shipping base in Myanmar.

LTTE frequently exchanged control of territory in north and east Sri Lanka with the Sri Lankan military. In 2002, they had a 15,000 sq km of real estate under their control. However after the breakdown of the peace process in 2006, the Sri Lankan military launched a full scale military offensive. Victory over the LTTE was declared on May 16, 2009 after 26 years of conflict. Several LTTE fighters committed suicide and defeat was conceded. The undisputed leader Prabhakaran was killed along with several other high ranking Tamils. It is currently proscribed as a terrorist organization by 32 countries including USA, UK, EU, Canada, Sri Lanka and India, but has extensive support amongst the Tamil diaspora.

Abu Sayyaf

Founded in 1991, Abu Sayyaf is one of the many militant groups based in southern Philippines in Bangsamoro and seeks independence of southern Philippines. The group finds support from Jemaah Islamiyah and *al Qaeda* and indulges in kidnapping and seeks ransom. Its strength is around 200 with an extended membership of 2000.

Lashkar Jihad

Laskar Jihad is an anti-Christian militia in Indonesia formed in 2000 by Jafar Umar Thalib, who had studied in Pakistan and fought along side the mujahideen in Afghanistan in the 1980s. Between 2000 and 2001, an estimated 10,000 people were killed and hundreds of thousands had to flee their homes as the Laskar burnt down churches and houses. During 2001 and 2002, it expanded its activities to the provinces of Aceh and Papua at opposite ends of the country.

Kumpulan Mujahideen Malaysia (KMM)

KMM envisages the creation of a pan Islamic state, comprising Malaysia, Indonesia, southern Thailand and southern Philippines. Malaysian police assess its strength as 70 to 80 members. Its financial resources are unknown, probably is self-sustaining.

Islamic Movement of Uzbekistan (IMU)

IMU was formed in 1991 with the objective of overthrowing President Islam Karimov of Uzbekistan, and to create an Islamic state. Operating out of bases in Tajikistan and northern Afghanistan, the IMU launched a series of raids into southern Kyrgyzstan in 1999 and 2000. However, in 2001 the IMU was largely destroyed fighting alongside the Taliban against coalition forces in Afghanistan. Since then the IMU has reportedly opened training camps in Waziristan and is now involved with other groups attempting to overthrow the Government of Pakistan. There is no reliable evidence indicating that the IMU remains an operational force in Central Asia. It is also affiliated with al *Qaeda* and embraces the latter's anti-west and anti-US agenda.

Islamic Jihad Group

Broke away from the Islamic movement in Uzbekistan and is active in Central Asia with links to al *Qaeda* and *Taliban*.

East Turkestan Islamic Movement (ETIM)

ETIM is based in China's Xinjiang province and aims at uniting the Turkic people of Turkey, Kazakhstan, Kyrgyzstan, Uzbekistan, Pakistan, Afghanistan and western China in to one Islamic state. The Movement has support of *al Qaeda.*

Jemaah Islamiyah Organisation

The Group is responsible for suicide bombing in Jakarta in 2003 and 2004; Bali in 2003 and 2005 and Manila in 2005. The Group follows the Darool

Islamic Movement and aims to unite South East Asia as an Islamic state.

Palestinian Liberation Organisation (PLO)

The PLO was considered by the United States and Israel to be a terrorist organization till 1991. It was created in 1964 in an effort to give a voice to a large number of Palestinians living in refugee camps in Lebanon. PLO was headquartered in Jordan, Lebanon, Tunisia and West Bank at different times. It is recognized as the sole legitimate representative of the Palestinian people by over 100 states with which it holds diplomatic relations, and has enjoyed observer status at the UN since 1974. In 1993 PLO recognized Israel's right to exist in peace, accepted *UN Security Council resolutions 242 and 338, and rejected violence and terrorism; in response Israel officially recognized the PLO as the representative of the Palestinian people.

Palestine Liberation Army

It comprises of elite Arab battalions based in host Arab countries. Formally under the PLO but practically are under the control of the host country. These forces have never been deployed as one formation. Palestinians living in these countries can opt to serve in these battalions in lieu of national service.

Palestine Islamic Jihad (Harakat al-Jihad al-Islami al-Filastini)

Broke away from Palestinian Muslim Brotherhood in Gaza Strip, it aims at destruction of Israel and creation of Palestine state. The group is currently based in Damascus and its financial backing is believed to come from Syria and Iran. It also has offices in Beirut, Tehran and Khartoum. It maintains connections with Hezbollah and HAMAS.

---

* Resolution 242, 1967 deals with

(i) Withdrawal of Israel armed forces from territories occupied in the 1967 Arab Israel war.

(ii) Respect for the sovereignty, territorial integrity and political independence of every state in the area.

Resolution 338, 1973, called for a ceasefire in the Yom Kippur War.

Hezbollah or Party of God or 'Islamic Jihad for Liberation of Palestine

It is a Shia Islamist political and militant organisation based in Lebanon. Its 1985 manifesto listed its four main goals as Israel's final departure from Lebanon as a prelude to its final destruction; ending any imperialist power in Lebanon; submission of the phalangists to 'just rule' and bringing them to trial; and giving the people the chance to choose the system of governance, but with commitment to the rule of Islam. Also seeks the return of Jerusalem to Palestine. It receives funds from Iran and Syria and in turn trains and funds Palestinian groups. A fearsome terror group is now a legitimate political party in Lebanon. Hezbollah also operates schools, hospitals, and agricultural services for thousands of Lebanese Shia.

Harakat-al-Muqawamat al-Islâmiyyah (HAMAS)

HAMAS is a Palestinian Sunni Islamist socio-political organization, with a military wing. It is classified as a terrorist organization by a number of countries, including Israel, the EU, USA, Canada and Japan. It seeks replacement of Israel by the Palestine state and is known for multiple suicide attacks against Israeli civilians in Israel, Gaza and West Bank. It has a military wing of around 10,000 professional soldiers. It indulges extensively in social and welfare work in Gaza and West Bank as well. HAMAS won the 2006 elections to the Palestine Legislative Council.

Fatah

Fatah is a Palestine movement which was created in 1959-60 by Yasser Arafat and his friends in Algeria with the aim of creating Palestine state and destroying Israel. By the end of the 1960s it was the largest and best funded of all the Palestinian organizations and had taken over effective control of the PLO. Backed by Syria, it began terrorist raids against Israeli targets in 1965, launched from Jordan, Lebanon and Egyptian-occupied Gaza. In 1967–1968, Fatah joined the PLO and won the leadership role in 1969. The grenade and crossed rifles, superimposed on the map of Israel is the emblem Fatah.

Al Aqsa Martyr's Brigade

Militant youth wing of Fatah, it targets Israelis in Gaza Strip, West Bank and those Palestinians who collaborate with the Israelis. Its primary weapon is suicide bombing and rockets and operates in concert with HAMAS.

Abu Nidal Organisation (ANO)

Founded in 1974 by Abu Nidal and a few others from PLO, has been a fearsome organization indulging in a number of high profile murders. On the decline, its present status is not very clear.

Asbat al-Ansar

Based in southern Lebanon and predominantly Palestinian, it follows an extreme Wahabist interpretation of Islam. It has connections with a*l Qaeda* and other extremist Sunni groupings.

Muslim Brotherhood

The Society of the Muslim Brothers is a transnational most influential Islamist movement. It was founded in 1928 in Egypt by a school teacher Hassan al-Banna. The Brotherhood's goal is to instill the Quran and Sunnah as the sole reference point for ordering the life of the Muslims and the state. The movement opposes violent means to achieve its goals, with a few exceptions. The Egyptian government, however, accused the group of a campaign of killings in Egypt after World War II. The Muslim Brotherhood is banned in Egypt.

Moroccan Islamic Combatant Group

It comprises Moroccan veterans from the Afghan war who aim at establishing an Islamic state in Morocco. It was responsible for the Casablanca attack in 2003. Its offshoot, *Salafia Jihadia* was blamed for the Madrid blasts in 2004. It has been banned worldwide.

Ansar al–Islam

The Group, comprising of Iraqi Arabs and Kurds, seeks Iraq as a Muslim state. Also known as Ansar al-Sunnah, Helpers of Islam and Kurdish Taliban, it is one of the fiercest groups against the US led coalition in Iraq.

Tanzim Qaidat al-Jihad fi Bilad al-Rafidayn (TQJBR)

The objectives of TQJBR with in Iraq are to overthrow the Interim Iraqi Government, expel the multi national forces and establish an Islamic state under Sharia law. Its strength is between 500 and 1000.

GIA

The GIA *(Group Islamique arme)* in Algeria has been a brutal organization killing those who worked for or supported the Government of Algeria. It aims to exterminate all Jews, Christians and infidels from the land of Algeria, as well as to overthrow the existing regime. GIA has killed more than 100 expatriates. It is considered a terrorist organisation by Algeria, France and USA. It decided in 1994 to enlarge the focus to waging global jihad against western culture and its encroachment on the Islamic society. The struggle aims at a worldwide Caliphate. Algerian authorities claim that GIA has been severely incapacitated.

The Salafist Group for Preaching and Combat (GSPC)

Broke away from GIA in Algeria, it has surpassed GIA in size and influence. GSPC observes a more strict and fundamentalist view of Quran. It maintains links with *al Qaeda*.

Libyan Islamic Fighting Group (LIFG)

LIFG is the most powerful radical faction waging Jihad in Libya against Colonel Qadhafi. It aims to establish an Islamic state in Libya. Shortly after the 9/11, LIFG was banned worldwide as an affiliate of *al Qaeda* by the UN.

Irish National Liberation Army (IRLA)

It aimed at liberating Northern Ireland from the British and unite the whole of Ireland and to turn the state in to Marxist-Leninist. The INLA declared a ceasefire in August 1998 and stated that there was no political or moral argument to justify a resumption of the campaign. In October 2009, the INLA formally declared its aims to pursue peaceful political means.

Provisional Irish Republican Army (PIRA)

It sought to expel the British from Northern Ireland and indulged in bombings in Northern Ireland and the mainland Britain. The Belfast Agreement of 1998 (de-escalation of violence) was signed by the British and Irish governments and endorsed by most Northern Ireland political parties. In 2005, the PIRA Army Council announced an end of the armed campaign to pursue exclusive peaceful means. Two small groups split from the PIRA, Continuity IRA and Real IRA. Both reject the Belfast Agreement and continue to engage in violence. Both organisations have been proscribed by UK and USA.

Ulster Volunteer Force (UVF)

UVF was founded in 1966 to oppose Northern Ireland's unification with Ireland, they believe in maintaining their ties with Great Britain and to remain a part of it. It declared a ceasefire in 1994, although sporadic attacks continued until it officially ended its campaign in May 2007. The group is a proscribed organisation in the Republic of Ireland and a designated terrorist organisation in the United Kingdom.

Loyalist Volunteer Force (LVF)

LVF is a paramilitary group in Northern Ireland, which is opposed to *Good Friday Peace Agreement, was formed in 1996 as a break away faction of the UVF. Composed largely of UVF hardliners, has been observing a cease-fire since 1998. The LVF decommissioned a significant amount of weapons in 1998, but has threatened in 2000 to resume its operations. It comprises of 300 cadres. The LVF is outlawed as a terrorist organization in the UK, Republic of Ireland and the United States. LVF is now a nonpolitical organization and indulges in crime and drug trafficking.

Ku Klux Klan (KKK)

KKK is a racist, anti-Semitic movement with a commitment to its goals of racial segregation and white supremacy. KKK is the name of three distinct past and present organizations in the United States, which have advocated extremist white supremacy and nationalism. The first KKK flourished in the South in the 1860s and died out by the early 1870s. The second KKK flourished

---

Good Friday Agreement was signed by the United Kingdom and Sinn Fein (along with USA as an intermediary) with the intent of ending the violence in Northern Ireland.

nationwide in 1920s. The third KKK emerged after World War II. Their white costumes consisted of robes, masks, and conical hat. The first and third KKK has a record of terrorism. It targeted blacks in particular, and the Catholics, Jews and recent immigrants in general.

Christian Patriots

A white group that seeks to cleanse USA of perceived inferior groups like Jews and others.

Covenant, the Sword, and the Arm of the Lord (CSA)

CSA is a militia style organization predominantly located in northern Arkansas, southern Missouri, and western Oklahoma. This organization is loosely affiliated with other white supremacist organizations within the United States, such as the 'Aryan Nations', 'The Order', and the 'Militia of Montana'. Between 1976 and 1985, CSA was involved in various illegal activities such as weapons procurement, counterfeiting, arson, robbery, homicide, and terrorist threats.

Revolutionary Armed Forces of Columbia (FARC)

Founded in 1964, this leading Latin American guerilla group, comprises 12,000 soldiers, is the military wing of the Communist Party of Columbia. It raises its finances through ransom, tax collection, hostage taking, drug trade and so on. FARC may have strayed from the Marxist path, it continues to receive aid from Cuba and Venezuela.

Action directe

Action directe was a French revolutionary group which intended to bring about the collapse of capitalism in Europe. It committed a series of assassinations and violent attacks in France between 1979 and 1987. Members of *Action directe* considered themselves anarchist communists who had formed an urban guerrilla organization. The French government banned the group. The group is presently dormant.

Basque Fatherland and Liberty (ETA)

ETA is a leftist group that indulges in violent activity to win independence for a Basque territory in northern Spain and southwestern France. They wish to govern this territory according to the principles of Marxism. The Basques have never had their own independent state, but have enjoyed varying degrees of autonomy over the centuries. ETA has killed over 850 people and carried out over 1,600 terrorist attacks. In 2005 the Spanish Parliament voted to restart talks if ETA lays down arms, the group is willing to talk but not disarm. There is no credible evidence of ETA having any links with the Muslim terrorist or *al Qaeda*. The group is proscribed as a terrorist organization by Spain, France, EU and USA. ETA has declared permanant ceasefire on 10 Jan 2011.

Special Purpose Islamic Regiment (SPIR)

SPIR is a Chechen militant organization formed in 1996, notorious for its role in the 2002 Moscow theater hostage crisis. It has approximately 100 cadres. It reportedly continues to conduct limited guerrilla operations in Chechnya and targets Russian soldiers and police personnel.

Tablighi Jamaat (TJ)

TJ is a Muslim Deobandi missionary and revival movement for facilitating spread of Islam. Leaders of *TJ* claim that the movement is non-political, pietistic and sends missionaries across the globe on conversion missions and functions at the grass root level to reach out to the masses. Reportedly, this missionary organization is becoming radicalized, and is being used as a cover to mask travel and activities of terrorists including members of the Taliban and *al Qaeda*.

Pan-Islamic Terror

Terrorists of this generation are younger, educated and exposed to modern outlook in life, yet radicalized by media, the internet and mobile phones. Dr Tanveer Ahmad, an Australia-based psychiatrist who specializes in the alienation of Muslim immigrants in the west, states "he (terrorist or jihadi) is likely to be of South Asian back ground – especially Pakistani – educated and informed – and sees himself as Muslim alone, without nationality". The growth of terrorism is not a spontaneous phenomenon. It is manufactured, deliberately planned and exploited by the big players who have loads of money to sway the gullible minds and scores to settle with the mighty. Big money involved in this business of terror includes narcotics, drug peddling, gun running, human trafficking and other international crimes. According to one estimate it is calculated to be worth around $ 1.3 trillion.

Madrassa is a significant feeder to the terror factory, A madrassa provides the breeding ground to terrorists with a facade of recognised education system of any country.

How is a jihadi motivated to sacrifice his life? The fundamentalist Islamic organizations generally follow Wahabism. They believe that Islam has no borders and that all countries once ruled by Muslims should be brought back to Islamic fold. In their interpretation of Islam, it is not difficult to motivate their followers to commit suicide to achieve martyrdom. Both Sunni and Shia have the highest place for martyrdom. Hadith literature preaches that martyrs are distinguished from other forms of death. Terrorism has found this new weapon, the fidayeen, which is difficult to counter except by education and materialism.

The way terrorism has spread across the globe indicates to a very intricate and scientifically structured organization which encompasses an appealing philosophy, dedicated do or die personnel and leadership, hi-tech training facilities, communications, networked intelligence, continuous availability of finance, technology on a wide canvas and support of a nation (s) with international standing. *Al Qaeda* number two, Ayman Al Zawahiri, is known to have once said that chemists, engineers and economists who were well-versed with Islam, had the same standing as the ulema or clergy. Ethnicity across the frontiers and democracy facilitate terror acts of the magnitude of 9/11 and Mumbai.

Al Qaeda has nearly all the ingredients of a super organization, but the time could be a major factor inflicting attrition, fatigue, break up of the leadership, demoralization due to lack of success, paucity of funds, character degeneration, frustration and so on. The counter terror operations are not hopeless at all but are time consuming. Counter-terrorism is a massive global industry involving governments at various levels, ranging from law and order, counter terror operations by the security forces, compromising on the democratic values and freedom, to conventional military operations on the escalatory ladder.

Analysis

Terrorism is not an end in itself, it is only a means to achieve political and religious goals. It is not idealism but a means to wear down a political or religious system in a desired direction. It is also a method to disrupt the daily life and wear down a population so as to frustrate it to rise against an established order. It is a method to publicize and draw attention to a cause. 1972 Munich, 1985 TWA flight, 9/11, attack on the Indian Parliament, 26/11 etc are some of the examples. Terrorism feeds on the hungry media which sensationalises the event at any cost. Treatment of terrorism defies the normal law and order mechanism of a state. It is an extra ordinary crime which requires extra ordinary measures to deal with it.

Terrorism has persisted all along in the recorded history. It all started with the expansionist states and civilizations like Egyptians, Greeks, Mongols, Muslims, Europeans and Americans in the twentieth century. Foreign rules and their departures left deep scars and divisions resulting in the present global unrest, tensions and greed. It has become glaring and intense ever since the advent of communication explosion, both electronic and aviation. Shrinking of the world adds to the greed.

From North Africa right up to Philippines, extending also in to Central Asia is one belt which clamours for Muslim rule/Caliphate which was demolished by the European invaders. Add to it is the western overbearing attitude in recent times. There is also the backlash in far off theatres resulting in globalization of the terror. Indian subcontinent is greatly affected by the Muslim terrorism and the backlash.

Terrorism acts are well planned and well rehearsed. These acts are neither impulsive nor ad hoc. The aims are well conceived and are normally not deviated. The terrorists are well trained over a period of time, even to the extent of training pilots formally. The process may involve selection of personnel, indoctrination, training and rehearsals and rewards. The planning is nearly always cellular with information voids between various components. In fact the operations have been corporatized with broad guidelines from the central leadership and franchisee type execution.

Democracy does not seem to be the panacea of all societal ills. In fact the democracy in the undeveloped and underdeveloped world is being exploited by the unscrupulous leaders elected by the poor, innocent and illiterate masses. The Communism and dictatorship is not all gone. They keep raising their head off and on through terrorism as alternative systems.

Why Terrorism

Terrorism is not a new phenomenon. Zealots, the Jewish terrorists in mid First century AD, were launching forays in the Roman cities and camps killing them and their collaborators *en masse* to cleanse the holy land. In India there were the Thugs between seventh and thirteen century who indulged in terrorism to please Goddess Kali. There are other examples during the French Revolution.

There is state terrorism, state sponsored terrorism or terrorism by the non state actors. Historically the violence by the state terrorism greatly surpasses the terrorism by the non state actors. Some of the examples are Lenin, Hitler and Mao, who killed 40 million plus, 35 million plus and 20 million plus respectively during their regimes. Today terrorism refers to non state actors either operating as a group or sponsored by a state and indulging in planned violence, notwithstanding the consequences to the target environment or on the perpetrators. Aim being to disrupt society, rupture public safety and spread fear and uncertainty. His actual aim is often beyond the immediate target. The magnitude of the consequences is only constrained by the logistics, technical knowhow and training, and not by the controllers and political considerations. He intends to cause fear, stress, depression, exhaustion, economic impact and loss of authority of the government to linger on for as long as possible. He is not so much concerned by the immediate and collateral damage as the long term impact. The terrorist wishes to be felt around the corner all the time.

There are two aspects, psychology of the terrorists and treatment of the victims of terror. What needs to be analysed is what makes the terrorist commit such heinous crimes as to kill *en masse* innocent people to include women, children and the old, and in some cases commit suicide to make the incident lethal. What is the motivation? It is the hammering of the person's mind that the job is noble and is the answer to the call of religion. The preaching is by the dedicated and proven teacher, the ulema, the fundamentalist hardliners, a colleague and the leader. The motivation is to become a martyr and go to heaven. Then is the lure for money that will be given if you survive and if you don't, to your loved ones. The entire system is portrayed as credible which has stood the test of time. The system is also seen and shown prevailing on a wide geographical canvas. The human resource is available in plenty in the third world, both qualified and semi literate.

Who are the perpetrators with such massive moral authority to order killing of the innocent and cause uncertainty in a nearly alien environment. These are the men and women who are convinced of a cause that must be eliminated at all costs for the sake of the society and the religion which are seen at grave risk. The reasons are both historical and current. Take the violence between the Muslims and the rest. There are historical religious reasons which were highlighted by the expansionist states in the medieval times and subsequent suppression and exploitation over the centuries.

Then was the industrial revolution which caused the world to shrink and gave rise to the phenomenon of the survival of the fittest. Might is right. How do the weak survive? Probably unconventional war was only affordable. The mechanics of this war has been discussed enough. A lot of money is needed to run the show. This money is available, accounted and unaccounted through sponsorship by the states, rich individuals, religious institutions, drugs, illicit means and also as part of the political process.

The third element is the flood of the markets with weapons, explosives and instruments of terror which are conceived and manufactured in the west. Their poor copies are manufactured in the third world countries, *albeit*, are effective for the purpose of terrorizing. These weapons are dual purpose and are traded by the west to the third world countries. Counter-terrorism has become a massive global industry involving governments at various levels; ranging from law and order agencies, counter-terror operations by the security forces and prosecution of the conventional military operations on the escalatory ladder. The same west now comes to the rescue of the third world countries. They provide them the same kind of weapons as they provided the terrorists, probably better at exorbitant profit. They also provide them the counter-terror training to fight their own creation. All this is engineered for greed and control of markets and natural resources. America's involvement in Afghanistan and creation of the Taliban is a classical example of this engineered cycle. Billions worth of weapons and equipment have been sold in the region and beyond. Thus the western countries are benefiting from both, the cause and effect of the terrorism.

The fourth element is the over bearing states, particularly in the west, who have triggered this uncontrolled chain reaction of terrorism. Let us take an example of the Russian invasion of Afghanistan in 1978. Americans moved in to oppose and safeguard their interests, but through proxy. Pakistan was involved with motivation of receiving military and civil aid from USA and other western countries. Saudis got involved to help their Pakistani brethren and also to spread Wahabism. More western nations joined in, which forced the Russians to withdraw leaving behind a vacuum. Hereafter it was free for all, the Americans, the European allies, Pakistanis and so on. A serious terror problem emerged for the Asians, for which the cause was Russia followed by America. Pakistan played the role of a surrogate, but suffered the most. The Indians get involved because the problem of Pakistan has to be externalized. The entire South Asia gets involved with ripple effect in Central and South East Asia. A serious digression from the poverty alleviation imperatives.

In the reaction, America suffered the 9/11, UK 7/7, 21/7, France 25/7, 18/10 and many more in Europe and other countries. Whistle has been blown for engagement of the west. Their own medicine is being administered to them in recent years. All efforts are being made in the reverse gear to carry the war to the developed world. The western nations must devise a method to extricate themselves and live contented. It is a tall order but well worth considering. While this book is being scripted, here is what Tony Blair has to say in a chat with TOI (Times of India):

> *"There are two major changes that have come home to me after I have left office. One is the shift of global power to east, to Asia, to countries like India and China. And west in the 21th century, including countries like mine will have to get used to the fact that we are going to have partners who will be equals, some times more than equals.*

It might be challenging for us actually, but we have to come to terms with that, and realize that in the end the geopolitics of the world has changed fundamentally, and for good. Secondly we have to acknowledge that the extremist threat is still there, it is real and it is not going away. We need to double our efforts to confront this. It is a global threat based on an ideology ...."

The third world also has to help itself. They should plan to come out of the technological dependence of the west. West is also beating the East and the Middle East with the stick of the democracy.

The system in its present form is not conducive to the peculiar quality of human resource in the third word. The leaders have to be visionary and dedicated. The uncertainty of the office and tenures diffuse the focus of the leaders. These tenures are seen as windows of opportunity by them. The leadership does not provide the right motivation to the bureaucracy, judiciary, scientists, police, armed forces and the business class. Out of frustration and need to survive they fall in line. The plans are not carried forward but are modified or scrapped with the change of leadership. All plans as such remain short term plans. Is democracy a system of consensus, if so it is a weak system in the third world, exploitable by its leaders and the west? The system of consensus makes the country porous to terrorism in all its forms and manifestations. The force with which the west propagates democracy in relation to all other forms of governance does not serve the concerned countries in an optimal manner. It allows the countries with low level of development to be exploited by the west to act as their tool. Other systems are not allowed to be examined. They are stigmatized. The prevailing systems need to be modified to suit the indigenous conditions. The corrupt must be brought to book without any protection from the Parliament and the governments. The third world countries must go proactive to serve their national interests now and in the long run.

Muslim Terrorism in South Asia

Over a billion people in the world follow the teaching of the Prophet Muhammad, who sincerely believe that His teachings are a divine message. Islam is a religious, political and cultural ideology followed by a large number of the Muslim sects, all following the Prophet. Islam is founded upon the fundamental principle that man, life, and universe are all the creations of the eternal, one and only one God who is known as Allah. It is not in the scope of the book to analyse whether terror is sanctified in Islam or not. But its goal is clear, it is to subjugate the world to itself or eliminate the infidel. It is also true that half the incidents of terror in the world are executed by the Muslims. Consequent to the acts of terror, more Muslims are killed than non Muslims. Yet all Muslims are not terrorists. Many of them reject the actions of the Muslims around the world. This moderate element gets subdued as Islam teaches world domination.

Islam is based entirely on what was revealed to Prophet Mohammad. The revelation has two forms. One form is the Quran, which comprises verses compiled into chapters. The wording and the meanings of the verses are written into the Quran exactly as revealed to Prophet Mohammad. The Quran was compiled and written during the life of the Prophet. The other part of the revelation is what is known in Arabic as the Sunnah, which comprises statements, actions, and endorsement of the Prophet. The Sunnah is also a revelation from God to the Prophet, except that the wording of the Sunnah is left to Prophet Mohammad. The Sunnah was compiled after the death of the Prophet based on written statements and verbal narrations. Hence, any view in Islam has to be validated by the Quran and the Sunnah.

Muslim terrorism in twentieth and twenty first century aims at achieving varying political ends like ending American military presence in the Middle East and the Arabian Peninsula, over throwing infidel regimes, and stopping

American support for Israel. It also aims to propagate Islamic culture, society and values in contrast to the western values and culture.

Muslim Terrorism is the direct offshoot of the fanatical Islamic cult known as Wahabism, which runs Mecca and believes in the destruction of non Islamic cultures and is financed by Saudi Arabia. The 9/11was executed by nineteen hijackers of whom fifteen were from Saudi Arabia. *Al Qaeda* was founded and run by a Saudi, Osama Bin Laden, who, as a teenager, joined the Wahhabi sect and served as the religious police to enforce sharia. The actions of Saudi Arabia, the centre of Islam, leads to the conclusion that Islam encourages terrorism.

Wahabis can garner the Saudi wealth and sponsor extremist mosques and educational institutions on a global scale. They created *al Qaeda* and radicalised the Taliban. They wield a great deal of influence on the extremist groups across the globe and sponsor Islamic radicalisation programs. Wahabis are protected by the Saudi state. Why the Western powers are not addressing the state of Saudi Arabia is another matter.

The Tablighi Jama'at (TJ) is probably one of the most popular and widespread missionary and revival Islamic movement in the world today. It has spread to over 165 countries and is active in almost every country where Muslims live. It is not a rigid philosophy, but is dynamic to the extent of subtle changes in emphasis and direction that are often not visible. But it sees the reform of Muslim society on the lines of the dictates of the Sharia as its ultimate goal. Reportedly, this missionary organization is becoming radicalized, and is being used as a cover to mask travel and activities of terrorists including members of the Taliban and *al Qaeda*. The immediate concern of the TJ is not to capture state power and the establishment of an Islamic state, but rather the moral reform of individual Muslims in to true Muslims. State power will follow. It is a bottom up approach than top down.

The Soviet invasion of Afghanistan led to convergence of the Muslim fundamentalists from across the world under the patronage of the USA, with Pakistan acting as the main coordinator. With the eviction of Russia from Afghanistan, the jihadis and the world realised the potential of the Muslim militants. This war seems to be the beginning of the present Muslim terrorism and emergence of *al Qaeda* and Taliban.

The territories of South Asian countries of Afghanistan, Pakistan and Bangladesh are being used for nurturing as well as providing safe haven to Muslim terrorists, in that order of intensity. India is a victim. Numerically India has the largest Muslim population in South Asia; it suffered over 40,000 killed so far, a large number of them being Muslims. While Afghanistan, Pakistan and Bangladesh are weak democracies with military and external support as major elements, India enjoys a stable democracy with a growth rate of around 8.6 per cent.

After eviction of the Soviets from Afghanistan, the terror outfits were dumped by those who created or supported them and the aid to Pakistan was reduced substantially. Taliban captured Kabul and most of Afghanistan in 1996. Their rule was harsh, rather primitive and ancient Islamist. Soon after 9/11, the Muslim terrorists were to be taught a lesson and annihilated. Taliban were ousted from power in 2001and multinational forces from west were inducted in Afghanistan with a clear sphere of influence in Pakistan. Pakistan now was a reluctant partner but had to go along despite internal pressures. Situation in Afghanistan became chaotic with multiplicity of the terror factions, some colluding and others colliding. *al Qaeda* and Taliban, however, consolidated when Iraq front was opened and attention of the allies was divided. Talibanisation was to include the Central Asian Republics and beyond to Pakistan's advantage and its image in the Islamic world.

Pakistan now had to deal with three broad areas of violence - those targeting the west in Afghanistan, those indulging in domestic violence and those operating against India. Resultantly, Pakistan had no choice but to be soft on the terror groups and yet strike them either to deal with internal violence or at the instance of USA. Pakistan's writ in its own country is rather compromising.

The situation in Bangladesh deteriorated after 9/11. When Afghanistan and Pakistan came under pressure, a good number of terrorists found Bangladesh as safe haven. Using religion for political gains, the Bangladeshi society has highly radicalized in concert with the happenings in Pakistan and Afghanistan. Notwithstanding recent anti terror actions of the Bangladesh Government at the request of India, Bangladesh society, even though moderate, is capable of supportig Islamic militancy. India is the prime target, the anti-US and anti-west feelings are also loud.

Islamic terrorism in India is a factor of terrorism in the neighbourhood except Kashmir, where Pakistan makes a major physical and mental dent. Some youth goes astray under temptations and go to Pakistan and Afghanistan for weapons training and religious discourses in the madrassas. The problem in Kashmir is serious. Pakistan has made it an issue of national import.

Nuclear Terrorism in South Asia

South Asia has two declared nuclear weapon states, Pakistan and India. While Pakistan remains in a constant state of instability due to indigenous terrorism and terrorism as state policy, India is a stable democracy.

Pakistan

Pakistan nuclear infrastructure at a glance is tabulated below:

Facility	Status	Safeguards
Mines and Processing		
Baghalchar	Uranium mine; closed	No
Dera Ghazi Khan	Uranium mining and milling; operating Uranium conversion (UF6); operating	No
Uranium and Nuclear Mineral Resource Development, Lahore	Runs ore pilot reprocessing plant; Production of reactor fuel bundles.	
CHASHMA/Kudian	Fuel fabrication; operating	
Heavy Water Production		
Multan	operating	No
Karachi	operating	No
Weapons R&D		
Khan Research Laboratories, Kahuta	Pakistan's main nuclear weapons laboratory as well as an emerging centre for long-range missile development. The primary Pakistani fissile-material production facility, employing gas centrifuge enrichment technology to produce HEU.	No

Facility	Status	Safeguards
Wah	Enrichment plant; status not known	No
Chagai Hills	Nuclear test site	No
Research Reactors		
PARR-1 Rawalpindi	Light water, originally HEU, modified to use LEU, 10 MWt; operating	Yes
PARR- 2 Rawalpindi	Light water, HEU, 30 KWt; operating	Yes
Khushab	Heavy water and uranium research reactor, also for production of plutonium and tritium for advanced compact warheads. Two more plutonium producing plants being completed.	No
Power Reactors		
Karachi (KANUPP)	Heavy water, natural uranium, 137 Mwe; operating; Also a site survey has reportedly been completed for the construction of a 300 megawatt KANUPP II nuclear power plant.	Yes
CHASHMA-1(CHASNUPP-1)	Light water, LEU, 310 Mwe; operating	Yes
CHASHMA-2 (CHASNUPP- 2)	Light water, LEU, 310/600 MWe/under construction with China's assistance; likely completion 2011	Yes
Uranium Enrichment		
Kahuta	See above under 'Weapons and R&D'	No
Sihala	Experimental scale ultracentrifuge facility; operating	No

Facility	Status	Safeguards
Golra	Ultracentrifuge reportedly being used as test facility; status not known	No
Wah	Enrichment plant; status not known	-
Plutonium Extraction		
CHASHMA, a possible site		Yes
New Labs, PINSTECH Rawalpindi	Pilot scale Hot Cell facility; 20 kg per year	No
PINSTECH, Rawalpindi	The Pakistan Institute of Science and Technology is responsible for fuel cycle research and development including nuclear materials, metallurgy and fuel development. The New Labs Reprocessing Plant, a not-yet-operational plutonium and solvent extraction plant, is also located here.	No
Isa Khel	Plutonium milling; planned	No

Source : Carnegie Endowment for International Peace, Tracking Nuclear Proliferation

Pakistan's Nuclear-Related Facilities

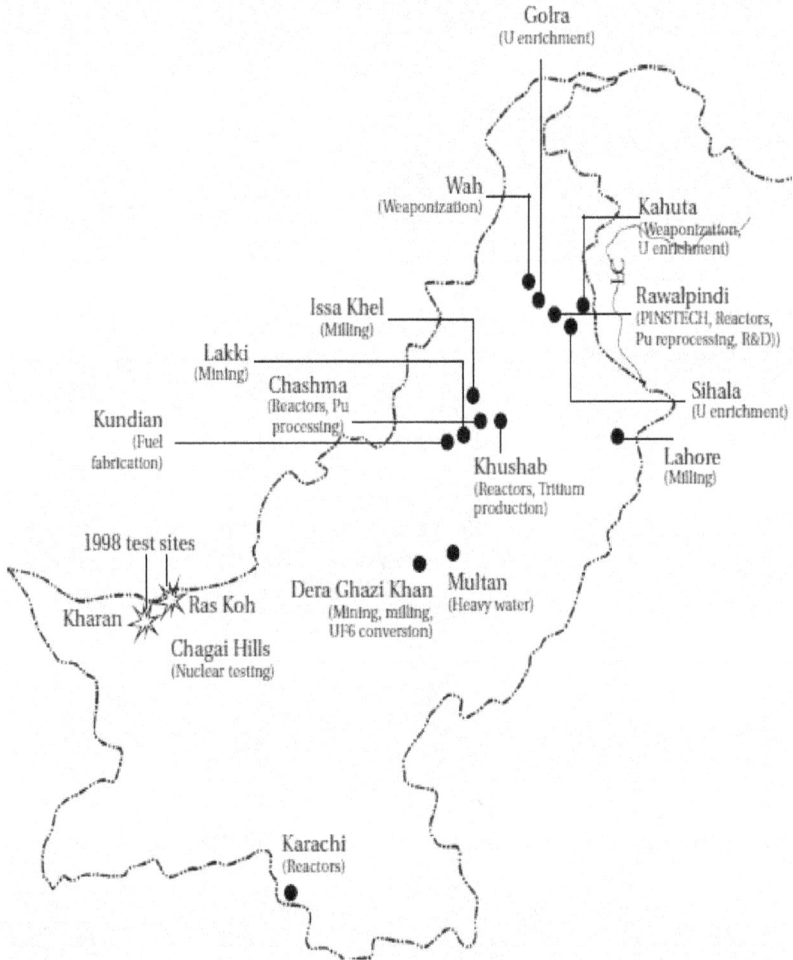

Golra
(U enrichment)

Wah
(Weaponization)

Kahuta
(Weaponization,
U enrichment)

Issa Khel
(Milling)

Rawalpindi
(PINSTECH, Reactors,
Pu reprocessing, R&D))

Lakki
(Mining)

Chashma
(Reactors, Pu
processing)

Sihala
(U enrichment)

Kundian
(Fuel
fabrication)

Khushab
(Reactors, Tritium
production)

Lahore
(Milling)

1998 test sites

Dera Ghazi Khan
(Mining, milling,
UF6 conversion)

Multan
(Heavy water)

Kharan

Ras Koh

Chagai Hills
(Nuclear testing)

Karachi
(Reactors)

Uranium development

Uranium development is overseen by the PAEC's Atomic Energy Minerals Centre Lahore, which also houses a pilot mill. PAEC has finalised a deal to acquire 6,000 tons of reasonably assured reserves of uranium by 2011 to fulfill one-third requirement of fuel for producing 8,800 MW of nuclear power in 2030. It is estimated that 350 tons of yellow cake (U3O8) will be required annually to meet the requirement of the planned nuclear power plants.

*The Baghalchar uranium mine, near Dera Ghazi Khan and a co-located mill, could produce up to 30 metric tons of yellow cake per year but has exhausted. It is now being used as an industrial and nuclear waste dumping ground.

There is a uranium mine at Qabul Khel in the NWFP with milling site at Issa Khel nearby, is possibly operative already*. A new uranium field has been developed by the PAEC at Tumman Laghari in the Dera Ghanzi Khan region of South Punjab. There are other efforts to increase the uranium production in Dera Ghazi Khan, Wahi Pandi; Karunuk (Sehwan); Rehman Dhora (Aamri) and the Shanawah Deposit, Karak,

Nuclear Power

Pakistan has Karachi Nuclear Power Plant (KANUPP), Chashma Nuclear Power Plant-1 (CHASNUPP-I) and CHASNUPP-II, which are operational; CHASNUPP-III and CHASNUPP-IV are being set up.

Pakistan's only uranium hexaflouride (UF6) plant located at Dera Ghazi Khan, is unsafeguarded. An un-safeguarded fuel fabrication facility is located at Kundian near the Chashma reactor.

Uranium Enrichment and Plutonium Extraction

Pakistan had no fissile material to produce a credible nuclear deterrent, delivery means, technology or the command and control elements. Not being a signatory of the Non Proliferation Treaty (NPT), covert means had to be adopted to acquire nuclear wherewithal.

---

*Andrew Koch and Jennifer Topping, Pakistan's Nuclear Weapons Program - A Status Report

Dr. Abdul Qadeer Khan, a German-trained metallurgist, brought with him knowledge of gas centrifuges and uranium enrichment technology that he had acquired while he was in URENCO Uranium Enrichment Plant in the Netherlands and from elsewhere in Europe. He was put in charge of building, equipping and operating Pakistan's Kahuta facility, which was established in 1976. Under Khan's directions, Pakistan set up an extensive clandestine network in order to obtain and develop uranium enrichment capabilities. Kahuta is the hub of Islamabad's nuclear weapons program and contains an un-safeguarded uranium enrichment plant using estimated 10,000 centrifuges. The plant can produce 55 to 95 kg of HEU per year (4-5 nuclear devices). Kahuta is most likely the site where HEU is formed into weapon cores. In addition to Kahuta, Pakistan has two smaller centrifuge facilities at Golra (ultracentrifuge facility for advance testing purposes before installation at Kahuta) and Sihala (reported 54 ultra-centrifuges cascade for testing and training).

The heavy water research reactor at Khushab is a prime institution of Pakistan's program for production of plutonium and tritium for advanced compact warheads. This facility, like that at Kahuta, is not subject to IAEA inspections. Khushab, with a capacity reported at between 40-50 MWt had gone critical in early 1998. The Khushab reactor provides Pakistan the ability to produce enough plutonium each year to fabricate at least one bomb. In support of the Khushab reactor, Pakistan has an un-safeguarded heavy water production facility with a capacity of 13 MT per year at Multan. In addition to Kahuta, spent fuel could also be extracted from other research or commercial reactors, even though they are under safeguards. The two small research reactors, called the Pakistan Atomic Research Reactors (PARR-I and PARR-II), at PINSTECH, are the centre piece of Pakistan's open nuclear research and development program. PARR-I is a 10 MWt pool type research reactor and has been converted to burn 20 per cent LEU fuel. PARR-I may also be producing tritium for advanced nuclear weapons. PARR-II is 27-30 kilowatt thermal (KWt) pool-type research reactor, went critical in late 1989.

In late 2006, the US Institute for Science and International Security reported construction of a new plutonium reactor at the Khushab nuclear site. The reactor is deemed to be large enough and assessed to produce enough plutonium to produce 40 to 50 nuclear weapons (?) a year.

*Command and Control

National Command Authority (NCA)

The NCA is responsible for policy formulation and will exercise development and employment control over all strategic forces and strategic organizations.

Employment Control Committee (ECC)

The head of the Government chairs the ECC. Other members include the ministers of foreign affairs, defense, interior; the Chairman JCSC, the three service chiefs; the Director General of the SPD, and technical advisors as required.

Development Control Committee (DCC)

The DCC also controls the development of the Strategic assets. The head of the government chairs DCC. The members include Chairman JCSC, the three service chiefs, DG of SPD, representatives of strategic community and scientists.

Strategic Plans Division (SPD)

Acts as the secretariat for the NCA and is responsible for establishing a reliable command, control, communications, computer, and intelligence network. The SPD is located in the joint services headquarters at Rawalpindi and is led by a senior army officer.

---

*Associated Press of Pakistan, 3 February 2000

In addition, there is a partially built plutonium reprocessing plant at Chashma that was started by France, but abandoned in 1979. Some US intelligence officials believe the facility is being completed, either indigenously or with Chinese assistance, and may be part of activities undertaken at 'New Laboratories'. The plutonium plant may be operational already but exact status is not known.

'New Laboratories', the experimental-scale plutonium reprocessing plant, located at PINSTECH, is capable of handling spent nuclear fuel from the first Khushab heavy water reactor and produces 10 to 20 kg of plutonium per year (1-2 weapons). 'New Laboratories' are an un-safeguarded facility. Bringing into operation a reprocessing facility at Chashma would significantly increase Pakistan's plutonium separation capability when clubbed with heavy water reactor at Khushab.

Pakistan appears to possess around 90 nuclear weapons of various yields. According to Pakistani authorities, these weapons are not kept assembled. The fissile cores are stored separately from the non-nuclear explosives initiators, and that the delivery means are kept unarmed.

Nuclear Weapons Security

Pakistan is believed to maintain tight control over its nuclear assets, and have instituted special security measures. Nonetheless, the world is concerned about their security. The precise threat, however, to Pakistan's stability or its nuclear weapons complex is difficult to forecast.

The Taliban in NWFP, FATA and part of Balochistan is in fair control of these areas. The Pakistani military and ISI are maintaining strong ties with the Taliban and *al Qaeda*. Depending on the course of the war in Afghanistan and the region, the relationship and ties may take a turn. Taliban is a force to reckon with, but not disciplined as the regular forces are.

Pakistan has the capability to produce both plutonium and HEU for nuclear weapons. Its main uranium enrichment facilities are at the Khan Research Laboratories at Kahuta. Pakistan also has another enrichment facility near Wah that the U.S. Government calls the Gadwal uranium enrichment plant. It may have other production-scale facilities. Pakistan also operates smaller enrichment facilities at the Sihala and Golra ultracentrifuge plants. These sites would be expected to have HEU and LEU stocks. The physical security arrangements at these facilities should be rigorous.

Pakistan operates the Khushab reactor, which is estimated to generate about 50 megawatts of power, large enough to produce plutonium for a few nuclear weapons per year. Separation of the plutonium is reported to occur at New Labs at Rawalpindi. This plant, next to PINSTEC, is large enough to handle all the irradiated fuel from the Khushab reactor. The storage arrangements for the separated plutonium are unknown, although they would include vaults and other security procedures.

Pakistan maintains facilities to produce metallic fissile material and shape the metal into nuclear weapons components. Such facilities would have fissile material in liquid, powder, and solid forms. Other facilities produce non-nuclear components and at least partially assembled nuclear weapons. The location of these facilities has not been reported extensively, although at least some of these facilities are located near Wah. The storage sites may well be in military bases.

To enhance the operational readiness, the fissile core and the rest of the device could be stored separately in vaults. The variation could also be that the weapon minus the fissile core is mounted on a delivery vehicle, and the fissile core is stored separately.

It is unknown if Pakistan has coded switch devices integral to its delivery systems (as opposed to the actual warheads). Such switches would act as hardware "gatekeepers" for ballistic missiles or aircraft. The need for a special code to arm and fire the missile or drop a gravity bomb would impede the ability of unauthorized personnel to carry out a nuclear strike. Such devices may be easier to master than PALs.

Little is known of the transportation arrangements for sensitive nuclear items in Pakistan. The type of transport containers or vehicles, or the extent of armed escorts, is unknown. The security of the nuclear material during move is of paramount importance. Insider threats could be a major problem.

Groups or individuals may violate security rules for a variety of reasons, including profit, settling a grudge, or religious or ideological motives. Violators may try to gain control over sensitive items for their own use or to transfer these items to non-state actors.

Shaun Gregory, a professor at Bradford University in UK, said in a paper published by the Combating Terrorism Center of the US Military Academy at West Point, that there were at least three known attacks on Pakistani nuclear facilities.

The first attack took place on the nuclear missile storage facility at Sargodha on November 1, 2007; the second was the attack on Pakistan's nuclear airbase at Kamra by a suicide bomber on December 10, 2007; and perhaps most significant was the August 20, 2008 attack when Pakistani Taliban suicide bombers blew up several entry points to one of the armament complexes at the Wah Cantonment, considered one of the main Pakistan's nuclear weapons assembly sites.

The threat of theft or diversion of fissile material or nuclear weapons falls into the following general areas:

- Outsider Threat—The possibility that armed individuals or groups from outside a facility gain access and steal weapons, weapon components or fissile material.

- Insider Threat—The possibility that individuals who work at a facility will remove fissile material, nuclear weapons, or weapon components without proper authorization.

- Insider/Outsider Threat—The possibility that insiders and outsiders conspire to obtain fissile materials, weapons, or weapon components.

- If Pakistan suffers extreme instability or civil war, threats to its strategic nuclear assets will substantially increase.

- Loss of Central Control of Storage Facilities—Clear lines of communication and control over weapons, weapon components, and fissile material may be broken or lost entirely.

- Coup—In the most extreme case, a coup takes place and the new regime attempts to gain control of the nuclear complex. Foreign governments may intervene to prevent hostile forces from seizing the strategic nuclear assets. The situation in that case will be messy in South Asia.

The security of nuclear weapons and the connected components entails physical security, security and verification of personnel, security of codes and prevention of unauthorized mating. In the current situation, Pakistan must also increasingly worry that experts from the nuclear complex could steal sensitive information or assist nuclear weapons programs of terrorist groups. The information could include classified nuclear weapons manufacturing data, exact storage locations of weapons or fissile material, security and access control arrangements, or operational details about the weapons.

India's Nuclear Facilities at a glance are shown on the map below:

Atomic Energy Establishment in India

SRINAGAR (Jammu & Kashmir)
Nuclear Research Laboratory (BARC)

GULMARG (Jammu & Kashmir)
High Altitude Research Laboratory (BARC)

NARORA (Uttar Pradesh)
Narora Atomic Power Station (NPCIL)

TURAMDIH (Jharkhand)
Uranium Mine (UCIL)

KOLKATA (West Bengal)
• Variable Energy Cyclotron Centre
• Regional Radiation Medicine Centre (VECC)
• Radio-pharmaceutical Laboratory (BRIT)
• Saha Institute of Nuclear Physis

AHMEDABAD (Gujarat)
Institute for Plasma Research

KASAN (Delhi)
Seismic Array Station (BARC)

BANDUHURANG (Jharkhand)
Uranium Mine (UCIL)

BARODA (Gujarat)
Heavy Water Plant (HWB)

DELHI
Radio-pharmaceutical Laboratories (BRIT)

DIBRUGARH (Assam)
Radio-Immunoassay Centre (BRIT)

KAKRAPAR (Gujarat)
kakrapar Atomic Power Station (NPCIL)

MOUNT ABU (Rajasthan)
for Astrophysical Science (BARC)

ALLAHABAD (Uttar Pradesh)
Harish-Chandra Research Institute

RAWATBHATA (Rajasthan)
• Rajasthan Atomic Power Station 1-4 (NPCIL)
• Rajasthan Atomic Power Project 5&6 (NPCIL)
• Heavy Water Plant-Kota (HWB)
• RAPPCOF-Kota (BRIT)

NARWAPAHAR (Jharkhand)
Uranium Mine (UCIL)

JADUGUDA/BHATIN (Jharkhand)
• Uranium Corporation of India (HQ)
• Uranium Mill & Mines (UCIL)

INDORE (Madhya Pradesh)
Raja Ramanna Centre for Advanced Technology
INDUS-1&2

TARAPUR (Maharashtra)
• Tarapur Atomic Power Station (NPCIL)
• Tarapur Atomic Power Project 3&4 (NPCIL)
• WIP / SSSF (BARC)
• Power Reactor Fuel Reprocessing Plant (BARC)
• Advanced Fuel Fabrication Facility (BARC)
• General Services Organisation

HAZIRA (Gujarat)
Heavy Water Plant (HWB)

NASIK (Maharashtra)
KRUSHAK (BARC)

THAL (Maharashtra)
Heavy Water Plant (HWB)

TALCHER (Orrisa)
Heavy Water Plant (HWB)
D2EHPA Plant

CHHATRAPUR (Orrisa)
Orrisa Sand Complex /
Thorium Plant (IRE)

BHUBANESHWAR (Orrisa)
Institute of Physics

MANUGURU (Andhra Pradesh)
Heavy Water Plant (HWB)

MUMBAI (Maharashtra)
• Nuclear Power Corporation of India Ltd. (HQ)
• Indian Rare Earths Ltd. (HQ)
• Heavy Water Board (HQ)
• ISOMED Plant (BRIT)
• Bhabha Atomic Research Centre
• Radiation Medicine Centre (BARC)
• BRNS / HBNI / NBHM (HQ)
• TIFR / TMC / AEES (HQ)
• DPS / DCS&EM (HQ)

GAURIBIDANUR (Karantaka)
Seismic Station (BARC)

HYDERABAD (Andhra Pradesh)
• Electronics Corporation of India Ltd. (HQ)
• Nuclear Fuel Complex (HQ)
• Jonaki Laboratory (BRIT)
• Centre for Compositional Characterisation pf Materials (BARC)
• Atomic Minerals Directorate for Exploration & Research (HQ)

NAVI MUMBAI (Maharashtra)
• Board of Radiation & Isotope Technology (HQ)
• Radio-pharmaceutical Laboratories (BRIT)
• Radiation Processing Plant (BRIT)
• Labelled Coupounds Laboratory (BRIT)
• Radiation Equipment Production Facility (BRIT)
• Beryllium Plant (BARC)
• Electron Beam Centre (BARC)
• ACTREC (TMC)

MYSORE (Karantaka)
Rare Materials Project (BARC)

BANGALORE (Karnataka)
Radio-pharmaceutical Laboratories (BRIT)

Chennai (Tamil Nadu)
• Institute of Mathematical Science

KALPAKKAM (Tamil Nadu)
• Madras Atomic Power Station (NPCIL)
• Bhartiya Nabhikiya Vidyut Nigam Ltd. (HQ)
• Indira Gandhi Centre for Atomic Research
• PFBR project (IGCAR)
• Nuclear Desalination Demonstration Plant (BARC)
• Kalpakkam Fuel Reprocessing Plant (BARC)
• General Services Organisation

KAIGA (Karnataka)
• Kaiga Generating Station 1&2 (NPCIL)
• Kaiga Atomic Power Project 3&4 (NPCIL)

TUTICORIN (Tamil Nadu)
Heavy Water Plant (HWB)

UDYOGMANDAL (ALWAYE) (Kerala)
Rare Earths Plant (IRE)

PALAYAKAYAL (Tamil Nadu)
New Zirconium Sponge Plant (NFC)

CHAVARA (Kerala)
Minerals Separation Plant (IRE)

KUDANKULAM (Tamil Nadu)
Kudankulam Atomic Power Project (NPCIL)

KOLLAM (Kerala)
Low Radiation Research Laboratory (BARC)

MANAVALAKURUCHI (Tamil Nadu)
Minerals Separation Plant (IRE)

Source: http://www.dae.gov.in/publ/indmap.htm

Perusal of the nuclear establishment layout will reveal that the establishments have been sited keeping the missile threat in view, need based and some consideration of internal security. In J&K there are only small research laboratories. In the Northeast, there is only one small centre. Very few establishments are there in the Naxal areas. In any case the Naxals are not anti national. They are trying to correct the internal social order and draw attention of the Central Government.

There are no indiginous threats to the nuclear establishments in India barring state sponsored external threats. The establishments are guarded physically, electronically and through codes. Some reports of accidents and nuclear sabotage have exposed weakness at regulatory mechanism, casting doubts upon their capability to avert proliferation, nuclear accidents and pilferage. The threat of pilferage of fissile material or components must be continuously updated. No comparison with Pakistan can be drawn.

In South Asia the threat of pilferage of the fissile material by the non state actors is real and maximum security measures must be co-opted in the nuclear fields. The international community needs to step in either directly through bilateral arrangements or through the UN.

Terrorism in India

Terrorism in India is primarily attributable to illiteracy, poverty, unemployment, disparity, political injustice, religious reasons, historical baggage and soft handling. The regions with long term terrorist activities today are Jammu and Kashmir, Naxalite areas in central India and the Northeastern states. These are being discussed in subsequent chapters separately.

Other Violence

Bihar

Existence of certain insurgent groups like the CPI-ML, Peoples War and MCC, is a major concern as they frequently attack local policemen and politicians. The root cause of the militant activities in the state is the disparity among different caste groups. Due to caste based divisive politics in the state, land reforms were never implemented properly. This led to growing alienation among the low caste. This also led to taking up lands of rich by force and killing the high caste people. The high caste people resorted to use of force by forming their own army *Ranvir Sena* to take on the naxalites. The Police remained a mute spectator to the killings as it lacked the wherewithal and motivation. There is also a strong suspicion that Bihar is also being used as a transit point for small-arms, fake currency, drugs, and terrorists entering through Nepal and Bangladesh.

With the backdrop of caste politics, high crime rate, low literacy levels at 47 per cent, poor healthcare and record of human development, Bihar state is now making all-round progress under the Chief Minister Nitish Kumar in his second tenure commencing November 2010. He has been credited with tackling crime and achieving an impressive annual economic growth rate of 11.3 per cent during his first five years in office commencing 2005. A fair amount of improvement in the law and order and counter terrorism is expected in the coming years.

Punjab

The insurgency intensified during 1980s when the movement for independence turned into widespread violence and led to fortification of the sacred Golden Temple in 1984. Operation Blue Star was conducted which involved flushing out of the militants from the complex. Eighty three army personnel were killed and 249 injured. Militant casualties were 493 killed and 86 injured. Indira Gandhi was assassinated as retaliation to operation Blue Star, which resulted in widespread anti-Sikh riots, especially in New Delhi. In 1985, Sikh terrorists struck an Air India flight from Canada to India, killing all 329 people on board.

The movement was crushed by effective counter insurgency and counter terror action by police backed by the army. The movement was short lived because it lacked a convincing stand and widespread support. Marginal simmering, however, continues by organisations like Babbar Khalsa International, Khalistan Commando Force, Khalistan Liberation Force and Khalistan Zindabad Force. Punjab is peaceful and progressive.

Mumbai

Mumbai has been the most preferred target for the militants from Pakistan. Since 1993, a series of attacks have led to over 700 killings. The most recent and unprecedented attacks of 26 November 2008, where two of the prime hotels, a landmark train station and a Jewish Chabad house, were brutally sieged. This was virtually attacking the Indian state.

New Delhi

On 13 December 2001 the Parliament of India was attacked resulting in a 45 minute pitched battle in which 9 policemen, a parliament staffer and all the five terrorists were also killed and were identified as Pakistani nationals.

Three explosions on 29 October 2005 killed more than 60 people and injured at least 200 others. It was followed by 5 bomb blasts on 13 September 2008.

Religious Violence

Ram Janam Bhumi/Babri Masjid structure, believed by the Hindus to have been built over the birthplace of the Hindu deity Ram, was demolished by Hindu *kar sevaks* on 6 December 1992. This action caused great anger in the Muslim community resulting in religious riots and 1200 deaths. Reprisals against Hindu minorities also occurred in Pakistan and Bangladesh, and other parts of India. 500 people died in Bombay. It is estimated that almost 200,000 people were displaced in the aftermath of the demolition and the resultant riots.

In the continuing violence, in 2002, a train burning incident took place in Gujrat. The coach, which was occupied by Hindu *kar sevaks*, returning from Ayodhya was set on fire resulting in death of 58 Hindu pilgrims. The fire was alleged to have been started by a Muslim mob, however an investigative panel led by Justice U C Banerjee claimed that the fire was accidental. This report was declared a sham report by Gujrat High Court and its finding and recommendations were not accepted in February 2011, special court convicted 31 people for the offence. In retaliation, the toll was around 1,500 dead. In 2005 elements of, Lashkar-e-Tayyiba attacked the disputed structure but were gunned down. In 2009 the Bharatiya Janata Party (BJP) released their Manifesto, again promising to build Ram Mandir at the disputed site.

A series of blasts took place across the holy city of Varanasi in 2006 resulting in the death of 28 and over 100 injured. Another low intensity bomb exploded in Varanasi in 2010 killing one. There have been more attacks on Hindu temples and Hindus by Muslim militants. Prominent among them are the Chamba massacre in 1998, the attacks on Raghunath temple Jammu in 2002 and attack on Akshardham temple in Gujrat in 2002 resulting in many deaths and injuries. In September 2008, Swami Laxmanananda, a popular regional Hindu Guru in Orissa, was murdered along with four of his disciples by unknown assailants.

More Religious Violence

In recent years, there has been a sharp increase in violent attacks on Christians, often perpetrated by Hindu fundamentalists. In Orissa, starting 2007 through 2008, there have been attacks on Christians, resulting in deaths and destruction of property including churches. Foreign Christian missionaries have also been targeted. The rise of anti-Christian violence has been allegedly linked to Vishwa

Hindu Parishad, Bajrang Dal, and Rashtriya Swayamsevak Sangh. The violence has also spread to Chattisgarh, Andhra Pradesh, Tamil Nadu and Kerala. However, there is some dialogue between the Sangh Parivar and the Christian community to resolve issues amicably.

Religion also plays a role in reinforcing ethnic divides among the militant separatist movements in Northeast India. National Liberation Front of Tripura (NLFT) seeks to convert all tribals in the state of Tripura, who are mostly Hindu or Buddhist, to Christianity. According to the Government of Tripura, the Baptist Church of Tripura is involved in supporting the NLFT.

Ethnic Cleansing of Kashmiri Pandits

In Kashmir, approximately 300 Kashmiri Pandits were killed between 1989 and 1990. In early 1990, all Hindus were asked by the militants to leave Kashmir or face death. Consequently, between 250,000 and 300,000 Kashmiri Pandits have migrated from Kashmir. The proportion of Kashmiri Pandits has declined from about 15 per cent in 1947 to, by some estimates, less than 0.1 per cent.

Hindu Fundamentalism

There is practically no history of Hindu terror. Hinduism is not a "one Prophet, one Book" religion like Islam and Christianity. Recent events (2005-2010) like Malegaon blasts, Mecca Masjid bombing, Samjhauta Express bombings and the Ajmer Sharif Dargah blast in India may well be attributed to some Hindus but only on the instance of Muslim fundamentalists supported by ISI. ISI targets moderate Muslims in India in addition to terrorism indiscriminately. The possibility of Hindu retaliation to the Muslim terror, however, cannot be ruled out in the future.

Northeastern India

Northeastern states comprise of seven states, also known as *the seven sisters* - *Assam, Meghalaya, Tripura, Arunachal Pradesh, Mizoram, Manipur, and Nagaland. The location of these states itself is part reason for them to be a hot bed of militancy. This region shares porous borders with China in the north, Myanmar in the east, Bangladesh in the southwest and Bhutan to the northwest. The region also assumes strategic importance as it shares approximately 4,500 km long international border with its four neighbours and is connected to the Indian mainland by a tenuous 22 km wide corridor at Siliguri.

These states accuse the Central Government of ignoring their development, as such, demand - ranging from secession to autonomy, self determination and special rights for their distinct identity. There are also ethnic and territorial disputes between Manipur and Nagaland. Because of anti national activities, insurgency and acts of terrorism, the following outfits from Northeast India have been proscribed:

- National Socialist Council of Nagaland - Isak-Muivah (NSCN-IM)

- Naga National Council-Federal (NNCF)

- National Socialist Council of Nagaland – Khaplang, NSCN (K)

- United Liberation Front of Asom (ULFA)

- People's Liberation Army (Manipur)

- Kanglei Yawol Kanna Lup (KYKL)

- National Democratic Front of Bodoland

---

*Articles 371A, 371B, 371C, 371G and 371H of the Constitution of India, in respect of Nagaland, Assam, Manipur, Mizoram and Arunachal Pradesh respectively pertain to the Special Provisions with regard to these States (Appendix)

- People's Revolutionary Party of Kangleipak (PREPAK)

- United National Liberation Front (UNLF)

- All Tripura Tiger Forces (ATTF)

- National Liberatrion Front of Tripura (NLFT)

- Kangleipak Communist Party (KCP)

- Manipur People's Liberation Front (MPLF)

- Revolutionary People's Front (RPF in Manipur)

- Achik National Volunteer Council (ANVC in Meghalaya)

Nagaland

There are about twenty tribes, who are commonly known as Nagas, but were never homogenous. Christianised in early 20th century, they preserved their distinct cultural tradition, dialect, custom and system of governance. Naga Hills became an integral part of British India in early 20th century, when all the rival tribes came under unified administrative control of the British. The British befriended the Nagas through Christian missionaries but encouraged their primitive psyche and isolation from rest of India.

The Naga National Council (NNC) submitted a memorandum to the Cabinet Mission in 1946 and demanded a separate state comprising of Naga inhabited areas of Nagaland, Assam, Arunachal Pradesh and Myanmar. NNC declared independence of Naga Hills on August 14, 1947. Angami Zapu Phizo took the lead role in this revolt, which however was suppressed by the Government. This was the beginning of the Naga insurgency. Phizo escaped to East Pakistan in December 1956, from where he migrated to London and continued supporting the secessionist movement in Nagaland till his death in London in 1990.

The National Socialist Council of Nagaland (Isak-Muivah) or NSCN (IM) continues to demand an independent Nagaland. Nagaland was formally declared as sixteenth state of Indian Union on December 1, 1963.

With a ban imposed on NNC, Nagaland Federal Government (NFG) and other militant outfits in 1972 by the Government of India, followed by strong counter insurgency measures, the insurgents were compelled to negotiate. Some of the rebel leaders who had joined political parties helped in the process of negotiations. The representatives of insurgents signed Shillong Accord in 1975 with Government of India by accepting Indian Constitution, and a sizeable section of China trained insurgents surrendered with arms to the security forces. The Government, on the other hand, released the arrested rebels and suspended counter insurgency operations. A section of hardcore militants, however, rejected the Shillong Accord. Their leaders Issac Swu Muivah and Khaplang formed a new underground party namely Nationalist Socialist Council of Nagalim (NSCN) in late 1970s with Isak Chisi, S.S.Khaplang and T.Muivah as Chairman, Vice-Presient and General Secretary respectively. They maintained the old stand of independence and revived hostilities. By late 1980s the NSCN split into two groups, one led by Issac and Muivah called NSCN (IM) and another by Khaplang called NSCN (K).

A Cease-Fire Agreement was signed between the Government of India and the NSCN (IM) in 1997 which received widespread approval and support. Terrorist outfits such as the Nagaland National Council-Federal (NNC-F) and the NSCN (K) also welcomed the development. The cease fire has been extended on yearly basis and is still in force in 2011.

There has been decline in violence during 2009-2010. This has been possible as a result of decrease in inter-factional violence between the NSCN (IM) and the NSCN (K), the success of the cease fire mechanism, talks with the Government of India and the civil society efforts. The Forum for Naga Reconciliation (FNR), an organization comprising the churches and the civil society groups, which was established in February 2008, had a role to play in controlling the violence. The FNR has been advising the general public to fly white flags on their houses and use stickers on their vehicles - 'A Journey of Common Hope'. This is a significant development as for the first time the leaders of two rival factions have got together and signed a peace covenant.

There seems to be a mood to end violence and focus on development. It is not to say that the basic issues have been resolved. Nagas, however, have been firmly intimated that there is no question of sovereignty and the adjoining areas of ethnic Nagas can only be considered for merger with them following the due process involving the states of Assam and Manipur. Autonomy, under Article 371A of the Constitution of India, as in the case of J&K under Article 370, can be considered. While the talks are in progress and ceasefire on, the conditionality is - no sovereignty.

Manipur

Manipur came under British rule as a princely state in 1891. It was the scene of fierce battles between the Japanese and the Allied forces during World War II. The Japanese were beaten back and this proved to be one of the turning points of the war.

After the withdrawal of the British, the Manipur Constitution Act of 1947 established a democratic form of government with the Maharaja as the Executive Head and an elected legislature. He signed the Instrument of Accession of the state to the Republic of India in October 1949 in Shillong. Consequently the legislative assembly was dissolved and Manipur became a Union Territory of India in 1956 and later, in 1972, a full-fledged state of India. The scope of the book does not permit any more discussion on the accession of the state to India. There are differing views leading to separatist movements since the 1970s, with several groups demanding independence. The Peoples Liberation Army (PLA), the United National Liberation Front (UNLF) and the People's Revolutionary Party of Kangleipak (PREPAK), all demand independence. This is notwithstanding the fact that a sovereign Manipur is neither the demand of all the people of Manipur, nor desirable, nor feasible.

All the nine districts of Manipur, four in the Valley and five in the Hills are affected by varying degree of militant activities. To turn the demography of the state favourable, the militant groups target outsiders to scare them away. Insurgents belonging either to the UNLF or the PREPAK are generally behind these attacks. In addition are the inter faction clashes and multiplicity of opinion when dealing with the Government of India. The multiple insurgent groups extract levies and ransoms from residents, transients, government offices, educational institutions, health centres, commercial establishments and the wider civilian population across the state.

There are 39 underground outfits/factions operating in Manipur; six Meitei based underground outfits banned by the Government of India since 2007 are Kangleipak Communist Party (KCP), Kanglei Yawol Kanna Lup (KYKL), Manipur People's Liberation Front (MPLF), PLA, PREPAK and UNLF. The UG groups mentioned have seriously affected the quality of life of a people so rich in culture and sports. There is rampant corruption in the government and the local bodies making the situation quite hopeless. The economic blockade of the NH 39 in 2010 for over two months by All Naga Students Association of Manipur (ANSAM) and other Naga groups was an example of apathy in the state and at the Central Governmental level.

Terrorist related violence in Manipur trebled since mid 2004 through 2009. *Just, with 8.52 percent of the territory and 6.12 percent of the Northeast's population, it accounted for around 45 percent of terrorism related fatalities in 2008 and 2009. The decline in terror has been noticed in 2010. This trend needs to be backed up by political and economic initiatives by the state and the Central Governments.

Assam

Beginning 1979, the people of Assam demanded that the illegal immigrants who had emigrated from Bangladesh to Assam be deported. The movement led by All Assam Students Union began non-violently with *satyagrahas*, boycotts, picketing and courting arrests in an escalatory mode.

In 1983 an election was conducted which was opposed by the movement leaders and led to widespread violence. The movement ended after the leaders signed Assam Accord with the Government of India on 15 August 1985. Under this Accord, anyone who entered the state illegally between January 1966 and March 1971 was allowed to stay in India but was disenfranchised for ten years, while those who entered after 1971 faced expulsion. A November 1985 amendment to the Indian Citizenship Law allows non citizens who entered Assam between 1961 and 1971 to have all the rights of citizenship except the right to vote for a period of ten years.

---

*Lt Col Anil Bhat, VSM (Retd), Manipur's Disturbing Downslide of Terrorism, Law and Order and Corruption 2009-2010

Bodos, despite the administrative autonomy, demand a separate Bodoland. There are several organizations which advocate the independence of Assam. The most prominent of them is the United Liberation Front of Assam (ULFA) with two main goals, the independence of Assam and the establishment of a socialist government.

The ULFA has carried out several terrorist attacks in the region targeting the Indian military and non-combatants alike. The group assassinates political opponents, attacks police and other security forces, blasts rail-road tracks, and attacks other infrastructure facilities. The ULFA has strong links with NSCN (IM), Maoists, the Naxalites and Kachin Independence Army in Myanmar. Military operations, against it by the Indian Army began in 1990; Operation Bajrang, Operation Rhino 1, Operation Rhino 2 and continuing operations till date resulted in some 10,000 militants killed in the clashes in last two decades or so. The ULFA, however, continues to be active in the region. In 2004, the ULFA targeted a school killing 19 children and 5 adults. Terrorism is still an issue in Assam. The anti insurgency operations continue till date.

ULFA uses Bangladesh, Bhutan and Myanmar as safe haven. The Indian government outlawed the group in 1986 and declared Assam a troubled area. In 1990, the ULFA had its Pakistani contacts (ISI) in place, who facilitated the crossover of a number of ULFA leaders, including Paresh Barua (C-in-C, ULFA), into Afghanistan. They met Gulbuddin Hekmatyar, a leading mujahideen leader of the time, for necessary guidance and coordination.

In cooperation with Indian Army, Bhutan carried out a massive operation in December 2003 to drive out the ULFA militants from its territory. Bhutan claimed that all the 30 camps of ULFA, NDFB and Kamatapur Liberation Organisation (KLO) had been smashed. Estimated 485 militants were killed and 3,000 fled the Bhutanese territory.

Bangladesh arrested several leaders of ULFA and handed them over to India. The government had directed the law enforcement agencies to crack down on ULFA bases in its territory. Bangladesh High Commissioner to India has indicated that Anup Chetia, general secretary of the banned ULFA, under detention in his country after serving a jail term, would be handed over to

India soon. He continues in the custody of Bangladesh as of now (December 2010). The crackdown on ULFA in Bangladesh has significantly weakened the organisation. In 2010, the following terror related accords between India and Bangladesh were concluded:

- Agreement on Combating International Terrorism, Organized Crime and Illicit Drug Trafficking,

- Agreement on Mutual Legal Assistance on Criminal Matters,

- Agreement on the Transfer of Sentenced Persons.

Though ULFA has lost most of its bases in Bhutan and Bangladesh, it has a few strong bases in Myanmar. At least 150 members of the outfit are staying in the camps there. It derives its strength and support from its sympathizers in Myanmar, which makes it difficult to distinguish the hard core cadres from the villagers. While some ULFA cadres in Myanmar have come forward with an offer of truce, there are others who are in touch with the Kachin Independence Army (KIA) in Myanmar and are making fresh recruitment in upper Assam.

Negotiations between the Government of India and ULFA leaders commenced in 2005 when ULFA announced setting up of a nine member People's Consultative Group comprising of journalists, rights activists, lawyers and academics, to clear the grounds for direct talks between the ULFA and the Government of India. The peace process is gaining momentum and seems on the right track as in January 2011. All indications are positive.

Tripura

The National Liberation Front of Tripura (NLFT) seeks to secede from India and establish an independent state, what they describe as the kingdom of God and Christ in Tripura. The NLFT is a proscribed organization in India.

The All Tripura Tiger Force (ATTF), the political wing of Tripura Peoples Democratic Front objectives are:

1. Expulsion of all Bengali-speaking immigrants who entered Tripura after 1956.

2. Restoration of land to tribals under 'Tripura Land Revenue and Land Reforms Act', 1960.

3. Removal of names of migrants who entered Tripura after 1956 from the electoral roll.

ATTF is a proscribed outfit. The other active group is Borok National Council of Tripura (BNCT).

There was a surge in terrorist activities in Tripura in the 1990s. Bangladesh territory is often used as a safe haven. The area under control of the *Tripura Tribal Areas Autonomous District Council* was increased after a Tripartite Agreement between the Government of India, the State Government of Tripura, and the Council. Consequent to dialogue and active measures, terrorism in Tripura has been largely tamed. The simmering, however, continues for more autonomy for the Council. There are also clashes between the Bengalis and the tribes. ISI is also active in Tripura.

Mizoram

After two decades of insurgency, the insurgents have seen light and have joined the mainstream political process of the country. The state is peaceful with marginal simmering.

Arunachal Pradesh

Arunachal Pradesh borders Bhutan, China, Myanmar, Assam and Nagaland. Myanmar provides safe haven for insurgents from Nagaland, the NSCN (IM) and NSCN (K), and ULFA from Assam. The state, as such acts as a transit for the insurgents. Besides, the arms from China are readily available from the PLA surpluses. The state primarily suffers the spill over of insurgencies from the rest of the Northeast.

Meghalaya

The state is bounded on the north by Assam and by Bangladesh in the south. About one third of the state is forested. The forests of Meghalaya are notable for their biodiversity of mammals, birds, and plants. Meghalaya is predominantly an agrarian economy. Meghalaya is by and large peaceful.

Assessment-Northeastern states

The Northeastern states are distinct, strategically important and sensitive. The Government of India is seized of the sensitivity of the issues. While states like Arunachal Pradesh, Meghalaya, Mizoram and Tripura have been peaceful for some years; significant developments towards peace in Assam and Nagaland have also taken place, though Manipur continues to reel under multiple insurgencies and demands independence. The media reports that India's Northeast burns, however, are not supported by facts.

Notwithstanding the improved situation, the insurgents in the Northeastern states continue to have links with the Naxalites and the Maoists elsewhere. Myanmar's northwest continues to be available as safe haven because of scanty administration. China continues to pump in its surplus weapons in the region. ISI of Pakistan is also active and supports some insurgent movements. Bhutan, Bangladesh and Myanmar are cooperating.

The Red Corridor: Naxal Affected Districts

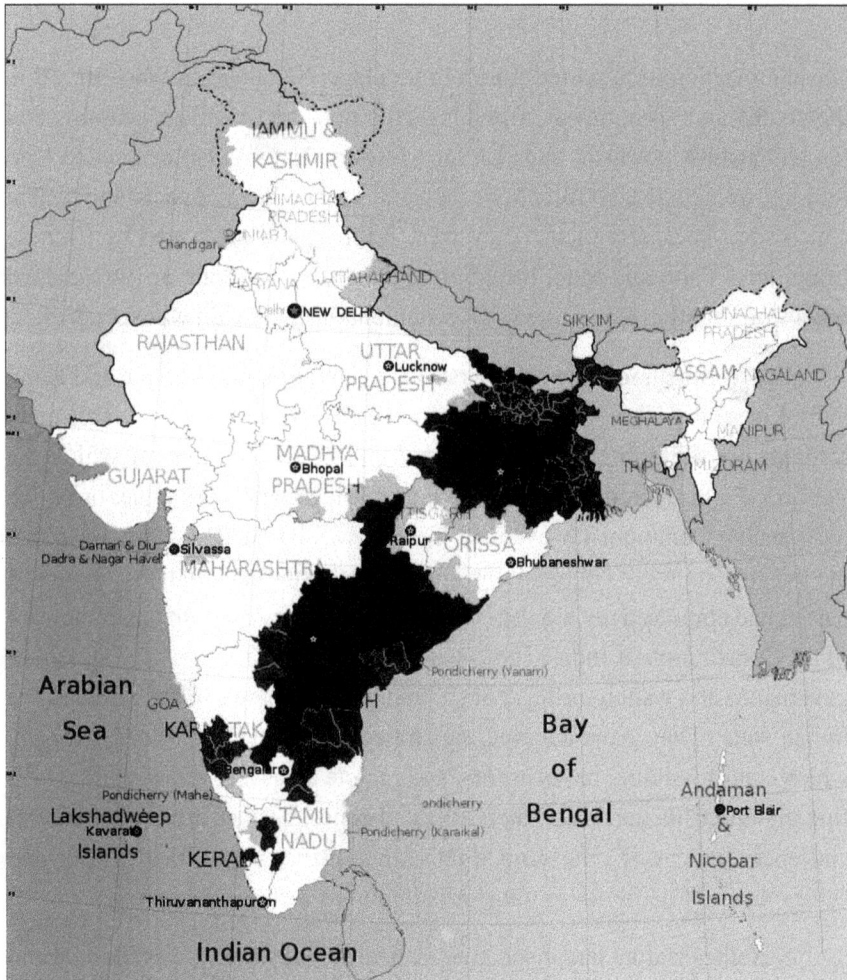

Naxal Movement

Naxal movement was started from a tiny village, Naxalbari in West Bengal in the sixties and seventies as a revolt of the poor and landless peasants and farmers against powerful and rich land owners. Naxals also demanded land reforms, to include land tiller to be the land owners. It was a social movement which soon became violent. They were inspired and motivated by Chinese Communist Party and Mao. Inception of the group was done in 1967 and All India Coordination Committee of Revolutionaries (AICCR) was set up.

Charu Mazumdar was the first head; Harekrishna Kongar and Kanu Sanyal were the other two main leaders. Charu spread the Naxal movement through his write-ups based on Marx-Lenin-Mao thoughts, of which the 'Historic Eight Documents' which outlined the ideological principles on which the Naxalite Communist Movement in India was based. They laid down that the Indian State was a bourgeois institution and that the main Indian Communist parties had embraced revisionism by agreeing to operate within the framework of the Constitution of India. The Naxalites reject the parliamentary system of governance and want to bring about a fundamental change in the nature of the Indian state. They have adopted the strategy of protracted armed struggle, which entails building bases in rural and remote areas and transforming them first into guerrilla zones and then liberated zones, besides area-wise seizures and encirclement of cities and finally, the seizure of political power and achievement of nation-wise transformation in to a classless society.

Naxalites started terrorist activities in different parts of West Bengal and looted landlords, money lenders and merchants, and distributed the wealth, so acquired, to the poor farmers and labourers. They also robbed weapons from the zemindars and police stations. As they became powerful and unpopular due to atrocities, Central Reserve Police Force (CRPF) and Army were deployed to deal with the movement. The joint operations and Charu Majumdar's death in 1972 led to a rapid decline of the Naxal movement, which was brought under control in late seventies.

Post Emergency PWG, CPI (ML), MCC and a few other smaller organizations gave a fillip to the revival of the Movement in Andhra Pradesh and Bihar. CPI (ML) decided to operate within the framework of the Indian Constitution, but did not rule out joining the armed struggle. PWG, on the other hand, decided on direct action. Their philosophy was given out in their document – 'Path of People's War in India':

"The program of our Party has declared that India is a vast 'semi-colonial and semi feudal country, with about 80 per cent of our population residing in our villages. It is ruled by the big bourgeois, big landlord classes, subservient to imperialism. The contradiction between the alliance of imperialism, feudalism and comprador-bureaucrat-capitalism on the other hand and broad masses of the people on the other is the principal contradiction in our country. Only a successful People's democratic revolution ie New Democratic Revolution and the establishment of People's Democratic Dictatorship of the workers, peasants, the middle classes and national bourgeoisie under the leadership of the working class can lead to the liberation of our people from all exploitation and the dictatorship of the reactionary ruling classes and pave the way for building Socialism and Communism in our country, the ultimate aim of our Party. People's War based on Armed Agrarian Revolution is the only path for achieving people's democracy i.e. new democracy, in our country".

CPI (ML), based on Marxisim-Leninism-Maoism thought, totally rejects the path of Parliamentarianism, peddled by the revisonitsts and neorevisionists of all hues and colours. Experience of all countries in the world has proved that the ruling classes, having total grip over the economic, political and cultural levels of the peoples will never allow the exploited and oppressed people to come to power through peaceful means. They always use various kinds of fascist repression to suppress the just struggles of the people. They use bourgeois parliamentary democracy as a cover to decieve the people, disrupt and destroy the just struggles of the people through bloody repression. The people are invariably forced to defend themselves against bloody repression, overthrough the dictatorship of the reactionary classes through revolutionary violence. This is the law of world's history

Hereafter the history of the internal dynamism of Naxalites is one of splits and mergers of various factions, more of the former. But Naxals continue to be a force

> ## Salwa Judum
>
> Salwa Judum (meaning peace march) is an anti-Naxalite movement in Chhattisgarh. Initially an uprising of local indigenous people in Chhattisgarh, the Salwa Judum movement later received support from both the opposition and ruling parties. A few years later the state government adopted the Salwa Judum movement in order to restore democratic rule to the regions where the Naxalites had established themselves. Chhattisgarh state has over the years trained a number of Special Police Officers (SPOs), from amongst the tribals, who are part of Salwa Judum. With its formation, the state has witnessed a marked rise in success against Naxalites. Chhattisgarh along with neighboring Jharkhand accounted for over 65% of the total Naxal violence in the country.

to reckon with, with an appealing ideology favouring the poor and deprived who form the mass of the population. The movement has spread to a large swathe in the central and the eastern parts of the country referred to as Red Corridor, covering 83 districts, mainly in the states of Bihar, Jharkhand, Chhattisgarh, West Bangal, Orrisa, Madhaya Pradesh, Maharashtra and Andhra Pradesh. The area from border with Nepal to Karanataka. *The movement now is spreading in other states like Haryana, Punjab, Uttrakhand, Assam, Kerala and Delhi. Incidents have increased from 1509 in 2006 to 1591 in 2008 to 2258 in 2009 and to 2212 in 2010.

More than 6,000 terrorists and the citizens have died so far. There are 40,000 IDPs. There is spatial as well as quantitative spread of violence. The left wing violence is spreading from the mineral rich region to other states and

---

Vikram Sood, New Face of Terrorism: Analysis of Asymmetric Threat from Land, Sea and Air, USI Journal July-September 2010

urban centres. It now encompasses around 200 districts, up from 160 a few years ago. They have amassed Rs 1,500 to 2,000 crores through extortions, drugs, robberies and such like activities. They have 10,000 assorted weapons to include AK series, INSAS and automatic weapons. They are also adept in handling IEDs and communication devices. Their cadres are well trained and are motivated. On the side of the government, there is political leadership deficit and inadequate para military force training and motivation. While there

Assessed Organisation of Naxalites

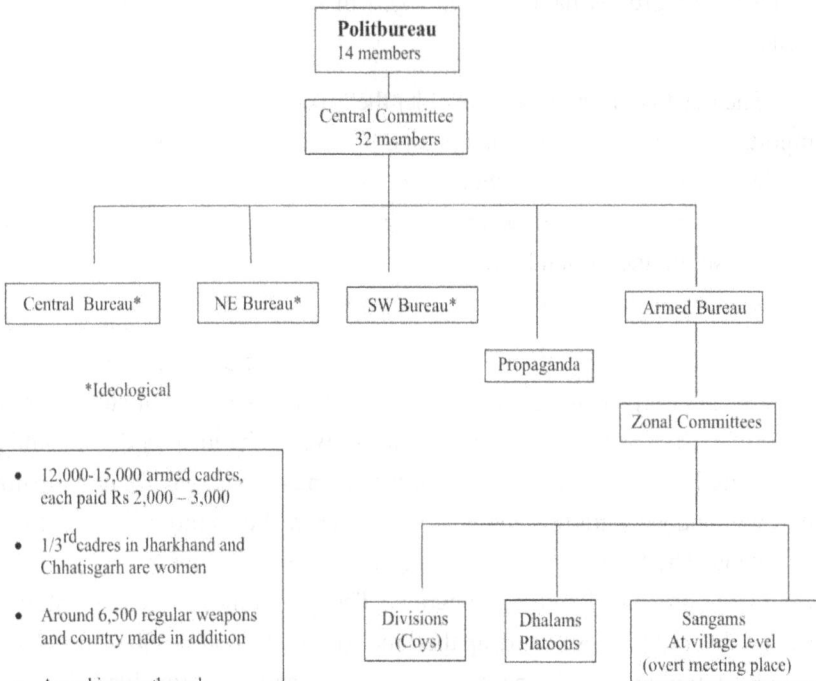

- 12,000-15,000 armed cadres, each paid Rs 2,000 – 3,000

- $1/3^{rd}$ cadres in Jharkhand and Chhatisgarh are women

- Around 6,500 regular weapons and country made in addition

- Annual income through extortion, drugs, developmental funds etc around Rs 2,000 crores

- 20 percent of the income is spent on welfare, 20 percent on treatment of injured and 60 per cent on arms procurement and training

is little hope of improving the political leadership, arming, training and motivation of the forces can be improved. The structure of the para military force needs a drastic change.

They meet at Dandakarnya and Abhujmarh. Abhujmarh is thickly forested and is mostly in Chhatisgarh. The area is totally undeveloped and not surveyed (10,000 sq km). Nearly 20,000 tribal families live in this forested area in 237 villages without any amenities.

In Chhattisgarh, the militia group Salwa Judum was formed as a reaction by tribals against Maoist atrocities. In Bihar, the *Ranvir Sena*, a proscribed terrorist organisation, is known to kill *Dalits* in retaliation to Naxalite activity. A number of groups have also emerged in Andhra Pradesh to counter the Naxalites.

The key to normalcy is to consider the Naxal problem an issue of national import, not only in making statements, but speedy action on ground. It is a politico-socio-economic-psychological issue covering a large swathe of the country. While CI operations are carried out by trained and motivated para military, simultaneous land reforms, education, health, employment and social management of the forest and mines must begin in right earnest.

It being an inter-state problem, there should be a coordinated approach with the Centre providing a platform. Andhra's experience of surrender and rehabilitate should be tried in other states as well. The local bodies should be empowered inclusively and the feudal system must make way for participatory management. Education is another field which will be a motivating factor for the tribals. The land, forest and mining wealth policies favouring the tribals should be announced and implemented. The government should go slow on mega industrial houses setting up their industry in the region. Since problem is complex involving tribals, the state governments should be flexible in initiation of the dialogues and avoid rigid conditionalities. The Centre and states must guard against those propounding rigid policies like 'dialogue only on cease fire' or 'development only if the violence is shunned'. It will not work as there are a number of factions at work. Another important aspect is the manning policies of the states. Dishonest officials must go. This will require political will above the party interests. 10 year perspective will be required both for the CI operations and the civic action. It is not a law and order problem. Its management approach must be inclusive.

Jammu and Kashmir

On transfer of power to India and Pakistan in 1947, the princely states acceded to one or the other dominion. Maharaja of Jammu and Kashmir needed time to decide whether to accede to India or Pakistan or claim independence. The State of Jammu and Kashmir went in to Stand Still mode in order to take a final decision. Whereas Pakistan accepted the Stand Still Agreement, India invited the Maharaja to negotiate. In the meanwhile, in September 1947, over 2000 tribesmen supported by Pakistan attacked the Jammu sector first and in October, the same year the Srinagar Valley. Feeling helpless, the Maharaja acceded to India and sought Indian military intervention which was promptly provided. On intervention of the UN, a cease fire line (CFL) came in to existence resulting in division of the State of Jammu and Kashmir. Ever since, India and Pakistan have fought two wars and a major border conflict in 1965, 1971 and 2001 respectively.

As a result of 1972 Simla Agreement, the cease fire line was converted in to Line of Control, a political line, not alterable by local military action. Line of Control may emerge in to an international border as a result of political negotiations.

Area of J&K

- Total Area   2,22,236 sq km

- Area under occupation of Pakistan   78,114 sq km

- Area ceded to China by Pakistan   5,180 sq km

- Area under occupation of China   37,555 sq km

- Area under effective control of India   1,01,387 sq km

The present state of affairs commenced in 1987 after an alliance between National Conference with the ruling Congress party for the elections was established. The elections were allegedly rigged in favour of National Conference. This led to an armed insurgency movement initiated in part by those who lost elections. Pakistan supplied these groups with logistic support, arms, recruits and training.

Beginning 2004 Pakistan began to taper its support for insurgents in Kashmir, possibly in the wake of attempts to assassinate Pakistani President by the terrorists. His successor, Asif Ali Zardari has continued the policy of calling insurgents in Kashmir 'terrorists'. The ISI, however, has its own agenda.

Besides the Pakistani supported of violence in J&K, there is domestic driven movement due to internal causes, in particular low level of development and corruption. Only a small part of the development funds from the Central Government reaches the masses. The insurgency in the state is a continuous process with the graph moving up and down. The Government of India, as such, maintains at least a third of its army and large para military forces in the state to manage the Line of Control and the internal security. There are widespread protests against Indian army presence in the state. The remedy becomes a cause as well.

Civilians bear the brunt both from the insurgents and the military, as inherent in any counter insurgency operations. It is assessed that up to 85,000 people have died, many more injured and maimed for life as a result of the insurgency. The resultant widows and orphans cause social problems adding to the unrest.

Fatalities in J&K, 2001-2010

Year	Civilians	SF Personnel	Terrorists	Total
2001	1067	590	2850	4507
2002	839	469	1714	3022
2003	658	338	1546	2542
2004	534	325	951	1810
2005	520	216	996	1732
2006	349	168	599	1116
2007	164	121	492	777
2008	69	90	382	541
2009	55	78	244	377
2010				475*
* Compiled from various sources				

Source: South Asia Terrorism Portal Database

In its year-end review, the Union Ministry of Home Affairs stated that, during 2009, the number of terrorism-related incidents had dropped by 27 per cent, killing of civilians by 17 per cent and of Security Force personnel by 19 per cent, compared to the corresponding period of 2008.

Incidents

Year	Incidents
2006	1667
2007	1092
2008	708
2009	460
2010	488 (compiled from various sources)

Source: J&K Police

Though militants suffered heavily in J&K, and the situation has improved gradually, there was a rise in infiltration bids by militants in 2009. Taking into account the overall improvement in the situation, the Government of India withdrew two army divisions from J&K. The announcement was made on December 17, 2009 by the Minister. Earlier in the month, the Government had announced withdrawal of a significant number of CRPF battalions as a confidence building measure, with a view to hold quiet dialogue with the separatist groups. However, the revocation of the Armed Forces Special Powers Act (AFSPA) was ruled out.

The Lok Sabha elections were held in the State in five phases, between April 16 and May 13, 2009 were by and large peaceful. In the first phase (Jammu-Poonch), the polling was 49 per cent; the second phase (Udhampur-Doda), the turnout was 45.3 per cent. The third phase (Anantnag) had a voter turnout of 26 per cent, nearly 11 per cent higher than the 2004 polls. The fourth phase (Srinagar) witnessed the lowest voter turnout, at 24 per cent, though this was also higher than the 2004 election. In the fifth phase, voting was held in Baramulla and Leh, and the voting percentage was 40 and 60 per cent respectively.

Union Home Minister P Chidambaram, on October 14, 2009, stated in Srinagar, that the Centre would start a dialogue process with every shade of political opinion in J&K for the resolution of the Kashmir issue, but that would be a quiet dialogue. He said the Centre would hold talks with mainstream political parties like the National Conference, People's Democratic Party, Congress and other smaller parties, and also other groups, which are not organized or are referred to as extremists. All efforts are being made to continue a genuine political process through polls, CBMs and softening of military posture.

Militancy in J&K is Pakistan sponsored with locals receptive to the sponsorship in the Valley. Pakistan's claim to J&K territory is as a result of an aggression in 1947. Any concessions should be equitably distributed between the three segments of the state ie the Valley, Ladakh and the Jammu region. The first step should be to put in place effective border guarding by the army and the para military forces. As far as possible, no infiltration should be permitted. The political corruption must cease and the developmental funds must reach the masses. More students from all regions should be given stipends and admission in rest of India. Conditions should be created for honourable return of the Kashmiri pandits. In trickle, some are returning. Employment opportunities for the Kashmiris should also be created both inside and outside the state. The communications with the rest of India should be improved including the extension of the railways. Dialogue with the people of the Valley will give rich dividends, but over a period of time. The dialogue with Pakistan should be maintained to reduce the suffering of the people of Jammu & Kashmir and with a hope of a solution. Even the resolution of Kashmir issue is unlikely to minimize militancy, as militants have no other occupation.

The situation is so intertwined and the players are so rigid that a cut and dry solution is unlikely to come by. A number of political solutions have been suggested from time to time. The dialogue between India, Pakistan and all political representatives of J&K should continue.

The Counter-Terror or Counter-Insurgency measures primarily imply political process, CBMs and softening of military posture in the state and with Pakistan. The border guarding, however, should continue to be as effective as possible. The level of corruption must be brought down and genuine welfare and fair play should be visible.

Terrorism in Pakistan

Pakistan the melting pot of terror

Nicolas Sarkozy President of France

"We will continue to insist to Pakistan's leaders that terrorist safe-havens within their borders are unacceptable, and that those behind the Mumbai attacks be brought to justice"

Barrack Obama,President of USA

The Islamic jihad gradually scaled up throughout 1990s and thereafter, and gained international proportions with growing cooperation and assistance amongst the terror groups, particularly in the Middle East and the Arab countries. Their grievances are against USA, European Union, Israel and the Hindu India. The terror war is getting more lethal with sophisticated weaponry and no holds barred targeting. The Islamic terror organizations and movements know no international boundaries and operate as a nation globally. Most Islamic groups have rallied around Osama bin Laden's *al Qaeda* organization in Afghanistan/Pakistan.

Pakistan employed unconventional methods of warfare ever since she was granted independence in 1947. Despite the Standstill Agreement with the state of Jammu & Kashmir, Pakistan launched tribals with the support of army to annexe Jammu & Kashmir. In all, 1,500 soldiers died on each side during the war and Pakistan was able to acquire roughly two-fifths of Kashmir, bulk of it, being barren and rocky Northern Areas, more of a liability for a developing country, strategic importance notwithstanding. In 1965, Pakistan employed large scale infiltrators to support its offensive against India. Pakistan attempted to initiate resistance movement by means of a covert infiltration, codenamed Operation Gibraltar. The operation ended in a complete failure. Nearly all infiltrators were killed or captured.

Pakistan suffers from identity crisis and insecurity. Its policies are not based on geo-political realities, but a desire to lead the Muslim world and avenge its defeat in the 1971 war. Its policies are not explicitly pro-poor, as such is not a welfare state. At the cost of national pride, it raised terror organizations at the behest of USA, then trains and pitches the same forces against USA and other western countries, and yet fights the same organizations she creates for more aid. She receives aid from democracies, communist countries and from the Muslim world. Without aid the country may collapse.

In the recent times, terrorism in and around Pakistan started with Soviet invasion of Afghanistan in 1979. In the war between anti-communist forces and the Soviet-backed Afghan Government, anti-communist guerrillas, jointly called the *mujahideen*, fought both the Soviet troops and the pro-Soviet Afghan Government led by President Babrak Karmal. The reason given by Pakistan for opposing the Soviets was to deny them a border with Pakistan and access to the Arabian Sea.

By 1983, the CIA was purchasing sophisticated small arms, totaling 10,000 tons, mainly from China, were channelled to Afghanistan via Pakistan. By 1985, the CIA began to supply intelligence, military expertise and advanced weapons to the rebel forces. They included satellite reconnaissance data of Soviet targets in Afghanistan, Soviet plans for military operations, intercepts of Soviet communications, covert communication technology; detonating devices for tons of C-4 explosives for urban targets, long-range sniper rifles, a targeting system linked to a US Navy satellite, guided anti-tank missiles and Stinger anti aircraft missiles. American-trained Pakistani officers were sent to Afghanistan to set up a secret *mujahideen* Stinger training facility, which was completed with a US made electronic simulator. By 1987, the CIA was sending a steady supply of 65,000 tons of arms to the *mujahideen*. USA maintained its oversight on the war by entrusting Pakistan's ISI to handle direct contact, which included training of the *mujahideen* and operations. In all, US provided over $2 billion in weapons and money in the 1980s.

Soviets announced the withdrawal from Afghanistan in 1988. What ensued was the fighting between the puppet government and the *mujahideen*, and amongst various factions. The *mujahideen* finally captured Kabul in 1992 but the guerrilla factions proved unable to unite, resulted in fragmentation of the control of the country.

The Taliban, a militia of Pashtun fundamentalist students, appeared in 1994 in Pakistan. These students had received training in madrassas in Pakistan along with the *mujahideen*. The Taliban captured Kabul in 1996, declaring themselves the legitimate Government of Afghanistan. Armed by religious zeal, the Taliban promised to end the civil war, corruption and lawlessness. As they rose in popularity, other Pashtun Afghans also joined them. The CIA training grounds became camps and safe havens for the militants. The situation became so murky that when the US launched cruise missile attacks at a camp near Khost in 1998, the training camps were found to be occupied by Pakistani military intelligence to train the Harkat-ul-Ansar, identified as a terrorist group by the US State Department.

On recognizing the oppressive nature of the Taliban, both the US and the United Nations lowered the level of interest in Afghanistan. US economic and military assistance to Afghanistan decreased after 1989. Afghanistan, its people, the Taliban and other militant factions, no more relevant to US, were dumped. Afghanistan suffered more than 1 million dead, millions injured, and more than 5 million became refugees in neighboring countries. The plan misfired both for USA and Pakistan. By the end of 2001, there were approximately 5 million Afghan refugees in Pakistan, which included the natural increase during the past 20 years and there were about 2.4 million Afghans in Iran. 7.4 million refugees in both countries and other devastations, were the price paid for the misadventure. A similar misadventure by India was arming and training of LTTE in 1980s against the government forces but misfired. India had to deploy a corps size force in Sri Lanka to disarm the same force, trained and armed by her. Indian Prime Minister, Rajiv Gandhi was assassinated at the behest of the same force. The lesson being, that the internal affairs of a state, if intervened militarily, are more likely to bounce back than accrue any dividends. The other examples being, Americans in Vietnam, American intervention in Iraq and the Russian offensive in Afghanistan itself.

Terrorism in Pakistan is mainly a result of Pakistan's support of terrorist activities in its neighbouring countries, India and Afghanistan through state funding of Islamic terrorists. Subsequent to 9/11, Pakistan had to do a *volte face* under extreme US pressure and had to fight the very own Islamic militants who had long been harboured and nurtured by her. All this was in return for American financial and military support as a part of the War on Terror. In 1987, 90 per cent of all reported terrorist activities worldwide were located in Pakistan.

The sectarian violence plaguing the country originated in the controversial Islamic policies of General Muhammad-Zia-ul-Haq initiated during his tenure from 1977 to 1988. These policies gave immense power to religious figures in the country, who, in turn, spread intolerant religious dogmas among the masses. The Shariat Courts were established to provide for overriding powers over the criminal courts and encouraged the fundamentalists and the jihadis.

ISI of Pakistan is an autonomous body as part of the army, exporting terror in the name of jihad. It is widely believed that in the incidents of 9/11; attack on the Indian Parliament; London bombing; Bombay, Hydrabad, Bangalore, Ahmedabad and Jaipur bombings; ISI had an active hand. There was similarity in the pattern of attacks in the Indian cities. Pakistan has become the epicentre of Muslim jihad and trains jihadis for Chechneya, Xinjiang, Phillipines, Indonesia, Sudan, Uzbekistan, Iraq, Lebanon, Palestine, Morocco, Libya, Egypt and other Muslim and Arab countries. The ISI also supports Taliban and *mujahideen* to fight in Afghanistan and Kashmir. In addition to sheltering and training the Taliban, Pakistan also provides funding, bankrolling operations, diplomatic support, planning and directing offensives, providing logistics and so on. Pakistan claims that even she is a victim of terror. But she is victim of her own terror while its neighbours are victims of Pakistan sponsored terror. Pakistan now perceives main threat to it from within, from terrorism, not from its neighbours.

Along its western borders and along Indo-POK border, and inside Pakistan, Pakistan has a large number of madrassas and jihadi training camps. *Madrassas

* Vali Nasr, an authority on Islamic fundamentalism, and Richard Holbrooke, former U.S. ambassador to the UN;

Suba Chandran, IPCS, Madrassas in Pakistan-1.

were established as institutions of higher studies, where law, Islamic sciences and philosophy were taught. Initially a part of the mosque but later emerged as seperate institutions. During the eleventh and twelfth centuries, madrassas specialised in law and jurisprudence. It was only after the introduction of western education under colonial rule that their curriculum underwent a change. In recent times, although the madrassas came in to being to fill a void in the education spectrum of Pakistan and Afghanistan, the religious influence and environment led to their use as ground for indoctrination and jihad training. During the Soviet invasion of Afghanistan, a new kind of madrassa emerged in the Pakistan-Afghanistan region, which was not so much concerned about scholarship as making war on the infidels. Many madrassas in Pakistan are funded by Saudi Arabia, particularly the ones that teach Wahabism, a particularly austere and rigid form of Islam which is rooted in Saudi Arabia. Most recruits are from the lower-middle and middle classes who do not have access to regular schooling or choose to go to a madrassa. Madrassas have also been used as shelters or meeting points for militants, bases for clandestine planning of operations by Taliban and *al Qaeda* supporters, or training grounds for their soldiers. Not all terrorists are a product of the madrassa, they could well be a technical graduate, post graduate or a doctor from a well to do family like Osama bin Laden himself.

A large number of madrassas do not impart jihadi training. According to the Human Rights Commission of Pakistan, about one third of these schools provide military training to their students and few madrassas send their students for training and participation in the Afghan civil war. However, they have very significant role in spreading terror. Their graduate is only good for madrassa and mosque services as maulvi, maulana or mullah, and not for the vibrant modern environment. They provide ready material for any kind of jihad any where for commitment to their perceived cause and also for monetary gains. Like all human beings, these unemployed youth also have responsibility towards the well being of their families, their security and comfort. The Zia's Islamisation policies, the Iranian revolution, the Soviet invasion of Afghanistan, the Kashmir issue and the jihad that followed with active Pakistan's involvement, were factors contributing to the sudden growth of madrassas and militancy in Pakistan. The madrassas adhere to different faiths such as Deobandi, Brelvi,

Ahle Hadith, Ahle Tashi etc. Most madrassas have permanent sources of income from land, buildings and other property. Invariably a madrassa is run by a waqf that takes care of the management of financial aspects. All practicing Muslims are supposed to pay zakat @ 2.5 per cent of personal income that must be devoted toward alms. Zakat produces almost $1-1.2 billion a year in private philanthropy, much of which goes toward the funding of madrassas. Besides, many of these madrassas receive funds from outside Pakistan, major contributors being Saudi Arabia and America. In addition, are the drug money and the remittances.

Anatomy of Islamic Jihad

According to a study carried out by Marc Sageman on behalf of CIA, a pan-Islamist jihadi is not poor. *Al Qaeda* attracts educated middle class, if not upper-crust. An engineering degree may well be a pre-requisite to become a terrorist. As per his findings, *al Qaeda* recruits are normally married, have plenty of children and see nothing wrong in entertainment available in the society. The first generation of Islamic terrorists, were the Arab veterans of the anti-Soviet jihad in Afghanistan, who worked with bin Laden. The second generation is pan-Islamic, with *al Qaeda* a source of inspiration only. They are more likely to be trained by any groups like Lashkar-e-Tayyiba, Jaish-e-Mohammad and so on. This generation of terrorists is more cosmopolitan than their predecessors. The prominent terror groups in Pakistan are:

Al Qaeda

Al Qaeda is an international Sunni Islamist movement founded in 1988. It is the umbrella group of militant Islam and has fostered a state of mind called *al Qaedism*. It has attacked civilian and military targets in various countries, the most notable being the 9/11, resulting in war on terror, world wide, by the US.

A fierce terrorist organisation, comprising individuals who have undergone training in one of the camps in Afghanistan or Sudan. *Al Qaeda's* objectives include the end of foreign influence in Muslim countries and creation of a new Islamic Caliphate. Reported beliefs include that a Christian-Jewish alliance is conspiring to destroy Islam and that the killing of bystanders is justified. Being on the run, following the war on terror, it operates from rugged terrain along

Pakistan-Afghanistan border, possibly from Waziristan in Pakistan and as such, is severely affected, which has led to the regional groups using the *al Qaeda* as brand or cover name. *Al Qaeda* has been labeled a terrorist organization by the UNSC, the NATO, the European Union, the US, Austria, India, Canada, Israel, Japan, South Korea, the Dutch, the UK, Sweden and the Swiss .

After 9/11, the linkages that emerged between the ruling elite in Pakistan and terrorists of *al Qaeda*, who destroyed the twin towers of New York, were undeniable. This finds mention in the 9/11 Commission report but not openly. The US legislation, following the report, makes special provisions to reform Pakistan into a moderate Islamic state. The plan is unfolding.

Taliban

Taliban means students. It is a Sunni Pashtun movement, primarily operating in Pakistan and Afghanistan. Originated as *mujahideen*, fighting the Soviet Union in Afghanistan, its rank and file comprises of Afghan refugees who were educated in madrassas along Afghan-Pakistan border. Its strength is estimated at 7,000-11,000 and ideology - Islamist fundamentalism and Pashtun nationalism. They wish to live a life like the Prophet lived and feel that jihad is their right and in the interest of the Afghans. Talibans are intolerant to other religions. The movement was started in 1994 by religious students under the leadership of Mullah Muhammad Omar, a local mullah and veteran commander of the anti-Soviet resistance. The origin of Taliban is not clear, however, these *mujahideen* seem to have started with the aim of ridding the Afghan society of corruption and crime. The CIA funds came in handy through ISI to arm and train them against the Soviet forces. In 1994 they took control of 12 provinces in Afghanistan and by 1996 they had captured Kabul. Taliban facilitated the entry and re-organization of *al Qaeda* in Afghanistan. Taliban governance was rather primitive, ancient Islamist and harsh. They were strict with the women and confined them to the burqa and did not encourage any education for them.

In 2001, the allied forces inflicted massive casualties on Taliban and drove them out of power. The remaining Taliban fled across the border into Pakistan to regroup and train. In 2006, a resurgent Taliban initiated their first offensive to take back Kandahar, their former stronghold. Even though, they were denied control of the south, they continue to be a force to reckon with. In Pakistan they run their writ in Swat, North and South Waziristan and are capable of striking any where in Pakistan. In February 2009, President Zardari of Pakistan made a statement:

> *"The Talibans are trying to take over the country. This fact was being kept under the wraps in Pakistan, but things seem to have become serious for the state of Pakistan."*

Taliban in Afghanistan and Pakistan have a long term agenda – to defeat the government forces, capture territory, enforce sharia and eventually take over the state. Taliban have formed a new alliance, Shura Ittihad-ul-Mujahideen, in North and South Waziristan in February 2009. The new alliance would comprise the groups led by chief of banned TTP, Baitullah Mahsud and the two reportedly pro-government powerful commanders Maulvi Nazir of South Waziristan Agency and Hafiz Gul Bahadur of North Waziristan tribal region.

Tehrik-e-Taliban Pakistan (TTP)

An umbrella group that would enable the numerous pro-Taliban groups operating in the FATA and NWFP to co-ordinate and consolidate their growing influence in the region. By early 2008, the most significant threat was posed by the forces under the command of Baitullah Mehsud in the South Waziristan, and the Tehrik-e-Nefaz-e-Shariat-e-Mohammadi (TNSM) forces under the command of Maulana Fazlullah in Swat. In both, South Waziristan and Swat, militants have demonstrated ability to upgrade from guerrilla warfare to holding territory and effectively questioning the writ of the state. The civilian government that came to power following elections in February 2008, sought peace with the group and accepted the terms and conditions of the TTP including imposition of the sharia in Swat. TTP has a strength of around 35,000 and plans to become a global player and attack Washington.

Harkat-ul-Mujahideen (HUM)

HUM was formed in 1985 to fight the Soviet forces in Afghanistan. It was formed by a group that separated out of another group, the Harkat-ul-Jihad-al-

Islami (HuJI). An Islamist militant group based in Pakistan, comprises several thousand armed personnel with support from Pakistan, Kashmir, Afghanistan and Arabs. It is based in Muzaffarabad, Rawalpindi, and several other places in Pakistan and Afghanistan. It collects donations from Saudi Arabia and other Gulf and Islamic states, and from Pakistan and Kashmir. With the Soviet withdrawal from Afghanistan in 1989, the outfit turned against J&K at the behest of Pakistan. HUM remerged with HuJI to form Harakat ul-Ansar (HUA). HUA has considerably weakened because of capture of its prominent leaders by the Indian security forces. HUA has links with the Kashmiri militant group, Al-Faran.

Jaish-e-Mohammed (JeM)

 Formed in early 2000 by Maulana Masood Azhar after the IC-814 hijack to Kandhar and his release. It comprises of several hundred armed personnel and supporters. Supporters are mostly Pakistanis and Kashmiris, and also Afghans and Arabs. It is funded by *al Qaeda*. It is based in Peshawar and Muzaffarabad, but primarily operates in Kashmir. JeM maintains training camps in Afghanistan. It aims to unite Kashmir with Pakistan.

Lashkar-e-Tayyiba (LeT)

Responsible for a string of attacks, including on Indian Parliament and the Mumbai blasts, its goal is to unite Kashmir with Pakistan, and also to destroy the Indian republic and annihilate Hinduism. It is based in Muridke (near Lahore) and Muzaffarabad, and trains militants in mobile training camps across POK/ AK and Afghanistan. Banned, but operates through the front organization, the Jamaat-ud-Dawa (JuD). JuD has also been banned post 26/11. It comprises of several hundred personnel and maintains ties with fanatic groups in Philippines, Middle East and Chechnya. LeT and JuD collect donations from the Pakistani community in the Persian Gulf and UK, Islamic NGOs, and businessmen from Pakistan and Kashmir. Its cadres are from Pakistan and Afghanistan, who are armed with sophisticated weapons and are well trained. It is the armed wing of the Pakistan-based religious organization, Markaz-ud-Dawa-wal-Irshad (MDI) and is anti US, anti India and opposes missionary groups from the US. It has carried out a number of successful operations in

Kashmir and in other states in India.

Lashkar-e-Jhangvi (LeJ)

LeJ is a Sunni-Deobandi organization formed in 1996. It is a break away group of radical sectarian extremists of the Sipah-e-Sahaba Pakistan. Post 9/11, it provided safe houses to *al Qaeda* men on the run. It was banned in 2001, but remains active nevertheless. LeJ was involved in the assassination of Iranian diplomat Sadiq Ganji in Lahore, killing of Iranian Air Force cadets visiting Pakistan in 1990s and also seems to be involved in the assassination of Benazir Bhutto along with the death of 20 others in Rawalpindi on December 27, 2007. The LeJ aims to transform Pakistan into a Sunni state through violent means.

Lashkar-e-Omar (LeO)

LeO (the Army of Omar) is believed to have its members derived from Harkat-ul-Jihad-al-Islami, Lashkar-e-Jhangvi, and Jaish-e-Mohammed. The Lashkar-e-Omar does not seem to exist as a formal entity, but the name is said to signify collection of proscribed terrorist groups. No formal structure has been detected. The outfit, however, is accused of:

- Attack on a church in Bahawalpur in 2002 resulting in 18 deaths and 9 injuries.

- Grenade attack on a church in 2002 in diplomatic enclave in Islamabad in which five persons, including a US diplomat's wife and daughter, were killed and 41 injured.

- Suicide bombing outside the Sheraton Hotel and the US Consulate in Karachi in 2002, in which 10 persons were killed and 51 injured.

Tablighi Jamaat (TJ)

*TJ is a Muslim missionary and revival movement. It was basically formed for facilitating spread of Islam. Belongs to Deobandi faith, but its activities are not limited to the Deobandi community alone. Leaders of TJ claim that the movement is strictly non-political, pietistic and sends missionaries across the globe on proselytizing missions and functions with the main aim to work at the grass root level and reaching out to all Muslim Deobandis of the world for spiritual development. Reportedly, however, this missionary organization is becoming increasingly radicalized, and is being used as a cover to mask travel and activities of terrorists including members of the Taliban and *al Qaeda*. The nexus between TJ, HUM, JeI and HuJI in spreading jihadi movement in different countries is a dangerous synergy. It gave birth to HUM in 1980. Almost all of the HUM's original members were Tablighis. It was also reported by a Pakistani journalist Kamran Khan, who quoted unidentified office-bearers of the HUM as saying:

> *"Ours is basically a Sunni organization close to the Deobandi school of thought. Most of our workers come from the TJ. We regularly go to its annual meeting at Raiwind. Ours is a truly international network of genuine jihadi Muslims. We believe that the frontiers can never divide the Muslims. They are one nation and will remain a single entity. We believe that Islam has no borders and that all countries once ruled by Muslims should be brought back to Islamic rule. We try to go wherever our Muslim brothers are terrorized, without any monetary consideration. Our colleagues went and fought against oppressors in Bosnia, Chechnya, Tajikistan, Burma, Philippines and of course, India".*

Tehreek-e-Nafaz-e-Shariyat-e-Muhammadi

It is a Wahabi outfit whose objective is imposition of sharia in Pakistan. It was founded by Sufi Muhammad in 1992 and was banned by Pakistan in 2002. The organization is active in the areas along the Pakistan-Afghanistan border, especially Swat and Malakand but including Dargai and Chenagai. It supports the Taliban forces in Afghanistan and has been described as "one of the most dangerous religious militant groups in Pakistan.

Hizb-I-Islami Gulbuddin (HIG)

Gulbuddin Hikmatyar founded HIG in 1977. HIG was one of the major *Mujahideen* groups in the war against the Soviets. Hikmatyar ran several terrorist training camps in Afghanistan and was also sending mercenaries to other Islamic conflicts. Hikmatyar offered to shelter Osama bin Laden after he fled Sudan in 1996. HIG also fights along side Taliban. Combined with *al Qaeda* and Taliban, HIG is a force to recon with, with the aim of forcing the coalition to withdraw, overthrow the Afghan Government and establish a fundamental Afghanistan.

There are 11 domestic terror groups, 32 trans-border terror groups and four extremist groups in Pakistan. Some of these have been mentioned above in some detail, it is, however, not possible to give details here of all the groups. All these groups have the objectives which range from anti US and anti west, eviction of the western forces and influence from the Muslim countries, anti Israel, Islamisation (Sunni) of Pakistan, anti India, Jammu and Kashmir, and Sunni-Shia conflict. All these groups have inter group linkages and linkages abroad. These groups are a regional threat and threat to Pakistan itself. The extremist groups are:

- Al Rashid - Described as a welfare organization with financial resources provided by public donations. It expanded its mandate to carry out relief activities in Chechnya, Kosovo and Afghanistan. Its other objective is to push Western NGOs out of Afghanistan.

- Al Akhtar Trust - Was formed in 2000 to provide financial assistance for Islamist extremists, including the Taliban and to feed, clothe and educate the children of religious martyrs.

- Rabita Trust – Charitable Trust, aims to spread Muslim culture, is reported to have links with *al Qaeda.*

- Ummah Tamir-e-Nau – Proscribed, has links with *al Qaeda* and JeM.

Madrassas

Madrassas have long been the centers of classical Islamic studies and the guardians of the orthodoxy in South Asian Islam. *They rose as learning institutes in the Islamic world in the 11th century and catered to the Islamic as well as secular education. The character of a large number of these institutes, over the years, has changed to cater also to the fundamentalist requirements in recent times. Pakistan has 50,000-65,000 madrassas with an estimated 2 to

---

*Madrassas in Pakistan, Wikipedia

2.5 million students in 2002, out of which most cater to the dominant Sunni sect and remaining 15 to 20 per cent to the Shia. The madrassa education is preferred by those who can not afford private or public school education. However, there are families, irrespective of their financial status, who send at least one of their children to a madrassa. Madrassa education in FATA and NWFP, particularly North and South Waziristan, is much more prevalent than in the other parts of the country.

There were few madrassas in 1947 but were expanded during General Zia-ul-Haq's regime (1977-1988). The expansion occurred both because of the growth in Pakistan's population, poverty and the need to employ the young to fight the Soviet Union during the Afghan war. The expansion of Taliban was fueled by funding from the Muslim and Arab countries and USA. There were five million Afghan refugees in hundreds of refugee camps in the NWFP and Balochistan. It is estimated that 40 percent of them were school-age children, many of them orphans. Often, these madrassas provided them with free food, shelter, and basic skills of how to read and write, along with Islamic and jihad education.

A large number of these, which were established for the purpose of fighting the Soviets, were in fact, military training camps, where some religious education was imparted to give them cover of being madrassas, to legitimize their operations and to extract funds from the Muslim world. After the Russian pull out, the facilities were reoriented for jihad in Kashmir and elsewhere, with the involvement of the Pakistan Government. Backed by ISI, they have become a force to recon with in Pakistan and internationally.

In addition to the South Asian Dars-i-Nizami curriculum (a standardised curriculum in South Asia), the students specifically study the texts of the sub sects they belong to. This process results in sectarian bias and the resultant social effects. Students are taught to refute western ideologies like capitalism, democracy, socialism, freedom, individualism, human rights, feminism, and so on. There are a number of books in simple Urdu in circulation on these themes, which are clandestinely sold to the students and others. Thus, while the Dars-i-Nizami teaches neither specifically sectarian nor anti-western ideologies, these madrassas and books perform this role. Some madrassas even invite fighters from active frontlines to motivate students to fight against oppression.

Many of the Taliban were educated in Saudi-financed madrassas in Pakistan that teach Wahabism. Saudi wealth and charities contributed to these madrassas during the Afghan jihad against the Soviets. In these madrassas, there have been students from Central Asia, Philippines, Indonesia, Nigeria and Arab region with funds from Persian Gulf and Saudi Arabia. As Richard Holbrooke sees, the Saudis exported their problems through these madrassas to the Muslim world.

The funding of these madrassas seems to have been institutionalized through a fund raised by Saudi Arabia, Pakistan, Egypt, Libya and Sudan. Some representatives from the World Assembly of Muslim Youth (WAMY) have also been incorporated who have identified areas for the new mosques in Jammu, Udhampur, Rajouri and Poonch districts. WAMY is a Saudi organisation. The fund collected so far is around Rs 3,000 crores. The plan is multifaceted and on a vide canvas. It is also reported that there are students of Pakistani origin from USA and other European countries in Jamia Binoria madrassa Karachi. They are being indoctrinated over a period of 1-3 years and sent back to the country they belong to.

A madrassa also trains clerics for the mosque and teachers for the madrassas, for the sysrem to go on. Madrassa is an all-in-one institution sanctified by Islam. It is a sensitive system which can not be addressed without repercussions by the law and order agencies or the counter terror operations. These are permanent institutions, part of the education system and must be controlled and directed both by the secular and the spiritual authorities. Most are located in west of Indus unstable areas and in POK/AK. Very suitable for promoting jihad operations in the periphery of Islamic Republic of Pakistan.

Most madrassas are simply schools providing religious education to students who would probably not get any education otherwise. Some are, however, associated with providing fighters. General Musharraf tried to bring them under his control through two laws he passed: one to create state-controlled madrassas; the other to register and control them (2002). The first had moderate success, as some religious institutions were registered in 2003 with the Pakistan Madrassa Education Board. The second was unpopular with the madrassas, but the government has been firm about removing foreign students.

In overall analysis, Pakistan has all ingredients of a state which manufactures terrorism, exports it and maintains it. ISI is the central nervous system of terror export, an authority in itself. In addition to ISI, the unstable areas of Balochistan, FATA, NWFP and Northern Areas are suitable breeding ground for terrorism to flourish. As a state, Pakistan does not care for its flip flop policies of, some time creating and some time destroying its own creations. The state will continue to simmer and terror will continue to bleed Pakistan, its neighbouring countries and pockets of the world. The Mumbai attacks of 2008, is a classical example of thorough involvement of ISI to kill 5,000 Indians, embarrass the Government of India and bring down its booming economy. The amphibious covert operation was launched from Karachi from a mother ship, landing in groups in smaller boats with ammunition and weapons. The operation entailed months of preparations by LeT, backed up by ISI.

Perhaps Pakistan forgets that she is frustrating and exploiting a giant like the USA and is being tolerated because of its location suitable for logistics for operations in Afghanistan and elsewhere in the vicinity. This is a temporary phase for the routes can be developed from the north in due course. USA has violated the territorial integrity of Pakistan by high-tech assault in Abbotabad and killing Osama bin Laden.She also forgets that she is also nibbling a tiger in the neighbourhood, which when hits back, will bring catastrophe to her, like in 1971. No nation with even a modicum of pride will accept terror attacks from a smaller neighbour again and again. Pakistan is a brittle state (East Pakistan has already seceded) and India has the potential and wherewithal to strike Balochistan, FATA and parts of NWFP (South Waziristan in Particular) surreptitiously. Balochistan with vital economic establishments, divided society and fissiparous tendencies, can be addressed in detail, to eventually slice it away from Pakistan and cripple its economy. Pakistan can not afford to export terror with impunity indefinitely and without far reaching disastrous consequences. Some such consequences are already staring in the face. The originator and breeder of the terror, Pakistan, today is on the brink of being swallowed by its own Frankestein jihadist creations, unless is bailed out.

NWFP, FATA, Balochistan and POK/AK are already witnessing large-scale violence and insurrection. Despite the deployment of 100,000 soldiers in FATA to confront the Taliban, *al Qaeda* and other militant groups who have created safe havens there, jihadis have achieved major strategic successes in all the seven agencies, resulting in gravitation of the allied forces. There are reports of demoralisation, desertions and the reservations by Punjabi regiments to serve in FATA and NWFP, and also of surrenders by the forces due to physical and mental pressure, as also soldiers being taken hostage. FATA has become *de facto* autonomous, a *fait accompli*. There are routine major incidents of violence in Peshawar, Rawalpindi, Lahore, Sindh, Gilgit and elsewhere, which are pointers towards efforts to destablise the Islamic Republic of Pakistan as an entity. Islamabad's writ is being seriously challenged in a wide swathe of the geographical areas, and on a multiplicity of issues. Whatever be the consequences, India and the world are bound to suffer. A failed Pakistani state with nuclear weapons is not desirable, nor should it be allowed to exploit the world.

Cautiously, the author wishes to report that since 2008, there seems to be an improvement in the terror environment in the region, probably because of internal situation in Pakistan and counter terrorism measures adopted by the countries. Hopefully the trend will continue. We have to wait till Pakistan is relieved from its commitments along the Durand Line.

Terrorism in Afghanistan

With the 1979 Soviet invasion of Afghanistan, the war between Soviet Army and the Soviet-backed Afghan Government; and anti-communist forces was well underway. The number of Soviet troops in Afghanistan reached 100,000 by 1980. The *mujahidin* fought both the Soviet troops and the pro-Soviet Afghan Government. The United States backed the anti-Soviet forces. The CIA supplied an extensive array of intelligence, military expertise and advanced weapons to the rebel forces. They included satellite reconnaissance data; Soviet military plans; communication technology for the rebels; long-range sniper rifles; a targeting system linked to a US Navy satellite; wire-guided anti-tank missiles, stinger anti aircraft missiles and sophisticated training facilities. The weaponry was mostly purchased from China and shipped to Pakistan for deployment in Afghanistan. All out support was provided to the *mujahideen through ISI.*

Soviets withdrew in 1988. With the Soviets out, the *mujahidin* focused next on fighting the Afghan puppet Government and captured Kabul in 1992. Another power struggle amongst the factions ensued. Afghanistan thus became a fragmented country of several independent zones, each headed by a warlord.

The Taliban movement was started in 1994 by religious students under the leadership of Mullah Muhammad Omar, a local mullah and veteran commander of the anti-Soviet resistance. It is a Sunni Pashtun movement, primarily operating in West Pakistan and Afghanistan. Originated as *mujahideen,* its rank and file comprises of Afghan refugees who were educated in madrassas along Afghan-Pakistan border. Its strength is estimated at 7,000-11,000 and ideology - Islamist fundamentalism and Pashtun nationalism. They wish to live a life like the Prophet lived and feel that *jihad* is their right and in the interest of the Afghans. Taliban are intolerant to other religions. In 1994 they took control of 12 provinces in Afghanistan and by 1996 they had captured Kabul. Taliban governance was rather primitive, ancient Islamist and harsh. They were strict with the women and confined them to the *burqa* and did not encourage any education for them.

In October 2001, the allied forces inflicted massive casualties on Taliban and drove them out of power. The remaining Taliban fled across the border into Pakistan to regroup. In 2006, a resurgent Taliban initiated their first offensive to take back Kandahar, their former stronghold. Even though, they were denied control, they continue to be a force to reckon with. They run their writ both in Pakistan and Afghanistan.

Taliban in Afghanistan and Pakistan have a long term agenda – to defeat the government forces, capture territory, enforce sharia and eventually take over the state. Taliban have formed a new alliance, *Shura Ittihad-ul-Mujahideen*, in North and South Waziristan, Pakistan in 2009.

Afghanistan provided perfect environment in 1996 for *al Qaeda* to relocate its headquarters after it was denied permission to return to Sudan. *Al Qaeda* was welcomed by the Taliban. Taliban Government had been recognised by Pakistan, Saudi Arabia and the United Arab Emirates.

Al Qaida is a multi-national Sunni network with a global reach, and supports Islamic militancy in Afghanistan, Algeria, Bosnia, Chechnya, Eritrea, Kosovo, the Philippines, Somalia, Tajikistan, Yemen and Kosovo. *Al Qaeda* has been linked to most high profile attacks the world over including 9/11. It is not possible to ascertain its exact strength, it may be several thousands. It relies on foreign donors for their funding, where as the Taliban also rely on the poppy trade. Poppy production has shot up ever since the US invasion. *Al Qaida* has shifted its headquartered from Afghanistan to Pakistan with growing integration between them and the Taliban, and the various networks like Jalaluddin Haqqani, Baitullah Mehsud, Gulbuddin Hekmatyar and the others. *Al Qaeda* is expanding its activities in other countries like Yemen and Somalia with the aim of providing global leadership to jihadis and targets Americans, Israelis and those regimes which support USA.

After elections in 2004, Hamid Karzai was declared the interim President and continues as President till date (2011). Afghanistan adopted its new constitution, establishing the country as an Islamic Republic with the Government consisting of a President, two Vice Presidents, and a National Assembly of two Houses: the House of People (Wolesi Jirga), and the House of Elders (Meshrano Jirga). There is also an independent Judiciary branch consisting of the Supreme Court (Stera Mahkama), High Courts and Appeal Courts.

The US holds Osama bin Laden responsible for the 9/11 attacks, and the Taliban for providing him safe haven. They operate in the eastern and southern regions. News reports indicate that the scattered Taliban have teamed up with Gulbuddin Hekmatyar, head of Hezbi Islami. It is not certain to what degree these groups are cooperating with one another, however, all three clearly want the United States and International Peace keepers to leave Afghanistan. The Taliban-al Qaeda-Hekmatyar alliance resorts to suicide bombings and deadly attacks on the aid workers to get their message across.

The War in Afghanistan began in 2001, as the US Operation Enduring Freedom was launched, along with the British military. In addition International Security Assistance Force (ISAF), which was established by the UN Security Council at the end of December 2001, was inducted to secure Kabul and the surrounding areas. NATO assumed control of ISAF in 2003. By 2009, ISAF had around 64,500 troops from 49 countries. The United States has approximately 29,950 troops in ISAF. As in November 2010, there are 130,000 NATO troops and 10,000 Enduring Freedom troops in Afghanistan. Another 30,000 are being inducted by May-June 2011. The induction includes high technology wherewithal of war in land, air and sea.

The aim of the invasion was to find Osama bin Laden and other high ranking al Qaeda members to put them on trial, to destroy the organization of al Qaeda, and to remove the Taliban regime which supported it. The US has stated that, as policy, it would not distinguish between terrorist organizations and nations or governments that harbored them.Osama bin Laden has been found and killed on 2 May 2011. Al Qaeda, however, lives on.

Afghanistan has been devastated by the Soviet invasion, the anti Soviet war and multi national force operations that followed. More than 1.2 million died due to violent reasons, 3.7 million Afghans died due to non violent avoidable causes, 5-10 million fled to Pakistan, Iran and Iraq. Another 2 million were internally displaced (IDPs) and 4.2 million were injured. US-backed Pakistani Army offensive in NW Pakistan generated another 2.5 million Pashtun refugees or IDPs. In addition to the human toll, economic and ecological damage was colossal. The writ of the Taliban and associated terror groups generally run in areas away from Kabul.

The present government in Afghanistan has overt support of USA. The forces in Afghanistan include from USA, UK, EU, ISAF, many other countries, the Afghan armed forces and Afghan police. The militants are the *al Qaeda*, Taliban, Jaish-e-Mohammed, Lashkar-e-Tayyiba, Hezb-ul-Mujahideen, Hezb-i-Islami, Jaish-e-Mohammed and Northern Alliance. Pakistan plays a major role in influencing the course of operations. It provides logistic support and air and sea space to the allied forces. Its ISI supports most of the terror groups in Afghanistan, despite denials. In addition are the reconstruction teams from various countries. The scene in Afghanistan is chaotic, like *sambar* or *khichri*. Afghanistan has become all the more important with the signing of 1,700 km pipeline agreement to carry Turkmen natural gas across Afghanistan to Pakistan and India. The agreement has been backed by USA.

Terrorism in Sri Lanka, Bangladesh, Nepal and Myanmar

Sri Lanka

After the military victory of May 2009 over LTTE, the President declared that he could look for a final solution of the Tamil issue only after he had secured a new mandate as the President, and a 2/3rd majority in Parliament, which would enable him to amend the Constitution. He has been elected President with 2/3rd majority with support of the Tamil National Alliance (TNA). The All Party Representatives Committee (APRC), constituted in July 2006, under the Chairmanship of Professor Tissa Vitharana to formulate a draft proposal for Constitutional reform, also provides the necessary direction for reform. The report, submitted in July 2010 includes the following salient recommendations:

- Adoption of a Parliamentary form of Government at the Centre.

- A Unitary structure for the Republic with power shared between the Centre and the Provinces.

- A three-tiered distribution of power (Central, Provincial and Local Governments).

- A mixed electoral system, combining features of the first-past-the-post and proportional representation systems.

- Creation of a Senate.

- Granting of foremost place to the Buddhist religion.

- Status of national language to both Sinhala and Tamil; use of English for official purposes.

- Securing in-built mechanisms to check any secessionist tendencies.

- Creation of two Community Councils, one for Indian Tamils and the other for Sri Lankan Muslims.

- Creation of a Higher Appointment Council for State Services and the Judiciary.

- *Retaining the substances of articles 82 (5) and 83.

The other post war issues to be addressed are:

- Rehabilitation of the IDPs, which is, by and large complete, quality notwithstanding.

- Rehabilitation of 11,000 LTTE cadres who had surrendered. 4,500 of these have been rehabilitated. The remainder are being screened and released in batches for rehabilitation in due course of time.

- De-mining, which is progressing well, over 300,000 mines have been cleared.

There are a few cells of the LTTE still active and are striving desperately to form a transnational Government for the Sri Lankan Tamils. Three broad groups are now assumed to be controlling the remaining pro-LTTE international factions:

- A US group said to be headed by V Rudrakumaran;

- A UK group, controlled by Aruththanthai Emmanuel of the World Tamil Forum; and

- A Norway group under Perinpanayagam Sivaparan *alias* Nediyavan.

There are no significant incidents of terrorism or threat to security in Sri Lanka since the hostilities have ceased. The Government's achievements in rehabilitation of IDPs, and surrendered LTTE cadre, have been significant. In the last budget, highest allocation to the Defence Ministry has been made. The

---

* Article 82 (5) requires any amendment of the Constitution to be passed by two-thirds of all members (including those not present);

Article 83 provides for approval of certain bills by a referendum.

Sri Lankan Government, however, is moving with caution. The past linkages of the LTTE need to be demolished effectively, particularly of the logistics. The Tamils in South India are particularly vulnerable to political machinations. The region also must watch that no LTTE cadres are imparting terror training in the neighbouring countries.

Bangladesh

Bangladesh suffers from abject poverty; 56 million live under poverty line. There is social inequality and deprivation with a large youth population and unemployment. Lack of freedom, democracy and political space deprives people of expressing their legitimate grievances. There is unregulated flow of money. Religion has been politicized. With all these deficiencies there is poor governance and the failure of the state to deliver.

Beginning 1984, the Jamaat-e-Islami, in coordination with its Pakistan counterpart and the ISI, recruited some 5000 madrassa alumni as *mujahideens* and sent them in batches to Afghanistan to participate in the jihad against the Soviets. Here, they came in close contact with the Afghan and Pakistani fundamentalists. On returning from Afghanistan, these cadres propagated for a transnational Muslim state comprising Bangladesh, Assam, Tripura, Muslim majority districts of West Bengal and the Rohingya Muslim dominated Arakan Hills of Myanmar.

Bangladesh has several terrorist and extremist groups which include Harkat-ul-Jihad-al-Islami - Bangladesh (HuJI-B), Jagrata Muslim Janata Bangladesh (JMJB), Jama'at-ul-Mujahideen Bangladesh (JMB) and Hizb-ut-Tahrir.

HuJI-B has links with a*l Qaeda* and Pakistani militant groups, and JMB has ties with it. Its leader Fazlul Rahman is believe to have signed bin Laden's 1998 declaration of holy war on the US. It has cadre of 2000 men. It has been implicated in the 2002 attack on the American Center in Calcutta. HuJI-B is on the US State Department's list of 'other terrorist organizations'. It is also banned in Bangladesh. The re-emergence of HuJI-B under the name "Conscious Islamic People" has been reported. Further, the political wing of HuJI-B will seek to enter politics under the name Islami Gono Andolon.

JMB seeks imposition of Sharia law in Bangladesh and is believed to be responsible for the widespread and coordinated August 2005 bombings in 63 out of 64 districts in Bangladesh killing 2 and injuring 50 in a series of nationwide blasts. JMB has 400 full time members and 50,000-100,000 part timers, and its own training camps. JMB is also reported active in three districts of West Bengal, India – Murshidabad, Malda and Nadia, where it maintains training camps. Reports indicate that there are about 100 full-time JMB cadres in these districts. It is suspected to be affiliated with *al Qaeda* and is a banned organization. The outfit suffered a major setback when six of its top leaders were executed in 2007 and a number of others were arrested recently (2010). Among those executed were its founder chief Shaikh Abdur Rahman and second in command Siddiq ul Islam Bangla Bhai.

JMJB is based generally in northwest of Bangladesh. It is suspected to be linked with *al Qaeda*. It is also responsible for a series of suicide bombings in Bangladesh. Reports indicated that the JMJB is supported by certain members of the BNP and police. JMJB is a banned organization.

Hizb-ut-Tahrir is an international Islamist political party founded in Jerusalem in 1953. Hizb-ut-Tehrir has three clear goals: to establish a community of like-minded Hizb-ut-Tehrir members in host states, to sway public opinion in one or more host states to facilitate change of government, and, finally, to establish a new government that will implement Islamic laws. Hizb-ut-Tahrir's goal is to establish a global Islamic Caliphate. It is a proscribed organization.

Shahadat-e-al-Hikma (SAH) is a group of Islamic extremists. Their leader Kowsar Hussain Siddique is alleged to be connected with Taliban and *al Qaeda* and is believed to be funded by Dawood Ibrahim. Although there is no authenticity about the strength of SAH, the group's leader Kowsar claimed that the outfit has 10,000 commandos and 25,000 fighters to bring Islamic revolution. The numbers have not been substantiated. The group is banned.

Left Wing Extremism (LWE) in Bangladesh, often described as *Sarbaharas*, is a highly dispersed, low-scale and criminalised movement, consisting of a multiplicity of minor groups, no combination of which constitutes any significant threat to the country's security as of now. The network of different active Left outfits survives in 10 southwestern districts, particularly Kushtia,

Jhenidah, Chuadanga and Meherpur. 13 factions of armed Communist groups, and as many gangs operate in 23 districts of the Khulna, Rajshahi, Dhaka and Barisal divisions. They, reportedly, indulge in murder, drugs trafficking, robbery, extortion, abduction and other unlawful activities. These outlawed groups possess a large number of sophisticated weapons.

The fundamentalist movements in Bangladesh are linked to *al Qaeda,* Taliban, other like organizations in India, Nepal, Sri Lanka, Myanmar, Indonesia, Malaysia, Pakistan and Afghanistan. ISI is attempting to convert Bangladesh into a regional hub for terror with reach into India and Southeast Asia. Bangladesh's riverine borders and the coast line need to be guarded effectively.

BNP coalition alliance with the Jamaat-e-Islami Party brought some JMB officials into the government. These officials facilitate fundamentalist influence over parts of Bangladesh. Madrassas further facilitate terrorist activity, making inroads into the armed forces and rigging of the elections.

The July 2006 series of coordinated bomb blasts that killed around 200 persons and injuring some 500 on commuter trains in Mumbai, were suspected to be handiwork of several individuals reportedly with ties to terrorist groups in Bangladesh and Nepal who were directly or indirectly linked to ISI.

With political stabilization in 2009, the activities of terrorists in Bangladesh, has registered a downward trend. No terrorist attack has been recorded in 2009, though radical groups, both Muslim and LWE continue to maintain a varying degree of presence across the country.

There are strong reasons for optimism in Bangladesh, given the current regime's initial steps against disruptive and radical forces. Nevertheless, the residual capacities of these forces, their deep linkages in the political establishment, and the complex dynamic that had thrown Bangladesh into the desruptive spiral in the past years, continue to exist. It will take years of sustained commitment at all levels of governance to restore the normalcy in the state. India also needs to amend its Immigrant laws and guard its borders more effectively. The vote bank politics must give way to the national interests.

Myanmar

Myanmar is grouped with Southeast Asia, but for its contiguity and influence on the countries of South Asia, the country study is included here. The border adjoining India and Bangladesh is hilly, thickly wooded and as such porous.

Terrorism in Myanmar primarily consists of anti-government militant activity. At least half a dozen militant groups from India's northeast, where numerous tribal and ethnic groups fight for greater autonomy or independence, have training camps in northern Myanmar's thick jungles under the patronage of the NSCN (K).

While ULFA and NSCN (K) have camps in the Kachin province bordering China, the other outfits have been operating from areas bordering India. There are also several Indian Insurgent Group camps in Shan and Chin States. The NSCN (IM) takes the help of the Karen National Union (KNU) for cross border smuggling of small arms from Southeast Asia and China's Yunnan. These are shipped to the Northeast via the Naf River in the Bangladesh-Myanmar border and through Chittagong port. Chinese arms also enter India's Northeast directly through Myanmar.

The arms from Thailand and Cambodia are first shipped to Myanmar's Arakan forest, repacked and then smuggled into Northeastern states to support insurgents of India and Bangladesh. Myanmar's opium cultivation has grown from 27,700 ha in 2007 to 28,800 ha in 2008 to 31,700 ha in 2009 to 38,100 ha in 2010.

India and Myanmar in July 2010 agreed on close cooperation between the security forces of the two countries in tackling terrorism. The two sides signed a treaty on mutual legal assistance in criminal matters that will be crucial in enabling India to get access to insurgents from the Northeastern states who continue to take shelter along the India-Myanmar border. The seven-nation BIMSTEC* grouping, in 2009 also adopted a convention to combat terrorism and insurgency against militancy, particularly in its northeast.

The situation in the northeast of India is improving because of positive

---

*Bay of Bengal Initiative for Multi-sectoral Technical and Economic Cooperation

initiatives by Bangladesh, Myanmar and BIMSTEC.

Nepal

A monarchy throughout most of its history, Nepal was ruled by the Shah dynasty from 1768, when Prithvi Narayan Shah unified its many small kingdoms. The Communist Party of Nepal (Maoist) resorted to an armed struggle in 1996, by attacking police stations and thereby declaring a People's War. They strongly believe in the philosophy of Mao Tsetung – 'political power grows out of the barrel of gun' and won the largest number of seats in the Constituent Assembly election held in April 2008, and formed a coalition government which included most of the parties. Nepal, thus, became a secular and inclusive democratic republic. Nonetheless, political tensions and consequent power-sharing battles continued, as inherent in any coalition.

In May 2009, the Maoist led government was toppled and another coalition government with all major political parties barring the Maoists was formed. The move came in the wake of opposition to the Prime Minister Prachanda's decision to sack Army Chief following the General's opposition to the Prachanda's demand for the integration of members of the PLA raised by the Maoists during their days in the insurgency into the Army. CPN (Maoist) leader and ex Prime Minister of Nepal, Prachanda has warned that the Maoist agitation that his party had launched, will be intensified. The following terrorist groups prevail in Nepal:

The CPN (Maoist)

The CPN (Maoist) currently a proscribed group was formed in 1995 following a split in the Communist Party of Nepal-Unity Centre. A radical faction led by Pushpa Kamal Dahal alias Comrade Prachanda and Baburam Bhattarai set up the CPN (Maoist) and denounced the Communist Party of Nepal (Unified Marxist-Leninists)* and other mainstream communist factions as rebels and revisionists due to their participation in the parliamentary process. It resorted to an armed struggle 1996 onwards by attacking police stations in the

---

*Communist Party of Nepal (Unified Marxist-Leninists) is one of the largest communist parties in Nepal. It was created in 1991 through the unification of the Communist Party of Nepal (Marxist) and Communist Party of Nepal (Marxist-Leninist) as a result of People's Movement.

northwestern Nepal and declaring a People's War.

They aim to establish a New Democracy in Nepal through a revolt against feudalism, imperialism and so-called reformists. They also draw inspiration from the Revolutionary Internationalist Movement and Peru's Left Wing Extremist guerilla movement. The radical communist parties from different parts of the world have provided ideological support. Their demands included the abolition of royal privileges and the promulgation of a new constitution, and the abrogation of the Mahakali Treaty with India dealing with the distribution of water and electricity and the delineation of the border between the two countries.

Government estimates indicated that there are approximately 5,500 combatants, 8,000 militia, 4,500 cadres, 33,000 hard core followers, and 200,000 sympathizers.

The main fighting and support forces consist of Magars, Tharus, Janjatis (Gurungs, Rais, Limbus, Tamangs, Dalits, Brahmins and Chhetris, the last two also providing the political and military leadership). Among the Maoist fighters – about 60 per cent are deployed in the mid-west and west, 10 per cent are in the far west with around 10 percent in Gorkha, the rest are located in Kathmandu valley and east of it. A considerable number of retired Gurkha soldiers of the British and the Indian Army inhabit many of the Maoist-affected areas and participate in the movement.

Available reports also indicate that one-fifth to one-third of the cadres and combatants may be women. The All Nepal National Independent Students' Union (Revolutionary), or ANNISU-R is the student wing of the Maoists. According to a report the ANNISU-R comprises approximately 400,000 members. Reportedly, weaponry in their possession include AK-47 rifles, self-loading rifles, .303 rifles, country guns, hand grenades, explosives, detonators, mortars, and light machine guns.

Young Communist League (YCL)

YCL was formed by the CPN (Maoist) during the People's War as an affiliate to provide support and energy to the revolution. The YCL is a fusion of the Party's military and political character, and it is composed of PLA members who have an interest in politics. As the party's youth wing, its role is to organise youth, be involved in events, conduct political awareness, and take part in development work as volunteers. Once the CPN (Maoist) was proscribed, the YCL was also forced to go underground. After the 2006 People's Movement and the subsequent over-ground role of the insurgents, the CPN (Maoist) revived the YCL.

At its first national convention in Kathmandu in February 2007, the YCL formed a 45-member new Central Committee with Ganeshman Pun as its Chairman. Most of the YCL members are reportedly combatants, also include an unspecified number of child soldiers. It is widely known that YCL cadres receive extensive military training. They openly carry knives, sticks, iron bars and other improvised weapons and swagger around the countryside and the Kathmandu region without fear or restriction.

The other face of the YCL is that it engages in a number of symbolic activities such as cleaning localities, cleaning rivers and planting trees. On occasions, they have involved themselves in quasi-policing activities like traffic management, night patrolling, demolition of illegal houses, and the capture of gangsters. Backed by the might of the Maoists, YCL cadres challenge Government authorities, including the Police, and are progressively establishing a parallel authority and system. The YCL is active in majority of districts across the country.

Janatantrik Terai Mukti Morcha – Goit (JTMM-G)

JTMM-G was formed in July 2004 by Jaya Krishna Goit after splitting from CPN (Maoist). Goit, formerly a leader of the Unified Marxist Leninist (UML), was also co-ordinator of the *Madhesi National Liberation Front of the CPN (Maoist). Gradually, as he came to believe that the Maoists were not serious about the development of the Terai region, he floated a separate outfit. Unconfirmed reports suggest strength of a thousand, including hard-core cadres and sympathisers.

---

* Madhesi implies Terai region of Nepal.

JTMM-G demands

- The Terai should be declared an independent state.

- There should be proportionate participation by determining constituencies on the basis of population.

- All the police, army and administration in the Terai should be evacuated and Madhesi people should be posted there.

- Population census should be conducted in Terai under the supervision of Madhesis.

- All the revenue collected from Terai should be spent for the development of Terai.

- All the Madhesi killed by the state and Maoists should be declared martyrs and NPR 1.5 million should be provided as compensation.

- Citizenship should be issued from the central to district level in coordination with the Madhesis.

- The land of Madhesis captured by Maoists should be returned.

- Maoists should end their donation drive and tax collection in Terai.

Janatantrik Terai Mukti Morcha – Jwala Singh (JTMM-J)

JTMM-J was formed by Nagendra Kumar Paswan aka Jwala Singh in August 2006 after he broke away from the Goit led JTMM-G. Jwala Singh, a former CPN (Maoist) cadre, developed differences with Goit over the strategies to be adopted for the liberation of the Terai and declared an independent Terai state. He stated that any talks with the Government will be to demarcate the border only. The group claims to have formed an armed militia in 12 of the Terai's 20 districts.

The terrorism in Nepal stems from a domestic conflict between the Government and the Marxist rebels who seek political, social and economic justice in the society. There are not only the Maoists, but are Madhesis, in addition to numerous small rebel groups who create law and order problems making the country soft towards the internal and external elements. The scenario will have telling effect in Nepal and the region, particularly Bhutan, India, Myanmar, Bangladesh and Pakistan, as the Nepal's territory and systems are being used by terrorists.

Assessment: South Asia

South Asia is a group of countries with common colonial past, long history of conflict, war, terrorism and trans-border ethnicity. Countries are sponsors as well as victims of terrorism. Nationalism, ethnicity and religion are powerful factors that contribute to terror. These countries, including India, at best are developing and far from achieving the status of developed countries. India, Pakistan and Sri Lanka should be considred developing, the remaining are least developed. The technological threshold is low despite claims of high technology. The per capita income is one of the lowest, over 40 per cent are illiterate, there is disease and human right abuse, unemployment and rampant corruption. Societies do not break free from the shackles of the past, and superstitions. A lot good human resource is frittered away in visits to places of worship, *yatras*, marriages and other family functions in addition to the strikes, layoffs, wanton destruction of the scarce resources and so on. The political class often ignores the aspiration of the people who vote them in. There is no bar in criminals becoming politicians and ministers. The judiciary will look for hard evidence against them in tune with the standards in the developed and educated world. The law, thus, is circumvented. Against these countries, the stick of democracy, human rights, environment and denial regimes, is often used by the developed world. Ethnicity is double edged, it is used to germinate and spread terrorism, and yet the same platform is used for communication and resolution of disputes. Media in India plays a pivotal role in checking the unfettered authority of the politician, particularly, where it comes to corruption at high places.

South Asia is the most terror affected area of the world. Each country suffers varying degree of insurgency and terror. In fact all countries are intertwined as far as terror networking is concerned. The major conflicts in the region between India and Pakistan keep the resolution of terror problem elusive. Pakistan continues to pursue its policies of exporting terror in its neighbourhood and the world over as the state policy. Pakistan is central to cause of terror problem in South Asia. *Al Qaeda*, Taliban and a large number of other terror groups operate in concert with anti West, anti Jew and anti India agenda. Anti India implies fermenting separatist movement in Jammu & Kashmir. Madrassa in Pakistan and Bangladesh provides a fertile ground for training, planning and indoctrination of the potential terrorists. Islamic terrorism is on the rise. In Pakistan, crackdowns on the jihadi and sectarian organizations have backfired, triggering large-scale militant Islamic consolidation. The war in Afghanistan has only aggravated the situation. Pakistan and Bangladesh are serving as major hubs for ideological and material support to the South Asian radical Islamic networks.

In India, homegrown jihadists are emerging. Terrorism in India is primarily attributable to illiteracy, poverty, unemployment, disparity, political injustice, religious reasons, historical baggage and soft handling. The regions with long term terrorist activities today are Jammu and Kashmir, Naxalite areas in central and eastern India, the northeastern states and metropolitan cities. A large swathe of India is affected by terrorism or insurgency movements.

Terrorism/insurgency related fatalities in India have declined from a peak of 5,839 in 2001 to 2,611 in 2008, 2231 in 2009 and 1891 in 2010 (SATP data). Fatalities in 2011, till February are 117. India experienced no major Islamist terrorist attack outside Jammu & Kashmir in 2009 and 2010 after series of attacks in 2008 culminating in 26/11 outrage, which killed 166 civilians. Union Home Minister Chidambaram revealed some 13 Islamist terrorist conspiracies were thwarted in 2009. The decline in Jammu & Kashmir, where fatalities have dropped to 374 in 2010, is also noteworthy. This may well be due to Pakistan's growing terror backlash and international pressure. The terror infrastructure in Pakistan, however, is being kept intact. There is an increase in the fatalities in the Left Wing Extremism. The fatalities increased from 638 in 2008, 997 in 2009, 1174 in 2010 and 103 (till March 2011).

Insurgency and terror related casualties across India's northeast have also declined over the years and continues as we have entered 2011. Bangladesh, Bhutan and Myanmar initiatives to crack down on the militant camps in their territories are having the desired effect. However, Manipur continues to be hot bed in the region. Some insurgent groups demand secession from the Indian state. These groups often also clash with each other. There have been renewed Governmental efforts and positive movement to bring almost all militant outfits in the Northeast to the negotiating table even though there are several contentious issues concerning post conflict repatriation, resettlement and disarming of cadres. With Manipur, the negotiations between the Government of India and the militants have yet to commence due to the conditionality of the militants, secession being the major issue.

As of June 2010, Indian Government has identified 83 districts in 9 states as Naxal hit in central and eastern parts of the country referred to as the Red Corridor. The Naxalites, however claim to operate in 182 districts, mainly in the states of Bihar, Jharkhand, Chhattisgarh, West Bengal, Madhya Pradesh, Maharashtra and Andhra Pradesh. Chhattisgarh is at the epi-centre. Despite the movement of additional para military forces in to the region, the Naxal related fatalities have been on the rise and there is reason to believe that they have expanded their areas of subversion. The Naxal problem in India is the most serious insurgency issue being faced by the Indian state.

In Nepal, the CPN (Maoist) resorted to an armed struggle in 1996, thereby declaring a People's War and won the largest number of seats in the Constituent Assembly election held in April 2008, and formed a coalition government. Nonetheless, political tensions and consequent power-sharing battles continued. In May 2009, the Prime Minister resigned in the wake of the Army Chief's refusal to integrate PLA members into the Army and for general insubordination. The Maoist led government was replaced by another coalition government. CPN (Maoist), now Unified Communist Party of Nepal – Maoist (UCPN-M), has warned that the Maoist agitation that the party had launched, will be intensified. The terrorism in Nepal stems from a completely domestic conflict between the Government and the Marxist rebels. However, there will be telling effect in the region, particularly Bhutan, India, Myanmar, Bangladesh and Pakistan as the Nepal's territory and systems are being used by terrorists.

In Bangladesh, since the election of the Sheikh Hasina Government in December 2008 with a clear majority, the regime moved strongly and swiftly against terrorist groups. This includes HuJI-B and Jamaat-e-Islami Bangladesh. Dhaka has also acted decisively against many other terrorist groups operating in India's northeast, who had found safe haven in Bangladesh. Their camps have been shut down, and most of their leaders have been handed over to Indian authorities or arrested. Measures have also been initiated to beef up the security apparatus to include formation of a 17 member 'National Committee on Militancy Resistance and Prevention, and a proposal for a South Asian Anti-Terrorism Task Force has been made.

Groups such as HuJI-B with links with *al Qaeda*, and the LeT, are currently dormant. The JMB, which was the principal architect of the serial blasts across the country in August 2005, has survived, despite the execution of its top leadership and the arrest of many second rung leaders. The security forces seem to be focusing more on the Left Wing Extremists than the Islamist groups as is evident from the casualties in the years 2008, 2009 and 2010. Regrouping of the Islamist groups should, thus not be ruled out. Madrassas need to be watched. India and Myanmar hold stakes in Bangladesh's stability and secular governance. As of now (2011), Bangladesh's secular roots are holding.

Terrorism in Myanmar primarily consists of anti-government militant activity. Myanmar's opium cultivation has grown by 50 per cent since 2006. More than 1 million people in Myanmar are now involved in producing opium. At least, half a dozen militant groups from India's northeast, have training camps in northern Myanmar's thick jungles. The NSCN (IM) takes the help of the Karen National Union (KNU) for cross border smuggling of small arms from Southeast Asia and China's Yunnan Province.

The situation in the northeast of India is improving because of positive initiatives by Bangladesh, Myanmar and *BIMSTEC.

In Sri Lanka, there is little possibility of a resurgence of terrorist violence

---

*Bay of Bengal Initiative for Multi Sectoral Technical and Economic Co operation (BIMSTEC) is an international organisation in South Asia and South East Asia. The member countries are: Bangladesh, India, Myanmar, Sri Lanka, Thailand, Bhutan and Nepal.

in the foreseeable future; however, Tamil separatism as a political ideology remains.

Pakistan has all ingredients of a state which manufactures terrorism, exports it and maintains it. ISI is the central nervous system of terror export. The originator and breeder of the terror now also suffers from the backlash of the jihadis. Its social fabric and attitudes, particularly of the religious leaders, will prevent a truly democratic form of governance to take roots. Military is another power centre.

Pakistan has a number of terror outfits like *al Qaeda,* Taliban, LeT, JeM and organizations with pan Islamic character which operates from its soil in the neighbouring countries, particularly South Asia. Madrassa provides motivated manpower for the terror factory to go on. J&K and Afghanistan have been effectively invested by Pakistan.

Afghanistan has been devastated by the turmoil since 1978. In addition to the human toll, the demographic upheaval and displacement, economic and ecological damage is colossal. The writ of the Taliban and associated terror groups generally continue to run in areas away from Kabul. Turbulence is likely to continue due to external factors and will have serious implications for South Asia.

It is no longer possible to divorce developments in Afghanistan from the Islamist terrorism in South Asia. The combine of Afghanistan and Pakistan has created nearly a hopeless situation in South Asia and elsewhere in the world. The situation in both countries has worsened steadily. 2009 was a year of escalating violence and widening disorder across this region.

The 'London Summit' (London Conference on Afghanistan, January 10, 2010), represented the consensual approach of the international community, led by the US and the UK, outlining the proposed strategy to support the Afghan Government to secure, stabilize and develop Afghanistan. It seems a plan to somehow walk away from the mess in Afghanistan. A face saving exit policy. The western withdrawal too soon will surrender Afghanistan to extremism and will be seen as the triumph of the radicals. The South Asia will be the worst sufferer as the jihadis will be released to operate in the neighbourhood. The US cannot simply turn its back on Afghanistan. The reconstruction teams from various countries must continue and complete their missions. The stability in Afghanistan has become all the more important with the signing of 1,700 km pipeline agreement to carry Turkmen natural gas across Afghanistan to Pakistan and India. The agreement has been backed by USA.

South Asia needs stability for development of its masses. Its western flank is turbulant which externalises its internal problems. The world has to watch out to the two belligerant nuclear neighbours. J&K is a major issue but its resolution is unlikely to calm down ambitious Islamic Republic of Pakistan.

Counter-Terrorism in South Asia

"The soul, mind, and meaning of a State lie in its Laws"

Marcus Tullius Cicero, Roman philosopher

"The freedom of individual must take second place to the security of the state"

Lord Denning

Terrorism is a disease which needs to be treated rather than fought. You are not fighting an enemy but mentally sick and misguided who must be brought on course by looking in to their grievances and aspirations. A tooth for tooth strategy is counterproductive and has never succeeded. No effort is being made to defend the actions of the terrorists; their actions are not being approved, nor encouraged. However, the states must follow the law and not retaliate indiscriminately. Negotiations should be the hallmark. Terrorism cannot be tackled by state terrorism. Despite actions by the armed forces of the states, the menace of terrorism has increased.

The UN must find an expression for the acts of terrorism so that the crimes may be dealt in a uniform manner in the international courts. It is not easy as a number of countries, political systems and religions sponsoring terrorism will not agree. The political systems in various countries will have variety of views on the subject. An expression legally acceptable must be found. Care, however, must be taken that some economic and technological powers are not allowed to abuse counter-terrorism. Response to 9/11 should have been internal rather than global. Libya uprising (2011) is an internal matter and the International response is not a counter-terror measure, but is an act of terror. Some countries have made it a habit of invading other countries on the smallest pretext to externalize their internal issues or in their economic interest. They hover around energy rich regions and cultures inimical to theirs. Such overbearing attitude of the west will continue to draw responses in the form of terrorism. Wouldn't it be so by any weaker country or an aggrieved party?

Counter-terrorism has broadly been discussed in the previous chapters concurrently with the text on terrorism. The first step must be to recognise the need to deal with the menace of terrorism holistically. Not an easy task but some visionary leaders may be able to veer around the narrow political, economic and egoistic goals of a few countries. The issue should lead to agreements, conventions and treaties. Simultaneously it should also be treated directly by the concerned countries.

If the aim of the states is the welfare of their people, it is time that cooperation, prosperity and development replaced conflicts. Terrorism being global in nature, *per force*, must be responded by attacking (read tackling) it at multi levels, viz developed countries, at the level of UN, and the third world countries to include NGOs and societies.

Terrorism being a global phenomenon with global linkages, global planning and decentralized execution, must be treated top down:

- The role that the developed countries must play since they have joined the ranks of the victims.

- Joint effort in conjunction with the UN.

- The role of the third world countries where terrorism has taken roots, and are easy and routine victims.

- The role of the societies and NGOs.

Presently the developed world is treating the symptoms back home and in the third world countries. They must not meddle in the affairs of the other countries. They should also not exploit the developing and under-developed countries. Neo-colonialism should not be allowed and all international business should be through the trading norms and not through arms twisting. Their technological exchange should also be without exploitative strings attached.

These should all be out of moral considerations and the fact that the world has given them enough or they have taken enough from the world. Developed world must draw out a matrix of international relations through treaties, MOUs and so on to help the world reduce/eliminate the menace of terrorism.

The UN Global Counter-Terrorism Strategy was adopted on 8 September 2006. The Strategy, in the form of a Resolution and an annexed Plan of Action, is a unique global instrument agreed for the first time by all the member states that will enhance national, regional and international efforts to counter terrorism. The instrument provides a common strategic and operational framework to fight terrorism. A clear message, that terrorism is unacceptable in all its forms and manifestation has been sent to the concerned quarters. Counter-Terrorism measures range from strengthening state capacities to dealing with terrorist threats and to better coordination at UN level. The full text of this Strategy is at Appendix. This document is a wholesome terrorism document to promote awareness, participation and preventive measures. It also deals with respect for human rights. References have been made of the chemical warfare and Chemical Weapons Convention. Although it does not add much to the thirteen pre-existing UN counter-terrorism resolutions (listed on page 9), the Strategy puts them together in to a single, coherent, and universally adopted framework document. It is a consensus document implementable on a wide canvas. It is a breakthrough as it broadens support for the UN counter-terrorism program to include the entire UN membership, thus will lead to solutions which address the needs and aspirations of all nations big and small, of the first world and the third world alike. The Strategy, however, does not have provisions for enforcement. It is a consensus document.

The Strategy takes in to account the short, medium and long term measures. It is not merely addressing the law and order issues of the countries but goes much beyond to addresses both preventive and long-term measures to check the spread of terrorism. According to the Strategy, conditions conducive to the spread of terrorism include - poverty, unresolved conflicts, lack of rule of law and violations of human rights, ethnic, national and religious discrimination, political exclusion, socio-economic marginalization and lack of good governance. The Strategy is also committed to the realization of the

*Millennium Development Goals, which are poverty, universal primary education, hunger, maternal and child mortality, disease, gender inequality, environmental degradation and the Global Partnership for Development to be achieved by 2015. Concurrently, the Strategy is also concerned about the imperative for respecting human rights across every proposal and decision. It also acknowledges the role of the NGOs and that of the society. To that extent it is holistic as far as its implementation is concerned. It is being implemented by all, including the aggrieved segments and not just by a few as in the case of the Security Council. How the NGOs and the civil societies will be co-opted or how they will operate and contribute is a matter of detail that has to be gone in to. It will take time before some mechanism is in place as regards participation and the role that will be played by the NGOs and the societies of various countries. The support, sponsorship and funds may freely and legitimately be available to the NGOs and the societies. Their involvement has improved the reach of the UN and the regional players to various segments of society like the social workers, religious teachers, educationists, women organizations, media and so on to disseminate programs and also to educate the masses.

Broadly the 'Plan of Action' of the UN Counter-Terrorism Strategy includes:

- Measures to address the conditions conducive to the spread of terrorism

- Measures to prevent and combat terrorism

- Measures to build State capacities to prevent and combat terrorism and to strengthen the role of the United Nations system in this regard

- Measures to ensure respect for human rights for all and the rule of law as the fundamental basis of the fight against terrorism

The plan has the approval of all states. It has all the ingredients to succeed to an appreciable measure if the developed countries cooperate and stop

---

*The Millennium Development Goals (MDGs) are eight international development goals that all 192 UN member states and 23 international organizations have agreed to achieve by the year 2015. They include eradicating extreme poverty, reducing child mortality rates, fighting disease epidemics such as AIDS, and developing a global partnership for development.

meddling in the affairs of other states. The third world countries should display resilience and not fall a prey to short term gains. The states should also not allow themselves to be engaged by bigger nations. Some South Asian countries seem to be falling to this game. It has to be remembered that the countries engaging the weaker or smaller nations do so only in their self interest. The state propagation of religion should also stop to make the world more tolerant. All these are tall orders but sincere efforts need to be made to make the world a happier place to live.

Spread of Terrorism

The UN Educational, Scientific and Cultural Organization (UNESCO) has a key role to check fundamental causes to spread of terrorism. It should ensure timely realization of the development goals and objectives agreed at the major UN conferences and summits, through a system of checks and balance. The capacity of the UN in areas such as conflict prevention, negotiation, mediation, conciliation and judicial settlement, rule of law, peace keeping and peace building should be fully utilized to strengthen the global fight against terrorism. This would be done through a process of dialogue, tolerance and understanding among civilizations, cultures, peoples and religions. At another level, promote a culture of human development by establishing and encouraging education and public awareness programs by involving all sections of society. Youth unemployment must be reduced to prevent circumstances that force them to join anti-social activities. In fact the youth should be involved to rehabilitate the victims of terrorism and their families and facilitate the normalization of their lives.

The Strategy is premised on the principles of universality, indivisibility, interrelation and interdependence of all human rights – civil, cultural, economic, political and social – reaffirmed by the Vienna Declaration and Program of Action, 1993, which recognises interdependence between democracies, development and human rights.

The UNESCO Integrated Strategy to Combat Racism, Discrimination, Xenophobia and Related Intolerance (32C/13) must be implemented in all earnest to reduce the causes of terrorism.

Prevention and Countering Global Terrorism

Amongst other measures, the first step is to deny weapons, explosives and tools of destruction to the terrorist outfits and individuals. The countries must maintain strict verifiable accounting of all items of combat. The international register of arms transfer must be meticulously maintained by the UN. The states must not indulge in unaccounted arms transfer like it happened in Afghanistan. This very first step will be most potent. Such transfers normally strike back with ripple effect like in the case of Afghanistan, Pakistan and the western world, USA in particular. The illegal and illicit weapons in circulation should also be taken stock of. All states have a major role to play towards this consensus agenda.

The states must deny safe haven to the terrorists and bring them to justice, on the basis of the principle of extradite or prosecute, including any person who supports, facilitates, participates or attempts to participate in the financing, planning, perpetration of terrorist acts or provides safe havens. The states should also be careful in granting asylum to an individual (s) to obviate abuse of the gesture. The border and customs controls should be more effective to forestall a terror act. The International Maritime Organization, the World Customs Organization and the International Civil Aviation Organization should strengthen their co-operation and prevent the misuse of their channels.

The states must exchange timely and accurate information concerning terrorism to include drug trafficking, illicit arms trade, money laundering and smuggling of nuclear, chemical, biological, radiological and other potentially deadly materials. The states should become parties to the United Nations Convention against Transnational Organized Crime and to the three protocols supplementing it.

The facilities provided by the United Nations Counter-Terrorism Committee, Executive Directorate, the United Nations Office of Drugs and Crime and the International Criminal Police Organization should be utilized for an integrated approach to counter-terrorism.

The states must ensure the implementation of the relevant provisions of national and international law, in particular, human rights law, refugee law and international humanitarian law. To that end the states should conclude and implement mutual judicial assistance and extradition agreements, and strengthen cooperation between law enforcement agencies.

An International Centre to Fight Terrorism should be formed where a comprehensive updated database on all forms of terrorism region-wise is available to the countries and the international police organizations. The UN should provide the necessary and effective coordination and guidelines to get best possible response and assistance to counter international terrorism.

Building States' Capacity to Combat Terrorism

Building of state's capacity to counter terrorism is a wide subject demanding political, diplomatic, technological, financial, military and police initiatives. The porosity of the state should be identified and addressed. The aspect of democracy and human rights should not be allowed to be abused, nor should these be allowed to be used as a stick by the developed world.

Member states should consider making voluntary contributions to the UN to create and sustain counter-terrorism institutions and projects. They should also take advantage of the framework provided by international and regional organizations to share best practices in counter-terrorism capacity building and to offer their expertise and facilities to other states. Member states must cooperate in all the projects and schemes mentioned to combat terrorism at the global level.

Every national and international session/seminar should commence with a brief on the terror situation and its condemnation. There should be frequent exchanges of information on cooperation and technical assistance among member states, UN bodies dealing with counter-terrorism, specialized agencies, international, regional and sub-regional organizations, and the donor community to develop states' capacities to implement relevant UN resolutions. UN Counter-Terrorism Committee, its Executive Directorate, UN Office on Drugs and Crime and International Criminal Police Organization are particularly relevant in this regard.

The International Atomic Energy Agency and the Organization for the Prohibition of Chemical Weapons should devise methods and disseminate them to all countries to help states build capacity to prevent terrorists from accessing nuclear, chemical or radiological materials and in the event of their use by the terrorists, provide mitigating measures.

Human Rights

The human rights, refugee law, international humanitarian law and fundamental freedoms must be protected while countering terrorism. The institution of United Nations High Commissioner for Human Rights must be supported. States should strengthen the international legal architecture by promoting the rule of law and effective criminal justice dispensation across the nations. While human rights is the hall mark of the modern societies, care must be taken that the system is not exploited by the terrorists, firstly to execute an act and then veer around the democratic legal systems to evade the punishment or get away with lighter punishment not commensurate with the crime committed. The terror trials should be speedily concluded and punishment awarded should be implemented as soon as possible. The entire concept of human rights and justice needs to be reviewed as far as terrorism is concerned so as not to allow abuse.

The 13 UN Conventions, the precursor to the Global Counter-Terrorism Strategy, emhasise civil aviation security, maritime security, hostages and other terrorist acts. These 13 Conventions together with the Global Counter-Terrorism Strategy should form the backdrop to all regional and national and counter terrorism initiatives. However, in the absence of a comprehensive UN Treaty, national criminal laws and bilateral arrangements remain the basic tools of counter-terrorism enforcement.

South Asia

The countries of South Asia have common colonial background, trans-border ethnicity, cultural commonality with accompanying tensions, opportunities and threats, poverty, illiteracy, disease and unemployment. 40 per cent of its people live below poverty line. Except Bhutan, all countries are densely populated. There is inter and intra region economic disparity. India, Pakistan and Sri Lanka should be considered developing countries, others are among the least developed, comparable with sub Saharan countries. India is the largest country with 80 per cent population and 80 per cent GDP of the region. Countries, particularly India and Pakistan, have fissiparous regions and are in conflict with each other as well. Both have fought three wars and a major border conflict since their independence. The countries have porous borders which facilitate trans-border anti-social activities including terrorism.

Apprehensions, mistrust and tension exist between and among various nationalities, communities and religions. Consequently, South Asia remains politically volatile and threatens peace and stability both within and beyond. Socio-economic disparity and deprivations act as catalyst in creating unrest and terror. Self-seeking political class is another factor which exploits this state of affairs as safe passages to their power and legitimacy. This political class often frustrates the very people who elect them. The region, as such, becomes prone to outside interference and exploitation. Interestingly, because of the common background and trans-border ethnicity, the same reasons which create animosity and divide, also provide a people to people contact platform to communicate, share their experiences and concerns within South Asia.

In South Asia, in parts it is insurgency, independence/secessionist/self-determination movements and other forms of violence involving mass of people. Terrorism in its classical understanding is in Afghanistan, Pakistan, Jammu and Kashmir and in patches elsewhere in the region. However, all violence that resembles terrorism has been considered in this chapter. Counter-Terrorism is being dealt with in South Asia by the following provisions:

The Constitution (Sixteenth Amendment) Act, 1963, was enacted empowering Parliament to impose, reasonable restrictions in the interest of sovereignty and integrity of India, on the freedom of speech and expression; right to assemble peaceably and without arms; and right to form associations or unions.

Anti-terrorism laws in India have always been a subject of controversy because of fundamental rights of citizens guaranteed in Part III of the Constitution. These have been enacted before by the legislature and upheld by the judiciary though not without reluctance. Because of continuing terrorist activities, the statutes have been reintroduced with requisite modifications.

At present, the legislations in force to check terrorism in India are:

- The National Security Act, 1980

- The Unlawful Activities (Prevention) Act, 1967, which was designed to meet the challenge to the territorial integrity of India. The Act is completely within the purview of the Central List in the 7th Schedule of the Constitution.

- Other major Anti-terrorist law in India is The Maharashtra Control of Organised Crime Act, (MCOCA) 1999. This law was specifically made to deal with rising organized crime in Maharashtra and especially in Mumbai due to the underworld. Under the MCOCA, a person is presumed guilty unless he is able to prove his innocence.

The anti terrorist laws in Pakistan, often, changed with the change of regimes. The law in force in 2011 is '1997 Anti-Terrorism Act', which included a broad definition of 'terrorism' was enacted after 1997 bombing by Mehram Ali, a member of the Shia militant organization. This Act created specials Anti-Terrorism Courts (ATC) as well as an Anti-Terrorism Appellate (ATA) Tribunal. The Supreme Court declared most of the Act unconstitutional. After addressing the Supreme Court's observations, in August 1999, Anti-Terrorism Act, was amended to authorize Anti Terrorism Courts again.

Pakistan Armed Forces (Acting in Aid of Civil Power) Ordinance, 1998 was declared "unconstitutional, without legal authority, and with no legal effect by the Supreme Court in 1999. As a result the Ordinance was repealed. However, "civil commotion" was included as a crime under the 'Anti-Terrorism Act of 1997'.

*Pakistan considers at least five elements in its definition of terrorism. First, it considers terrorism a threat to humanity and human civilization and in principle condemns all acts of terrorism anywhere in the world. Second, it maintains that the root causes of terrorism should be addressed as part of the international campaign against terrorism. Third, the fight against terrorism should include state terrorism, (possibly implying case of Kashmir). Fourth, a distinction should be drawn between freedom struggles and terrorism. Fifth, a distinction should be made between the Islamic religion and terrorism.

Here is what the Ambassador Shamshad Ahmad, Permanent Representative of Pakistan to the United Nations has to say on 2 October 2001:

"No matter what actions we might contemplate against terrorism, this faceless enemy, which lurks in the shadows of fear and frustration, breeds on hatred and disillusionment and fed by ignorance and poverty, will not disappear unless we build global harmony and stability through mutual tolerance and shared prosperity. It will continue to haunt us if the roots of terrorism which lie in the inequality of societies, in the exploitation of downtrodden, in the denial of fundamental rights and in the sense of injustice are not addressed. It would be too simplistic to merely focus on the symptoms or their ugly manifestations. Terrorism has now emerged as a different challenge which has to be dealt with a resolute and measured manner.

Terrorism is the negation of human dignity. Human dignity can neither be achieved nor guaranteed in an environment of abject poverty and denial of inalienable rights. Most countries, if not all, represented here today have at one point in history or another chosen their own destinies based on the principle of self-determination of peoples. Yet, in contravention of this universal principle, there are peoples even today who remain deprived of their fundamental right of self-determination. The Security Council resolutions pertaining to their destiny and future remain unimplemented in the archives of this Organization. It is time for courageous decisions, for correcting historic wrongs and for redressing endemic injustices."

(Ambassador Shamshad Ahmad, it appears was presenting the Kashmir issue rather than defining the acts of terrorism).

Bangladesh has not clearly spelt out its position and covers the acts of terrorism under the Law and Order Disruption Crimes (Speedy Trial/Amendment) Act 2005, Money Laundering and Terrorist Financing Prevention

---

*Pakistan Defence Gallery, War on Terrorism & Kashmir issue

Bill 2005, Anti-Terrorism Bill 2005 and Bangladesh Tele-communications (Amendment Ordinance) 2005.

The Prevention of Terrorism Act of 1978 is a law in Sri Lanka. It provides the police with powers to search, arrest, and detain suspects. It was first enacted as a temporary law in 1979, then made permanent in 1982.

Terrorist and Disruptive Activities (Control and Punishment) Ordinance 2004 is in force in Nepal to deal with terrorism. Clause 9 of the latest TADO states that if a security official feels the need to prevent a person from carrying out any terrorist activity, such a person can be kept under house arrest for a maximum period of one year, six months at security official's discretion and another six months with permission from the home ministry. The Ordinance is under severe criticism.

Afghanistan, Bhutan, Myanmar and Maldives follow the law of the land to deal with terror issues.

Bilateral Agreements

India's predominant size and common borders with the South Asian states leads to psychological projection to the smaller nations. At times India's overbearing approach, though not so often, like suspension of free movement of goods to Nepal and training of the LTTE cadres add to this feeling. However, India has concluded treaties of friendship with all of its neighbours. Where required, India has also concluded river water treaties as an upper riparian state. India and Pakistan have concluded agreements not to attack each other's nuclear installations, provide advance notice while holding large scale military exercises, and prevention of air space violations. Between India and Pakistan there are issues which need to be resolved. Kashmir is one which has been dealt with separately. Because India-Pakistan relations affect the entire South Asian subcontinent, the conflictual issues in some details are at Appendix which can be resolved by give and take.

SAARC

It is dedicated to economic, technological, social, and cultural development emphasizing collective self-reliance. Meetings of heads of states are usually scheduled annually and the meetings of foreign secretaries, twice in a year. Sixteen Summits have been held so far (2010). The SAARC Secretariat is based in Kathmandu. It coordinates and monitors implementation of activities, serves as a channel of communication between the Association and its member states, as well as other regional organizations and provides support for various events of SAARC.

The area of cooperation on security aspects are:

- SAARC Coordination Group of Drug Law Enforcement Agencies

- SAARC Drug Offences Monitoring Desk (SDOMD) Colombo

- SAARC Convention on Narcotic Drugs and Psychotropic Substances

- SAARC Terrorist Offences Monitoring Desk (STOMD) Colombo

- SAARC Regional Convention on Suppression of Terrorism and its Additional Protocol.

- SAARC Conference on Cooperation in Police Matters

- Meeting of the SAARC Interior/Home Ministers

Drugs Law Enforcement

The SAARC Coordination Group of 'Drug Law Enforcement Agencies' deals with matters relating to progress in the implementation of the SAARC Convention on Narcotic Drugs and Psychotropic Substances, provision of training, equipment and know-how, creating awareness of the problems posed by drug abuse and drug trafficking, cooperation between SAARC and United Nations Office on Drugs and Crime (UNODC) as well as between SAARC and ASEAN and strengthening of SAARC Drug Offences Monitoring Desk (SDOMD) located at Colombo.

Terrorist Offences Monitoring

The objectives of the Terrorist Offences Monitoring Desk are to collate, analyze and disseminate information on terrorist offences, tactics, strategies and methods. Some of the initiatives taken by the SAARC in this regard are:

- Working paper presented by Bangladesh: SAARC Study Group Meeting on Terrorism, June 12-14, 1986 Dhaka.

- Report on Study Group Meeting on Terrorism, June 12-14, 1986 Dhaka.

- Report of SAARC Expert Group Meeting on Terrorism, Sept 20-21, 1986 Dhaka.

- Second SAARC Summit in Bangalore, Nov 17, 1986, Draft Declaration to Combat Terrorism.

- Third SAARC Summit in Kathmandu, Nov 4, 1987, SAARC Regional Convention on the Suppression of Terrorism.

In the Eleventh Summit at Kathmandu, January 2002, the leaders of the SAARC took a pledge to make collective efforts to stamp out terrorism. An additional clause was added to the SAARC Convention on Suppression of Terrorism in the 12th SAARC Summit which in brief states that all member states are committed to extradite or prosecute alleged terrorists thus denying them safe havens. Exchange of information, intelligence and expertise are among the areas identified for mutual cooperation under all conventions. Cooperation among Liaison Officers (Anti Terrorist Law Enforcement Officers) has been devised through holding international meetings at regular intervals to monitor, evaluate and improve counter-terrorism strategies.

At Thirteenth, fourteenth, fifteenth and sixteenth Summits, emphasis was laid for effective implementation of SAARC Convention on Suppression of Terrorism and the proposed UN Comprehensive Convention on International Terrorism.

At the thirty first Session of the Council of Ministers of SAARC nations, it was agreed to undertake the following anti-terrorism measures of cooperation:

1. Commitment to implement measures against organising, instigating, facilitating, financing, fund raising, encouraging, tolerating and providing training for or otherwise supporting terrorist activities.

2. Commitment to ensure the apprehension and prosecution or extradition

of persons connected, directly or indirectly, with the commission of terrorist acts.

3. Deal with the terrorists according to the law of the land.

4. Commitment to support the promotion of cooperation and exchange of information, consistent with respective domestic legal and administrative regimes, improve immigration and customs control measures to detect and prevent the international movement of terrorists and their accomplices, and trafficking in arms, narcotics and psychotropic substances or other materials, intended to support terrorism and also agreed to consider the development of an integrated border management mechanism.

5. To share expertise and information about terrorists, their movements, support facilities and weapons, bearing in mind in particular, the threats posed to maritime and coastal security and to share information regarding the investigation and prosecution of terrorists.

6. Contribute to the efforts in the UN General Assembly for the early adoption of the UN draft Comprehensive Convention on International Terrorism.

7. Urgently ratify and effectively implement the SAARC Convention on Mutual Legal Assistance in Criminal Matters, signed at the Fifteenth SAARC Summit in Colombo.

The theme of Counter-terrorism in all resolutions, obviously, is the recognition that terrorism is a regional security issue. Then is the requirement of full cooperation among states to serve as respective region's central clearing houses of terrorist and terrorist data, to assist in capacity-building and training programs, and creation of anti-terror strategy and execution for the region.

Regretfully the member states of the SAARC have not progressed enough to achieve its objectives. One of the reasons is the size and potential of India and Indo-Pak relations. One school of thought is that countries should refrain from raising bilateral issues in the forum. If it is not prevented the organization may not remain meaningful. The other school is that unless bilateral issues are resolved, the organization may not be able to function smoothly, particularly in the field of counter-terrorism.

The bones of contention like Kashmir and other Indo-Pak disputes should either be resolved or set aside to address the agenda of the welfare of its people and provide security in its wider meaning to include terrorism in particular. Every region has peculiarities, they should be factored in and SAARC must succeed in its mission like ASEAN and Asia-Pacific (Apac).

The Organisation has also not made any serious effort to implement the SAARC Conventions on Terrorism. There is a need for commitment to these conventions to stamp out terrorism from the region and the world. The experiences of other regions and states need to be taken in to account.

Equating terrorism with Islamic militancy, extremism or fundamentalism is an issue which needs to be debated. This feeling has come about in the wake of 9/11 and its Muslim actors. In most terror acts, the countries involved are Muslim, but it is not a war against all Muslims. Surely all Muslims are not terrorists and all terrorists are not Muslims. But most terrorists are Muslims. *Al Qaeda* is spreading its tentacles in many parts of the world making lives difficult for Muslims and also for non-Muslims. *Al Qaeda* is inching towards east. Muslim world has to watch out that the intensity of Muslim terrorist acts, with the passage of time, does not brand them as suspects, which is not yet the case.

International and regional cooperation is required to fight terrorism. One of the most effective measures taken by the UN against terrorism so far is Resolution 1373 dated 28 September 2001 of the Security Council through which a number of mandatory decisions were taken on terrorist financing, obligating states to refrain from providing support to terrorists and denying them safe haven. With this resolution, the Counter-Terrorism Committee has been established, to which all member states report on the steps they have taken to implement this Resolution. Resolution 1373* needs to be supported by the SAARC countries.

---

*Resolution 1373 (2001) calls for international cooperation to counter terrorism

The Organisation of American States has formed an Inter-American Committee against terrorism in 1999 which facilitates information exchange, creating proposals for strengthening anti-terrorism legislation, assisting members in compliance with all relevant international conventions and treaties, and capacity building. The Commonwealth of Independent States has taken a more direct approach to combat terrorism. Its Anti-Terrorism Centre houses a data base of terrorists, terrorist organisations, and terrorist financing structures and is to coordinate counter-terrorist operations. Another regional organization comprising of 13 members, Southeastern European Cooperative Initiative, adopted the Bucharest Declaration on the Suppression of Terrorism, which created a working group – Anti Terrorism Task Force (ATTF) with three sub-groups dealing with trans-national anti-terrorism, small arms and light weapons, and weapons of mass destruction. SAARC needs to learn from their experiences.

The role of the state needs to be supplemented through social movements that champion human rights, environmental protection, social justice, conflict resolution and peace building outside the political structure. The Forum for Naga Reconciliation (FNR), an organization comprising the churches and the civil society groups, established in 2008 in India, had a significant role to play in controlling violence in Nagaland. Salwa Judum is another organization in Chhattisgarh which operates like an NGO against the Maoists. Another social group, People's Consultative Group, was set up by ULFA in Assam, comprises nine members to include journalists, rights activists, lawyers and academics, to clear the grounds for direct talks between the ULFA and the Government of India. Such social movements can also act as powerful bodies to highlight the need to bring awareness on the issue of terrorism in the region.

Long-drawn and concerted efforts are required to combat terrorism in the age of globalisation and communication revolution. South Asia should join the global community as a group to identify international terror networks and should take strong initiatives. They should develop effective intelligence and counter-intelligence systems. Religious extremists should be countered. In fact, religions may contribute positively in influencing public attitudes against terrorism in South Asia.

Intelligence in Counter-Terrorism

Terrorism is a danger to the security of the international community, including the western world. Intelligence in the field of counter-terrorism is different, and in many aspects a more arduous task, than the classical intelligence. The intelligence network has to function without a break and in sync with other networks. Despite best efforts and equipment, countries and security agencies have faced strategic surprises, the most prominent being the sarin gas attack in Tokyo in March 1995, 9/11 and 26/11.

Trends

- While the number of international terrorist attacks has decreased, the lethality of the attacks has increased. Suicide and car bomb attacks are among the main methods used, like the truck-bombs used in Nairobi and Dar-es-Salam against the American embassies in August 1998. Since then, there were a large number of car or truck bombimgs in Pakistan and Afghanistan.

- Terrorism as a tool in political or ethnic conflicts has spread to new regions, mainly to Russia and the ex-Soviet republics, the states of former Yugoslavia, Tunisia and Libya.

- The threat from Sunni Muslims has grown, and we now see large countries like India, China and Russia confronting this kind of terrorism. The overwhelming majority of the Sunni has led to international networks of Islamist terrorists.

- The sarin gas attack by the Japanese cult Aum Shinrikyo in March 1995 in the Tokyo sub-way, has broken the taboo in the use of WMDs.

- The 9/11, the attack on Indian Parliament and 26/11 display the mammoth terrorist capability and networking.

- Iran, Syria, Lebanon, Sudan, Saudi Arabia, Pakistan and Afghanistan have emerged as states sponsoring or supporting terrorism.

- For the moment it seems that the various security services have not found the right operational response to suicide attacks.

- Osama bin Laden, the main sponsor and financier of the Sunni Islamist networks is dead. His network has also suffered a setback due to the finance and motivation provided by him when he was alive. He had a mesmerizing personality.

- From the organizational point of view, the security and intelligence agencies have taken serious steps to improve their capabilities:

- The FBI has tripled its counter-terrorism force since 9/11.

- The CIA has created a Counter-Terrorism Center at the highest civilian and military level.

- The Germans have greatly enhanced the police and security units.

- International cooperation has improved, mainly on the bilateral level:

  - The Arab League countries have arrived at an agreement to coordinate their intelligence and security activities.

  - Russia and China are coordinating to fight Islamic radicals in Central Asia. They participated in the first meeting on the subject with Uzbekistan, Kyrgystan, and Tajikistan.

  - Russia has upgraded and enhanced its intelligence cooperation with the United States, Great Britain, Turkey, and Israel, in the wake of the serious Chechen threat.

  - A new European body, Europol, is also a step in the right direction.

Future Terrorist Threats

- In south Asia, there will be international realignment. Pakistan will further tilt towards China. USA-Pakistan relations will be diluted.

- Taliban may adopt an independent policy in Afghanistan.

- *Al Qaeda* may be destabilized for next 1-2 years.

- In an year's time we may witness thinning out of the NATO and ISAF forces from Afghanistan.

- Psy war will greatly help.

- In the current decade terrorism will continue to be a serious threat on both the strategic and tactical level.

- The level of muslim militancy is likely to continue, Osama's disappearance not withstanding. Madrassa will continue to play an important role to keep militancy going.

- The threat of assassination of important leaders will continue.

- Incompetent and corrupt political leaders will provide right environment for terrorism to continue.

- The anti-globalization movement will focus its efforts against corporates, large multi-nationals and UN organisations.

- The Internet and computer networks will represent a major challenge in future.

- The WMD threat is real and will require technological knowledge and intelligence sharing to prevent its occurrence and damage control if it takes place.

Intelligence in Countering Future Terrorism

- The threat of large scale acts of terror and the potential of non-conventional terrorism will enhance the need to prevent terrorist schemes and give warning before such acts happen.

- Need to expand HUMINT and counter-terrorism expertise, the cultural knowledge and the language aptitudes.

- Penetration of known terrorist groups in South Asia by the intelligence services will become inescapable.

- Trans-border movement will increase requiring more vigil and controls.

- The terrorist ideologies, doctrines and strategies should become the curriculum of higher learning in conjunction with military professionals.

- The security services will have to deal with the encoding and decoding of communications between terrorist leaders, terrorist groups and cells.

- The proliferation of conventional weapons will need to be checked as the same weapons and equipment is being used by the terrorists as the security forces.

- In the fields of restructuring the intelligence agencies, there is much that needs to be done. The fight against terrorism will require much higher national priorities. There is a need to train and maintain a pool of capable and highly professional intelligence officers to monitor and interfere with the terror networks.

- The co-operation on the bilateral, regional and international levels will become inescapable in preventing and neutralizing not only international terrorism, but also internal terrorism in many countries.

Finance

Finance is a major driver for terrorism to go on. The kind of finance required can only be state sponsored. It is estimated that US$ 1.3 trillion is laundered every year to support terrorism. Zakat, drugs and gun running are major contributors to this fund apart from the funds provided directly by the states like Saudi Arabia, some Gulf countries, Pakistan and USA. It is assessed that within a 10-year period, the financial support to *al Qaeda* or its associates, received through direct donations, Zakat funds or through various schemes range between US$300 and $500 million for an annual income of around US$ 50 million. The 2009 United Nations World Drug report indicates that the illicit drug market worldwide has now become a US$ 320 billion per year industry. Unfortunately the states who are financially and technologically sound are the ones involved in state sponsorship and money laundering. The UN and the member states must pressurize them to refrain from employing terrorism as a weapon of coercion and violence without resorting to the norms of war. UN '1999 International Convention for the Suppression of the Financing of Terrorism' must be implemented in its correct spirit. World should also strive for another super power or multi-polarity.

Madrassas

Pakistan has over 50,000 to 65,000 madrassas with an estimated 2-2.5 million students, out of which most cater to the dominant Sunni sect and remaining

15 to 20 per cent to the Shia. They are chartered to impart religious as well as secular education. The private and public schools also provide the same kind of education, but with an emphasis on secular education. It should also be noted that not all terrorists are madrassa educated; they could be from private or public schools, and graduates from the universities.

The expansion occurred during the period 1977-1988 both because of the growth in Pakistan's population, poverty and because their students were employed to fight the Soviet Union during the Afghan war. The Afghan refugees also joined these madrassas and were readily available to fight in Afghanistan and elsewhere. Many of the Taliban were educated in Saudi financed madrassas in Pakistan that teach Wahhabism. In these madrassas, there have been students from Central Asia, Philippines, Indonesia, Nigeria and the Arab region. The funding of these madrassas seems to have been institutionalized through a fund raised by Saudi Arabia, Pakistan, Egypt, Libya and Sudan.

There are 69,000 Koranic Madrassas in Bangladesh imparting secular and jihadi training to Taliban returned from Afghanistan, Kashmir, Palestine and Chechnya with the agenda of creating a Caliphate in Bangladesh. There are madrassas in other states in South Asia as well, but they do not seem to be contributing to terror directly. These madrassas are sensitive religious institutions, normally attached to mosques. Countries must ensure that they do no impart jihadi training to the students, nor are they used as a facility by the terrorists.

Drugs

Afghanistan produced 6,900 tons of opium in 2009 and is the world's primary opium producer, supplying 92 per cent of the world's opiates. Afghanistan alone produces around US$ 64 billion worth of opiates every year.

The mountains of Myanmar, Laos, Vietnam and Thailand are the other area producing significant drugs in the vicinity of South Asia. Myanmar is the second highest producer of opium in the world after Afghanistan.

The SAARC Coordination Group of 'Drug Law Enforcement Agencies' deals with matters relating to progress in the implementation of the SAARC Convention on Narcotic Drugs and Psychotropic Substances, provision of training, equipment and know how, creating awareness of the problems posed by drug abuse and drug trafficking, cooperation between SAARC and United Nations Office on Drugs and Crime (UNODC) as well as between SAARC and ASEAN and strengthening of SAARC Drug Offences Monitoring Desk (SDOMD) located at Colombo.

Nuclear Security

Pakistan's facilities from mining and processing to heavy water production to nuclear research labs to power reactors and to uranium enrichment at Kahuta and Sihala must be watched for pilferage of fissile material or components by the undesirable elements to prevent them from producing a dirty bomb.

Pakistan's current stockpile of around 90 nuclear weapons and related facilities is also considered to be at risk, given the presence of *al Qaeda,* Taliban and other terror elements in Pakistan and the country's internal security scenario.

As regards India's nuclear facilities, the security is as good as it could be, however, precautions must be taken along the entire nuclear processing chain. In the case of both Pakistan and India, the transportation of the nuclear waste or the spent fuel needs to be watched in particular.

Cyber Security

Cyber terrorist has many advantages:

- It is cheaper than traditional methods.

- The action is difficult to track.

- There are no physical barriers to cross.

- It can be executed remotely.

- A number of targets can be addressed simultaneously.

Incidents of cyber terrorism can be reduced by adopting some of the following measures:

- All accounts passwords should be changed often.

- Change the network configuration in case of a doubt.

- Check with vendors for upgrades and patches.

- Audit systems and check logs to help in detecting and tracing an intruder.

- If you are ever unsure about the safety of a site, or receive suspicious email from an unknown address, don't access it.

- The methods the terrorists use to conceal their plans, their communication systems, codes and multiplicity of web sites must be studied for adopting counter-measures. This is a highly specialized task for which South Asia will need help from the developed countries.

- Cyber security laws must be enacted in all South Asian countries.

Hijacking

In 2005, India adopted its new anti-hijacking policy. The main points of the policy are:

- Any attempt to hijack will be considered an act of aggression against the country and will prompt a response fit for an aggressor.

- Hijackers, if captured, will be sentenced to death.

- Hijackers will be engaged in negotiations only to bring the incident to an end, to comfort passengers and to prevent loss of lives.

- The plane will be shot down if it is deemed to become a missile heading for strategic targets.

- The plane will be escorted by fighters and will be forced to land.

Maritime Piracy

*Sea piracy hit a record high of 142 attacks in the first quarter of 2011. 70 per cent of the attacks occurred off the coast of Somalia. International Maritime Organisation (IMO) was established in 1958 by the UN and became effective

---

*International Maritime bureau's Piracy Report Centre Kualalumpur.

in 1974. IMO is responsible for drafting conventions concerning maritime safety. Merchant vessels transiting through areas like Gulf of Aden, Southern Red Sea and Bab-el-Mandeb Straits are advised self-protection.

Hostage Taking

Hostage taking means someone who is seized by an abductor in order to compel another party such as a relative, employer, law enforcement agency or government to act, or refrain from acting, in a particular way, often under threat of serious physical harm to the hostage (s) after expiration of an ultimatum.

Taking hostages is a crime and an act of terrorism. Hostages are kept in a building, a vehicle, an air craft or in any confined space. Hostage taking may be politically motivated or to raise a ransom or to enforce an exchange against other hostages or even condemned convicts. Counter-terror operations is a specialized field, for which specialized forces must be raised, trained and deployed by all countries.

Money laundering

Money laundering is the practice of disguising the origins of illegally obtained money. It is the process by which the proceeds of crime are made to appear legitimate. The money involved can be generated by any number of criminal acts like drugs, corruption, accounting fraud, and tax evasion. The methods by which money is laundered are varied. The exact amount of money that is laundered worldwide is difficult to assess. However, it may be anywhere from US$ 600 billion up to US$ 1.5 trillion amounting to 2-5 per cent of global GDP.

In India, the Prevention of Money Laundering Act (PMLA), 2002 was enacted on 1 July 2005. The amended PMLA will address India's international obligations by accepting Financial Action Task Force (FATF) to address the problem appropriately at the global level. The money laundering in India is often through political parties, corporate companies, individuals and share market.

It is estimated that around US$ 2 billion are laundered in Pakistan every year. The underground economy consists of illegal business, drug trafficking, smuggling, illegal arms sale, organized crime, bribery, embezzlement, extortion, computer fraud and so on. The banks, insurance companies, non-banking financial institutions, investment companies, money transmitters and real estate agents are all targets of money launderers.

The major Anti Money Laundering laws in Pakistan are:

- The National Accountability Ordinance of 1999

- The Anti-Terrorism Act of 1997.

- The Control of Narcotic Substances Act of 1997.

- Anti-Money Laundering Act, 2010.

The Anti-Money Laundering Act 2010 has established a National Financial Intelligence Centre (NFIC) in the State Bank of Pakistan. The NFIC will operate under the Minister of Finance.

In Bangladesh, this issue has been dealt with by the Prevention of Money Laundering Act No. VII of 2002. The Act was last amended in the year 2009 and all the Financial Institutes are following this act. A counter-terrorism centre that would be the focal point of exchange between South Asian nations, is also expected to come up in Bangladesh, with both India and Pakistan reaching a consensus on the issue.

Counter-Terrorist (CT) Weapons and Equipment

The complete range of counter-terror weapons and equipment in the international markets are available on the internet. The western countries must be liberal in making them available at affordable prices to the needy and affected countries. Simultaneously, such equipment and offensive assault equipment should be denied to the suspect customers.

Counter-Terrorism in India

All that has been recommended in the preceding chapters is valid for India and is not being repeated. India, however, has to provide a lead and regional role in South Asia without being overbearing. India also has to ensure that all South Asian conventions, particularly, those referring to security are implemented. India and Pakistan should continue people to people contact like commerce, trade, culture, social and sports. *Aman ki Asha* is a shining example of cultural exchange. Efforts should continue to discourage export of terror from Pakistan's soil to neighbouring countries.

Nearly 40 per cent of India is affected by the menace of terrorism. The areas affected are J&K, Naxal areas, Northeast and metros. All these areas need different treatment, barring intelligence. Terrorists exploit the openness and freedoms provided in the Indian state. Coupled with it is the digressive political scene, coalition, corruption and the legislators in the Parliament and the state assemblies with criminal record. A lot of time is wasted in allegations, counter allegations and clarifications. Coalition partners hold the government under threat of withdrawal of support leading to short term, narrow, compromised and delayed decisions. Real issues could be addressed in a much more professional and committed manner.

Militancy in J&K is Pakistan sponsored with locals receptive to the sponsorship. Pakistan's claim to J&K territory is the result of an aggression despite the Stand-Still Agreement with the state in 1947. Any concessions should be equitably distributed between the three segments of the state ie the Valley, Ladakh and the Jammu region. The first step should be to put in place effective border guarding by the army and the para military forces. As far as possible, no infiltration should be permitted. The political corruption must cease and the developmental funds must reach the masses. Students from all regions should be given stipends and admission in rest of India. Employment opportunities should also be provided. Conditions should be created for honourable return of the Kashmiri pandits. In trickle, some are returning. Employment opportunities for the Kashmiris should also be created both inside and outside the state. The communications with the rest of India should be improved including the extension of the railways. While dialogue with Pakistan should be maintained, not much should be expected. Even the resolution of Kashmir issue is unlikely to minimize militancy, as militants have no other occupation. Dialogue with the people of the Valley will give rich dividends, but over a period of time.

Naxalism is an indigenous movement which is non-secessionist. They want a better life and inclusive development of the region. The Government of India should develop the area without taking away their lands for mega projects. They love their forests and the rich mineral resources. Corruption is another factor. Because of uneven development, they prefer Maoism. The tribals should be co-opted in all matters concerning their land and mineral resources. Along with the civic action, direct and meaningful military counter-measures also must continue.

The Northeastern states are connected by a tenuous 22 km wide corridor with the rest of India. While states like Arunachal Pradesh, Meghalaya, Mizoram and Tripura have been peaceful for some years; significant developments towards peace in Assam and Nagaland have also taken place, though Manipur continues to reel under multiple insurgencies and demands independence. The territories of Bangladesh, Bhutan and Myanmar can provide safe haven to the insurgents from Northeast. These territories must be denied to them. While Bhutan and Bangladesh are cooperating, Myanmar's northwest continues to be available as safe haven because of scanty administration. The insurgents in the Northeastern states also have links with the Naxalites, the Maoists and possibly militants from Southeast Asia. China continues to induct its surplus weapons in the region. ISI of Pakistan is also active.

Bangladesh, Bhutan and Myanmar should be engaged to deny the insurgents safe havens. Simultaneously the Northeastern states should be developed and aspirations of the people addressed. Counter-terrorism military operations where required should continue along with the civic action and engagement of the neighbouring states.

The controls should start from the borders including air space and maritime zones and off shore establishments. The controls should be organized in depth to nab the intruders early before they become effective. The border management responsibility should be well defined. The border management should also include the customs with additional responsibility. Since it is not possible to guard all borders physically in a foolproof manner, physical security should be supplemented by high-tech surveillance. The off shore establishments should have dedicated security including air support with delegated authority.

Religious Militancy

Hindus and Muslims suffer historical prejudices and events. While Pakistan continuously bombards the Muslim minds, they have shown remarkable resilience, and by and large are unaffected, barring a few who fall a prey to propaganda and other motivations. The demolition of Ram Janam Bhumi/Babri Masjid structure caused great anger in the Muslim community resulting in religious riots and 1200 deaths in India and South Asia. A lot that is happening can be attributed to this demolition.

There is practically no history of Hindu terror but for recent events (2005-2010) like Malegaon blasts, Mecca Masjid bombing, Samjhauta Express train bombings and the Ajmer Sharif Dargah blast. There are differing views with regard to perpetrators of such violence, ranging from the Abhinav Bharat, HuJI, Lashkar-e-Tayyiaba and *al Qaeda*. The possibility of Hindu retaliation to the Muslim terror has afairly strong evidence.

In recent years, there has been a sharp increase in violent attacks on Christians, often perpetrated by Hindu fundamentalists in Orissa in 2007-2008. Foreign Christian missionaries have also been targeted. The rise of anti-Christian violence has been allegedly linked to some fundamental Hindu organisations. The violence has also spread to Chattisgarh, Andhra Pradesh, Tamil Nadu and Kerala.

The religious militancy is encouraged by vote bank politics and by the fanatic leaders. Religion in India is a great driving force and can provide an effective platform to garner the support of the masses, either for votes or for deciding issues. The religious divide, often, can be exploited by the anti-social elements including planning of acts of terrorism and their execution. The religious divide is created by the politician.

Trans-Border Movement

In South Asia trans-border movements take place more for political reasons than economic. Economic movements take place due to less land use in the receiving country, more employment and better incomes. The porosity of the borders facilitates such movements. Such movements often diminish heterogeneity of the country of origin and increases heterogeneity in the receiving country leading to social disequilibrium and undesirable activities. Trans-border exodus has taken place from India to Pakistan and vice versa, from Burma to India and East Pakistan, from Afghanistan, Bangladesh, Nepal, Bhutan and Sri Lanka to India, from Nepal to Bhutan and vice versa leading to turbulence and political implications. Such movements in South Asia provide undesirable linkages across the frontiers, facilitating terrorism. The mass exodus of refugees in 1971 from East Pakistan to India led to a major war and break up of Pakistan. All states of South Asia are neither parties to 1951 Refugee Convention nor the 1967 Protocol, but uphold the spirit of these provisions. To obviate motivated and inconsistent responses, a refugee provision needs to be enacted in South Asia. It would help counter-terrorism measures.

Counter-Terror Provisions in India

- The Unlawful Activities (Prevention) Act 1967

- The National Security Act, 1980

- The Maharashtra Control of Organised Crime Act, 1999 (MCOCA)

- Unlawful Activities (Prevention) Amendment Act, 2004 (Enacted after POTA 2002 was repealed)

- Unlawful Activities (Prevention) Amendment Act, 2008*

- National Investigation Agency Act, 2008*

---

*Enacted after 26/11 Mumbai attacks.

- Armed Forces Special Powers Act, 1958 (applicable in areas declared as disturbed).

Hostage taking, hijacking and terrorism in a confined space will demand similar anti-terror operation. The National Security Guard (NSG) in India meets this requirement. It has two cutting edge army units which deal with hijacking, hostage relief and terror in a confined space. In addition are the supporting elements provided by the para military and technical elements. Technical support comprises of a communication sub unit and a high tech sub unit. High tech comprises of sophisticated gadgetry, primarily for surveillance. There is a large logistic staff for provisioning etc. The force has inbuilt mobility except air mobility which comes on requisitioning.

There is a training centre, which is well equipped and well organized. Overall the force is effective but for the flab which could be reduced and cutting edge sharpened and enlarged. This force could play a national as well as regional role by suitable deployment so as to meet India's internal requirement as also of South Asia. Composite self-contained elements could be located at Udhampur (J&K), Mumbai, Chennai, Kolkata, Patna and Delhi. The concept could be further refined. Speed of application would be of essence for which decision making will have to be streamlined. Any delay will harden the target.

In addition to above, all the three defence services have their specialized forces - Army has special force units, para brigade, and a commando platoon at each infantry battalion level; Navy has MARCOS and the Air Force commandos, GARUD Commando Force; each para military organization has its own commando force; and each state has commando forces. Out of these the special forces of the defence services should be counted out and left to perform their basic role. The para military and state special forces need more training and training facilities. What is left is the National Security Guard (NSG) which is world class, but not large enough to be effective in the entire country. Its application procedures also need to be fine-tuned.

Army has effective systems of training commandos in the Infantry School Mhow and two Counter Insurgency & Jungle Warfare (CIJW) Schools. These institutions should be enlarged to take on the training requirement of other organizations.

Counter-Terror Intelligence Restructuring

Effective and timely intelligence is the backbone of counter-terror measures. Like most countries, India also has many intelligence agencies, but they tend to function in their respective fields. Efforts to coordinate them fall prey to turf. The present setup comprises of external intelligence with Cabinet Secretariat (R&AW), internal intelligence with IB, Defence Intelligence Agency, Defence Services have their own intelligence with tactical and operational intelligence responsibility and the para military forces have their own small setups. Other border authorities like customs, drug enforcement, anti-money laundering and so on also have a lot to contribute. "Reforming National Security Structures" prepared by a Group of Ministers is a comprehensive national security document de-classified so far. In so far as the Intelligence is concerned, following recommendations have been made:

- Along with collection of intelligence, analysis and dissemination is equally important. The government has set up a Multi Agency Centre (MAC) which seeks to coordinate and analyse the intelligence coming from different sources and channels. This is an important step which requires space-based surveillance, open source intelligence (OSINT), cyber space, media, etc as important sources of intelligence. The interface between National Technology Research Organisation (NTRO) and other intelligence agencies needs to be improved.

- Strengthen HUMINT and penetrate various terrorist groups.

- National Counter-Terrorism Centre (NCTC)

Acts of terrorism are quick in time and space. Successful counter-terror operations will require speedy and surgical strikes. The need is to take speedy decisions which will require some modification to the existing laws governing the Centre and State role in the law and order matters.

There is a considerable overlap between Terrorism and the law and order issues. That is why a definition of terrorism is difficult to decide. NCTC will only lengthen red tape and diffused decision making. This may well be another super intelligence organisation. On the instance of a terrorist incident, the need is to take a quick political decision and execute counter violence speedily and efficiently. An empowered Counter-Terror department directly under the Home Minister should meet the requirement. This department should control the deployment and movement of the Special Forces.

International Co-operation in Counter-Terrorism

The Government of India has decided to set up a Counter-Terrorism division in the Ministry of External Affairs to handle the diplomacy involved in the International terrorism:

- India and Bangladesh concluded three agreements on mutual legal assistance on criminal offences, the transfer of sentenced persons and combating international terrorism, organised crime and illegal drug trafficking.

- India-Myanmar Treaty of cooperation in combating transnational organized crime, terrorism, drug trafficking, money laundering and smuggling of arms and explosives.

- India-Myanmar Treaty on mutual legal assistance in criminal matters that will be crucial in enabling India get access to insurgents from India's northeast states who continue to shelter along the India-Myanmar border.

- India and the US signed a Counter Terrorism Initiative in 2010 that includes steps to check financing of terror activities, joint probe in cases of bomb blasts besides cooperation in cyber and border security.

- A bilateral agreement between India and US on Counter-Terrorism is on the cards as a result of Home Minister's visit to US in April 2011.

- India-Germany Agreement on Expansion of Counter-Terror Cooperation, 2011.

- India-Indonesia Extradition Treaty and Mutual Legal Assistance Treaty that will expand counter-terror cooperation.

- Two MOUs setting up a joint working group (JWG) on Counter-Terrorism.

- Agreements on defence and security cooperation with Qatar and Kuwait.

- India-EU Agreement to cooperate in counter-terrorism.

Conclusion

There is a paradigm shift in the security perceptions. Firstly, the security includes economic development, human resource development, science and technology development, river water sharing, societal tolerance, political systemic security and comprehensive national strength. The security provided by the armed forces and the paramilitary forces is the sum total of all these factors for peace to prevail. There is another paradigm shift in which international terrorism blurs the international boundaries and compels consideration of security at regional levels. Many current problems of South Asian countries are beyond the control of any individual country. These problems are terrorism, environment, river waters, trans-border crimes, drugs, smuggling, human trafficking and many more. Reduction of these problems by mutual aid and understanding will add to internal and societal security of all these countries. Cooperative rather than competitive security is the need of South Asia. India, with borders with all South Asian countries, China and Myanmar, can play a pivotal role because of its comprehensive national strength, which includes democracy. India, however, must improve its procedures for speedy application of counter-terror force when required. Counter-terror force application must become seamless between the Centre and the states.

Conclusion

Conditions that prevail in South Asia are conducive to spread of terrorism. The demands from insurgents range from secessionism, self determination and quest for better living conditions. The major factors being poverty, inter and intra regional disparity, multiplicity of religions with conflictual past, political opportunism, heterogeneity and porosity. The region is flanked by Muslim states with terror footprints. One of them exports terror as a state policy. Indonesia, another major Muslim state towards southeast is moderate but inroads have been made by the fundamentalists. Balochistan, J&K and Manipur display fissiparous tendencies. There are tribal and autonomous regions in the NWFP and northwest of Myanmar. Major terrorist organizations like *al Qaeda*, Taliban, LeT, HUM and many more fiery groups are active in South Asia with their bases in Pakistan and Afghanistan. Most of poppy of the world is also grown on both flanks of South Asia.

The region is being engaged by major powers in their national interests and also to act as a countervailing to India. China has made access to Indian Ocean through development of major roads in Pakistan and Myanmar. China has also developed Gwadar on the Makran as a major port and is also financing development of Yangon as a major port on Indian Ocean in Myanmar. Oil and gas pipelines also feed the region from both the flanks.

Along with long term measures of the UN and SAARC, direct prophylactic measures should be adopted. Countries of the region must guard their borders to include maritime boundaries and air space, in a holistic manner by effective management. This should include intelligence, prevention of drug smuggling, gun running, money laundering, and infiltration from low guarded areas and legal channels. Intelligence should become effective from as far away from the assessed targets as possible and as such, should be organized in depth with in-built redundancy. HUMINT continues to be relevant along with hi-tech intelligence. All institutions of SAARC must exchange data in near real time.

A Regional Counter-Terror Institute should come up in Bangladesh, as proposed. This institute should act as a mother Counter-Terror institute in South Asia. Its role should be to coordinate with training institutes of the region and also develop concepts and doctrines. It should also act as a data bank for the terror network of the world, South Asia in particular.

National Counter-Terror institutes should also come up in India, Bangladesh, Sri Lanka and Pakistan. Other South Asian countries should be covered by these institutes. Depending on the national priorities, these institutes should be run by army, police or a combination of both. The deployment of NSG of India should be considered for regional employment.

Political integrity can be ensured by amendment to Constitutions, whereby individuals with criminal record are disqualified for holding any political office. Such disqualification should be unambiguously defined. Political leaders with clean record will clean up the bureaucracy as well.

Aspiration of the tribals and the locals should be kept in mind while initiating mega projects, so as not to disturb the ecology and cultural traditions. A happy population is a counter-terror measure by itself.

NGOs and Societies have an important role to play in creating awareness and information system, and preventing terror incidents, least make such incidents prohibitively expensive by way of finance and human toll. The Forum for Naga Reconciliation (FNR), comprising the churches and the civil society groups, had a significant role to play in controlling violence in Nagaland. Salwa Judum is another organization in Chhattisgarh which operates like an NGO against the Maoists. Another social group, People's Consultative Group in Assam, comprises journalists, rights activists, lawyers and academics, was setup to clear the grounds for direct talks between the ULFA and the Government of India. Such social movements can also act as powerful bodies to highlight the need to bring awareness on the issue of terrorism in the region.

All SAARC countries should support the UN Global Counter-Terrorism Strategy and all the 13 Conventions on countering terrorism. The UN Global Counter-Terrorism Strategy provides a clear message that terrorism is unacceptable in all its forms and manifestations to the concerned quarters. Counter-Terrorism measures range from strengthening state capacities to dealing with terrorist threats and to better coordination at UN level.

SAARC Coordination Groups of Drug Law Enforcement Agencies, Drug Offences Monitoring Desk, Convention on Narcotic Drugs and Psychotropic Substances, Terrorist Offences Monitoring Desk, Cooperation in Police Matters and other SAARC instruments should be implemented with commitment, despite bilateral differences.

There is enough scope for cultural exchanges because of common heritage and ethnicity. Such exchanges facilitate progress in political and diplomatic initiatives. The inter regional connectivity like the oil and gas pipelines, river waters and trade and industry will create dependence on each other leading to cooperation.

As it stands, the Organisation has not made significant effort to implement the SAARC Conventions on Terrorism. There is a need for commitment to these conventions to stamp out terrorism from the region and the world.

Post Script

Killing of Osama

Osama bin Laden has become a legend after he was killed in a blitzkrieg raid by the American special forces in Abbotabad, Pakistan on 2 May 2011. Osama is cut above others of his kind like Jarnail Singh Bhinderanwale, Prabhakran, Che Guera and so on. Osama was son of a billionaire, had his primary, secondary and university education in Jeddah. He had a degree in Public Administration in 1981 from King Abdul-Aziz University, Jeddah. Countries of the Arabian Peninsula, Syria, Pakistan, Afghanistan, and Sudan were the only countries he had visited. He gave up the life of glamour and comfort and became a fugitive in the cause of Muslims and Muslim religion, Sunni in particular. He was leading a life of total denial for over 20 years in the rugged mountains of Afghanistan and Pakistan, despite medical problems. 400,000 troops including NATO and ISAF with most sophisticated wherewithal, hunted for one man, Osama, for 10 years at an approximate cost of US$ 1.3 trillion. He will be an inspiration for all Muslim youth taking to violence in support of religion. Osama bin Laden was a great organizer and motivator. He was the greatest terrorist in support of Sunni Muslims, not likely to be replicated.

The killing of Osama bin Laden in Pakistan was a great embarrassment and humiliation for Pakistan leading to further mistrust with USA. China has already engaged Pakistan by constructing Karakoram Highway, developing Gwadar port on the Arabian Sea, providing defence equipment, nuclear reactors and knowhow. The relationship will become more intense, creating disequilibrium in South Asia.

USA, however, will need Pakistan to address terrorism and West Asia.

USA will simultaneously not find it easy to continue with substantial aid to Pakistan due to pressure from Congress and the American public.

In the Muslim eyes, Pakistan has played a pivotal role in promoting the cause of the Muslims and the Muslim religion. Pakistan may develop further immunity to the international opinion about its role of providing safe havens on its soil.

Internationally, Pakistan seems to have crossed the Rubicon leading to inviting military response from international forces. America carried out a military operation deep inside Pakistan displaying no respect for its integrity and capability as a nation. America has stated that more such operations may be launched as part of counter-terrorism.

Muslim terrorists are not going to relent or ease the intensity of their operations. They have already killed 80 in Pakistan on 13 May 2011. There may well be a pause to realign command and control.

There may yet be another angle. The operation may have been conducted with intelligence and concurrence of Pakistan. If that be so, it will become public sooner than later. Pakistan, in that case, may get overtaken by the anger and frustration of the masses and the indigenous militants alike. We have to wait and watch for the macro effects.

ARMED FORCES (SPECIAL POWERS) ACT,1958

(ACT 28 OF 1959)

An Act to enable certain special powers to be conferred upon members of the armed forces in disturbed areas in the States of Assam, Manipur, Meghalaya, Nagaland and Tripura and the Union Territories of Arunachal Pradesh and Mizoram

Be it enacted by Parliament in the ninth year of the Republic of India as follows:

1. Short title and extent:

    (1) This Act may be called the Armed Forces (Special Powers) Act, 1958.

    (2) It extends to the whole of the States of Assam, Manipur, Meghalaya, Nagaland and Tripura and the Union Territories of Arunachal Pradesh and Mizoram.

2. Definitions: In this Act, unless the context otherwise requires,

    (a) "armed forces" means the military forces and the air forces operating as land forces, and includes any other armed forces of the Union so operating;

    (b) "disturbed areas" means an area which is for the time being declared by notification under S. 3 to be a disturbed area;

    (c) All other words and expressions used herein, but not defined and defined in Air Force Act 1950 or the Army Act 1950, shall have the meanings respectively attached to them in those Acts.

3. Power to declare areas to be disturbed areas. — If, in relation to any State or Union Territory to which this Act extends, the Governor of that State or the Administrator of that Union Territory of the Central Government in either case, is of the opinion that the whole or any part of such State or Union Territory, as the case may be, is in such a disturbed or dangerous condition that the use of armed forces in aid of civil power is necessary, the Governor of that State or the Administrator of that Union Territory or the Central Government, as the case may be, may, by notification in the Official Gazette, declare the whole or such part of such State or Union Territory to be disturbed area.

4. Special Powers of the armed forces -------- Any commissioned officer, warrant officer, non commissioned officer or any other person of equivalent rank in the armed forces may, in a disturbed area:

   (a) if he is of the opinion that it is necessary so to do for the maintenance of the public order, after giving such due warning as he may consider necessary, fire upon or otherwise use force, even to the causing of death, against any person who is acting in contravention of any law or order for the time being in force in the disturbed area prohibiting the assembly of five or more persons or the carrying of weapons or things capable of being used as weapons or of fire arms, ammunition or explosive substances;

   (b) if he is of the opinion that it is necessary so to do, destroy any arms dump, prepared or fortified position or shelter from which armed attacks are made or are likely to be made or are attempted to be made or any structure used as a training camp for armed volunteers or utilised as a hideout by armed gangs or absconders wanted for any offence;

   (c) arrest without warrant, any person who has committed a cognisable offence or against whom a reasonable suspicion exists that he has committed or is about to commit a cognisable offence and may use such force as may be necessary to effect the arrest;

(d) enter and search without warrant any premises to make any such arrest as aforesaid or to recover any person believed to be wrongfully restrained and confined or any property reasonably suspected to be stolen property or any arms, ammunition or explosive substances believed to be unlawfully kept in such premises, and may for that purpose use such force as may be necessary.

5. Arrested persons to be made over to police.— Any person arrested and taken into custody under this Act shall be made over to the officer in charge of the nearest police station with the least possible delay, together with a report of the circumstances occasioning the arrest.

6. Protection to person acting under Act.—No prosecution, suit or other legal proceeding shall be instituted, except with the previous sanction of the Central Government, against any person in respect of any thing done or purported to be done in exercise of the powers conferred by this act.

7. Repeal and Saving:

   (1) The Armed forces (Assam and Manipur) Special Powers Ordinance, 1958, is hereby repealed.

   (2) Not withstanding such repeal anything done or any action taken under the said ordinance shall be deemed to have been done or taken under this act, as if this had commenced on the 22nd day of May, 1958.

Footnote: The Armed Forces (Jammu and Kashmir) Special Powers Act, 1990 (21 of 1990) pertains to the state of J&K and is generally on the same lines. The text is available in the authors' book 'Security and Defence Related Treaties of India'.

The United Nations Global
Counter-Terrorism Strategy

Resolution

The General Assembly,

Guided by the purposes and principles of the Charter of the United Nations and reaffirming its role under the Charter, including on questions related to international peace and security,

Reiterating its strong condemnation of terrorism in all its forms and manifestations, committed by whomever, wherever and for whatever purposes, as it constitutes one of the most serious threats to international peace and security,

Reaffirming the Declaration on Measures to Eliminate International Terrorism, contained in the annex to General Assembly resolution 49/60 of 9 December 1994, the Declaration to Supplement the 1994 Declaration on Measures to Eliminate International Terrorism, contained in the annex to General Assembly resolution 51/210 of 17 December 1996, and the 2005 World Summit Outcome, in particular its section on terrorism,

Recalling all General Assembly resolutions on measures to eliminate international terrorism, including resolution 46/51 of 9 December 1991, and Security Council resolutions on threats to international peace and security caused by terrorist acts, as well as relevant resolutions of the General Assembly on the protection of human rights and fundamental freedoms while countering terrorism,

Recalling also that at the 2005 World Summit Outcome world leaders rededicated themselves to support all efforts to uphold the sovereign equality of all States, respect their territorial integrity and political independence, to refrain in our international relations from the threat or use of force in any manner inconsistent with the purposes and principles of the United Nations, to uphold resolution of disputes by peaceful means and in conformity with the principles of justice and international law, the right to self-determination of peoples which remain under colonial domination or foreign occupation, non-interference in the internal affairs of States, respect for human rights and fundamental freedoms, respect for the equal rights of all without distinction as to race, sex, language or religion, international cooperation in solving international problems of an economic, social, cultural or humanitarian character and the fulfillment in good faith of the obligations assumed in accordance with the Charter,

Recalling further the mandate contained in the 2005 World Summit Outcome that the General Assembly should develop without delay the elements identified by the Secretary-General for a counter-terrorism strategy, with a view to adopting and implementing a strategy to promote comprehensive, coordinated and consistent responses, at the national, regional and international levels, to counter terrorism, which also takes into account the conditions conducive to the spread of terrorism,

Reaffirming that acts, methods and practices of terrorism in all its forms and manifestations are activities aimed at the destruction of human rights, fundamental freedoms and democracy, threatening territorial integrity, security of States and destabilizing legitimately constituted Governments, and that the international community should take the necessary steps to enhance cooperation to prevent and combat terrorism,

Reaffirming also that terrorism cannot and should not be associated with any religion, nationality, civilization or ethnic group,

Reaffirming further Member States' determination to make every effort to reach an agreement on and conclude a comprehensive convention on international terrorism, including by resolving the outstanding issues related to the legal definition and scope of the acts covered by the convention, so that it can serve as an effective instrument to counter terrorism,

Continuing to acknowledge that the question of convening a high level conference under the auspices of the United Nations to formulate an international response to terrorism in all its forms and manifestations could be considered,

Recognizing that development, peace and security, and human rights are interlinked and mutually reinforcing,

Bearing in mind the need to address the conditions conducive to the spread of terrorism,

Affirming Member States' determination to continue to do all they can to resolve conflict, end foreign occupation, confront oppression, eradicate poverty, promote sustained economic growth, sustainable development, global prosperity, good governance, human rights for all and rule of law, improve inter cultural understanding and ensure respect for all religions, religious values, beliefs or cultures,

1. Expresses its appreciation for the report "Uniting against terrorism: recommendations for a global counter-terrorism strategy" (doc. A/60/825), submitted by the Secretary-General to the General Assembly;

2. Adopts the present resolution and its annex as the United Nations Global Counter-Terrorism Strategy ("the Strategy")

3. Decides, without prejudice to the continuation of the discussion at its relevant committees of all their agenda items related to terrorism and counter-terrorism, to undertake the following steps for the effective follow-up of the Strategy:

    (a) To launch the Strategy at a high-level segment of its sixty-first session; To examine in two years progress made in implementation of the Strategy, and to consider updating it to respond to changes, recognizing that many of the measures contained in the Strategy can be achieved immediately, some will require sustained work through the coming few years, and some should be treated as long term objectives;

    (b) To invite the Secretary-General to contribute to the future deliberations of the General Assembly on the review of the implementation and updating of the Strategy;

(c) To encourage Member States, the United Nations and other appropriate international, regional and sub-regional organizations to support the implementation of the Strategy, including through mobilizing resources and expertise;

(d) To further encourage non-governmental organizations and civil society to engage, as appropriate, on how to enhance efforts to implement the Strategy.

Decides to inscribe in the provisional agenda of its sixty-second session an item entitled "The United Nations Global Counter-Terrorism Strategy".

Plan of Action

We, the States Members of the United Nations, resolve:

To consistently, unequivocally and strongly condemn terrorism in all its forms and manifestations, committed by whomever, wherever and for whatever purposes, as it constitutes one of the most serious threats to international peace and security.

1. To take urgent action to prevent and combat terrorism in all its forms and manifestations and, in particular:

   a. To consider becoming parties without delay to the existing international conventions and protocols against terrorism, and implementing them, and to make every effort to reach an agreement on and conclude a comprehensive convention on international terrorism;

   b. To implement all General Assembly resolutions on measures to eliminate international terrorism, and relevant General Assembly resolutions on the protection of human rights and fundamental freedoms while countering terrorism;

   c. To implement all Security Council resolutions related to international terrorism and to cooperate fully with the counter-terrorism subsidiary bodies of the Security Council in the fulfillment of their tasks, recognizing that many States continue to require assistance in implementing these resolutions.

2.   To recognize that international cooperation and any measures that we undertake to prevent and combat terrorism must comply with our obligations under international law, including the Charter of the United Nations and relevant international conventions and protocols, in particular human rights law, refugee law and international humanitarian law.

I. Measures to address the conditions conducive to the spread of terrorism

We resolve to undertake the following measures aimed at addressing the conditions conducive to the spread of terrorism, including but not limited to prolonged unresolved conflicts, dehumanization of victims of terrorism in all its forms and manifestations, lack of rule of law and violations of human rights, ethnic, national and religious discrimination, political exclusion, socio-economic marginalization, and lack of good governance, while recognizing that none of these conditions can excuse or justify acts of terrorism:

1.   To continue to strengthen and make best possible use of the capacities of the United Nations in areas such as conflict prevention, negotiation, mediation, conciliation, judicial settlement, rule of law, peacekeeping and peace building, in order to contribute to the successful prevention and peaceful resolution of prolonged unresolved conflicts. We recognize that the peaceful resolution of such conflicts would contribute to strengthening the global fight against terrorism.

2.   To continue to arrange under the auspices of the United Nations initiatives and programs to promote dialogue, tolerance and understanding among civilizations, cultures, peoples and religions, and to promote mutual respect for and prevent the defamation of religions, religious values, beliefs and cultures. In this regard, we welcome the launching by the Secretary-General of the initiative on the Alliance of Civilizations. We also welcome similar initiatives that have been taken in other parts of the world.

3. To promote a culture of peace, justice and human development, ethnic, national and religious tolerance, and respect for all religions, religious values, beliefs or cultures by establishing and encouraging, as appropriate, education and public awareness programmes involving all sectors of society. In this regard, we encourage the United Nations Educational, Scientific and Cultural Organization to play a key role, including through inter-faith and intra-faith dialogue and dialogue among civilizations.

4. To continue to work to adopt such measures as may be necessary and appropriate and in accordance with our obligations under international law to prohibit by law incitement to commit a terrorist act or acts and prevent such conduct.

5. To reiterate our determination to ensure the timely and full realization of the development goals and objectives agreed at the major United Nations conferences and summits, including the Millennium Development Goals. We reaffirm our commitment to eradicate poverty and promote sustained economic growth, sustainable development and global prosperity for all.

6. To pursue and reinforce development and social inclusion agendas at every level as goals in themselves, recognizing that success in this area, especially on youth unemployment, could reduce marginalization and the subsequent sense of victimization that propels extremism and the recruitment of terrorists.

7. To encourage the United Nations system as a whole to scale up the cooperation and assistance it is already conducting in the fields of rule of law, human rights and good governance, to support sustained economic and social development.

8. To consider putting in place, on a voluntary basis, national systems of assistance that would promote the needs of victims of terrorism and their families and facilitate the normalization of their lives. In this regard, we encourage States to request the relevant United Nations entities to help them to develop such national systems. We will also

strive to promote international solidarity in support of victims and foster the involvement of civil society in a global campaign against terrorism and for its condemnation. This could include exploring at the General Assembly the possibility of developing practical mechanisms assistance to victims.

II. Measures to prevent and combat terrorism

We resolve to undertake the following measures to prevent and combat terrorism, in particular by denying terrorists access to the means to carry out their attacks, to their targets and to the desired impact of their attacks:

1. To refrain from organizing, instigating, facilitating, participating in financing, encouraging or tolerating terrorist activities and to take appropriate practical measures to ensure that our respective territories are not used for terrorist installations or training camps, or for the preparation or organization of terrorist acts intended to be committed against other States or their citizens.

2. To cooperate fully in the fight against terrorism, in accordance with our obligations under international law, in order to find, deny safe haven and bring to justice, on the basis of the principle of extradite or prosecute, any person who supports, facilitates, participates or attempts to participate in the financing, planning, preparation or perpetration of terrorist acts or provides safe havens.

3. To ensure the apprehension and prosecution or extradition of perpetrators of terrorist acts, in accordance with the relevant provisions of national and international law, in particular human rights law, refugee law and international humanitarian law. We will endeavour to conclude and implement to that effect mutual judicial assistance and extradition agreements, and to strengthen cooperation between law enforcement agencies.

4. To intensify cooperation, as appropriate, in exchanging timely and accurate information concerning the prevention and combating of terrorism.

5. To strengthen coordination and cooperation among States in combating crimes that might be connected with terrorism, including drug trafficking in all its aspects, illicit arms trade, in particular of small arms and light weapons, including man-portable air defence systems , money laundering and smuggling of nuclear, chemical, biological, radiological and other potentially deadly materials.

6. To consider becoming parties without delay to the United Nations Convention against Transnational Organized Crime and to the three protocols supplementing it, and implementing them.

7. To take appropriate measures, before granting asylum, for the purpose of ensuring that the asylum seeker has not engaged in terrorist activities and, after granting asylum, for the purpose of ensuring that the refugee status is not used in a manner contrary to the provisions set out in paragraph 1 of this section.

8. To encourage relevant regional and sub-regional organizations to create or strengthen counter-terrorism mechanisms or centres. Should they require cooperation and assistance to this end, we encourage the United Nations Counter-Terrorism Committee and its Executive Directorate and, where consistent with their existing mandates, the United Nations Office of Drugs and Crime and the International Criminal Police Organization, to facilitate its provision.

9. To acknowledge that the question of creating an international centre to fight terrorism could be considered, as part of the international efforts to enhance the fight against terrorism.

10. To encourage States to implement the comprehensive international standards embodied in the Financial Action Task Force's Forty Recommendations on Money Laundering and Nine Special Recommendations on Terrorist Financing, recognizing that States may require assistance in implementing them.

11. To invite the United Nations system to develop, together with Member States, a single comprehensive database on biological incidents,

ensuring that it is complementary to the International Criminal Police Organization's contemplated Bio-crimes Database. We also encourage the Secretary-General to update the roster of experts and laboratories, as well as the technical guidelines and procedures, available to him for the timely and efficient investigation of alleged use. In addition, we note the importance of the proposal of the Secretary-General to bring together, within the framework of the United Nations, the major bio-technology stakeholders, including industry, scientific community, civil society and governments, into a common program aimed at ensuring that bio-technology's advances are not used for terrorist or other criminal purposes but for the public good, with due respect to the basic international norms on intellectual property rights.

12. To work with the United Nations, with due regard to confidentiality, respecting human rights and in compliance with other obligations under international law, to explore ways and means to:

    a. coordinate efforts at the international and regional level to counter terrorism in all its forms and manifestations on the Internet, and;

    b. use the Internet as a tool for countering the spread of terrorism, while recognizing that States may require assistance in this regard.

13. To step-up national efforts and bilateral, sub-regional, regional and international co-operation, as appropriate, to improve border and customs controls, in order to prevent and detect the movement of terrorists and to prevent and detect the illicit traffic in, inter alia, small arms and light weapons, conventional ammunition and explosives, nuclear, chemical, biological or radiological weapons and materials, while recognizing that States may require assistance to that effect.

14. To encourage the United Nations Counter Terrorism Committee and its Executive Directorate to continue to work with States, at their request, to facilitate the adoption of legislation and administrative measures to implement the terrorist travel-related obligations, and to identify best practices in this area, drawing whenever possible on those developed by technical international organizations such as the

International Civil Aviation Organization, the World Customs Organization and the International Criminal Police Organization.

15. To encourage the Committee established pursuant to Security Council resolution 1267 (1999) to continue to work to strengthen the effectiveness of the travel ban under the United Nations sanctions regime against Al-Qaida and the Taliban and associated individuals and entities, as well as to ensure, as a matter of priority, that fair and transparent procedures exist for placing individuals and entities on its lists, for removing them and for granting humanitarian exceptions. In this regard, we encourage States to share information, including by widely distributing the International Criminal Police Organization-United Nations Special Notices concerning people subject to this sanctions regime.

16. To step up efforts and co-operation at every level, as appropriate, to improve the security on manufacturing and issuing identity and travel documents and to prevent and detect their alteration or fraudulent use, while recognizing that States may require assistance in doing so. In this regard, we invite the International Criminal Police Organization to enhance its database on stolen and lost travel documents, and we will endeavour to make full use of this tool as appropriate, in particular by sharing relevant information.

17. To invite the United Nations to improve co-ordination in planning a response to a terrorist attack using nuclear, chemical, biological or radiological weapons or materials, in particular by reviewing and improving the effectiveness of the existing inter-agency co-ordination mechanisms for assistance, delivery, relief operations and victim support, so that all States can receive adequate assistance. In this regard, we invite the General Assembly and the Security Council to develop guidelines for the necessary co-operation and assistance in the event of a terrorist attack using weapons of mass destruction.

18. To step up all efforts to improve the security and protection of particularly vulnerable targets such as infrastructure and public places,

as well as the response to terrorist attacks and other disasters, in particular in the area of civil protection, while recognizing that States may require assistance to that effect.

III. Measures to Build States' Capacity to Prevent and Combat Terrorism and to Strengthen the Role of the United Nations system in this regard

We recognize that capacity-building in all States is a core element of the global counter-terrorism effort, and resolve to undertake the following measures to develop State capacity to prevent and combat terrorism and enhance coordination and coherence within the United Nations system in promoting international cooperation in countering terrorism:

1. To encourage Member States to consider making voluntary contributions to United Nations counter-terrorism cooperation and technical assistance projects, and to explore additional sources of funding in this regard. We also encourage the United Nations to consider reaching out to the private sector for contributions to capacity-building program, in particular in the areas of port, maritime and civil aviation security.

2. To take advantage of the framework provided by relevant international, regional and sub-regional organizations to share best practices in counter-terrorism capacity-building, and to facilitate their contributions to the international community's efforts in this area.

3. To consider establishing appropriate mechanisms to rationalize States' reporting requirements in the field of counter-terrorism and eliminate duplication of reporting requests, taking into account and respecting the different mandates of the General Assembly, the Security Council and its subsidiary bodies that deal with counter terrorism.

4. To encourage measures, including regular informal meetings, to enhance, as appropriate, more frequent exchanges of information on cooperation and technical assistance among Member States, United Nations bodies dealing with counter terrorism, relevant specialized agencies, relevant international, regional and sub-regional organizations,

and the donor community, to develop States' capacities to implement relevant United Nations resolutions.

5. To welcome the intention of the Secretary-General to institutionalize, within existing resources, the United Nations Counter-Terrorism Implementation Task Force within the Secretariat, in order to ensure overall co-ordination and coherence in the United Nations system's counter-terrorism efforts.

6. To encourage the United Nations Counter-Terrorism Committee and its Executive Directorate to continue to improve the coherence and efficiency of technical assistance delivery in the field of counter-terrorism, in particular by strengthening its dialogue with States and relevant international, regional and sub-regional organizations and working closely, including by sharing information, with all bilateral and multilateral technical assistance providers.

7. To encourage the United Nations Office on Drugs and Crime, including its Terrorism Prevention Branch, to enhance, in close consultation with the United Nations Counter-Terrorism Committee and its Executive Directorate, its provision of technical assistance to States, upon request, to facilitate the implementation of the international conventions and protocols related to the prevention and suppression of terrorism and relevant United Nations resolutions.

8. To encourage the International Monetary Fund, the World Bank, the United Nations Office on Drugs and Crime and the International Criminal Police Organization to enhance cooperation with States to help them to comply fully with international norms and obligations to combat money-laundering and financing of terrorism.

9. To encourage the International Atomic Energy Agency and the Organization for the Prohibition of Chemical Weapons to continue their efforts, within their respective mandates, in helping States to build capacity to prevent terrorists from accessing nuclear, chemical or radiological materials, to ensure security at related facilities, and to respond effectively in the event of an attack using such materials.

10. To encourage the World Health Organization to step up its technical assistance to help States improve their public health systems to prevent and prepare for biological attacks by terrorists.

11. To continue to work within the United Nations system to support the reform and modernization of border management systems, facilities and institutions, at the national, regional and international level.

12. To encourage the International Maritime Organization, the World Customs Organization and the International Civil Aviation Organization to strengthen their co-operation, work with States to identify any national shortfalls in areas of transport security and provide assistance upon request to address them.

13. To encourage the United Nations to work with Member States and relevant international, regional and sub-regional organizations to identify and share best practices to prevent terrorist attacks on particularly vulnerable targets. We invite the International Criminal Police Organization to work with the Secretary-General so that he can submit proposals to this effect. We also recognize the importance of developing public-private partnerships in this area.

IV. Measures to ensure respect for human rights for all and the rule of law as the fundamental basis of the fight against terrorism

We resolve to undertake the following measures, reaffirming that the promotion and protection of human rights for all and the rule of law is essential to all components of the Strategy, recognizing that effective counter-terrorism measures and the protection of human rights are not conflicting goals, but complementary and mutually reinforcing , and stressing the need to promote and protect the rights of victims of terrorism:

1. To reaffirm that General Assembly resolution 60/158 of 16 December 2005 provides the fundamental framework for the "Protection of human rights and fundamental freedoms while countering terrorism".

2. To reaffirm that States must ensure that any measures taken to combat terrorism comply with their obligations under international law, in

particular human rights law, refugee law and international humanitarian law.

3. To consider becoming parties without delay to the core international instruments on human rights law, refugee law and international humanitarian law, and implementing them, as well as to consider accepting the competence of international and relevant regional human rights monitoring bodies.

4. To make every effort to develop and maintain an effective and rule of law-based national criminal justice system that can ensure, in accordance with our obligations under international law, that any person who participates in the financing, planning, preparation or perpetration of terrorist acts or in support of terrorist acts is brought to justice, on the basis of the principle to extradite or prosecute, with due respect for human rights and fundamental freedoms, and that such terrorist acts are established as serious criminal offences in domestic laws and regulations. We recognize that States may require assistance in developing and maintaining such effective and rule of law-based criminal justice system, and we encourage them to resort to the technical assistance delivered, inter alia, by the United Nations Office on Drugs and Crime.

5. To reaffirm the United Nations system's important role in strengthening the international legal architecture by promoting the rule of law, respect for human rights, and effective criminal justice systems, which constitute the fundamental basis of our common fight against terrorism.

6. To support the Human Rights Council, and to contribute, as it takes shape, to its work on the question of the promotion and protection of human rights for all in the fight against terrorism.

7. To support the strengthening of the operational capacity of the Office of the United Nations High Commissioner for Human Rights, with a particular emphasis on increasing field operations and presences. The Office should continue to play a lead role in examining the question of

protecting human rights while countering terrorism, by making general recommendations on States' human rights obligations and providing them with assistance and advice, in particular in the area of raising awareness of international human rights law among national law-enforcement agencies, at States' request.

8. To support the role of the Special Rapporteur on the promotion and protection of human rights and fundamental freedoms while countering terrorism. The Special Rapporteur should continue to support States' efforts and offer concrete advice by corresponding with Governments, making country visits, liaising with the United Nations and regional organizations, and reporting on these issues.

Issues with Pakistan

Sir Creek Dispute

Originally the dispute started in 1907-08 on the border of the two principalities, Kutch and Sind. The dispute was referred to the Government of Bombay and subsequently resolved by the Government of India in 1914. It resulted in a document (Map No B 44) and implemented in the form of Map No B 74 in 1925, which became a landmark document. The award was accepted, both by the Rao of Kutch and Commissioner of Sind. In compliance with this award boundary pillars were erected along the land boundary from the head of Sir Creek towards east to a point referred to as Western Terminus and from Western Terminus at right angle towards north to Eastern Terminus generally covering the entire Rann. Thereafter the dispute remained dormant but resurfaced in 1960s as the 1914 award was questioned by Pakistan in its entirety. The matter was referred to arbitration and Indo-Pakistan Western Boundary Tribunal's Award on 19 February 1968, upheld 90 percent of India's claim to the entire Rann, conceding small sectors to Pakistan. The Award was ratified by both the countries and resulted in placement of boundary pillars. However what the Tribunal did not do was to demarcate a small portion of the land boundary at the head of Sir Creek and the Creek itself.

Pakistan's stand has been that the boundary should run along the eastern bank of the Sir Creek, thereby claiming the entire Creek. Pakistan quotes the map accompanying the 1914 Resolution in which the boundary has been shown along the eastern bank of the Creek. Indian stand is that the boundary should run through the middle of the Creek as per the internationally recognised Thalweg principle. India also accepts the main text of the 1914 Resolution which indicates that the boundary runs along the middle of the Creek. Between the main paper and the appendix (map), internationally the main text of a document is considered more authentic.

Linked with the issue is the establishment of the maritime boundary between India and Pakistan. Once the end point of the land boundary at the mouth of Sir Creek is decided, the maritime boundary can be drawn as per the Law of the Sea.

Siachen Dispute

Siachen Glacier is situated in North Ladakh, north of NJ 9842, the northern most delimited point of the Line of Control between India and Pakistan Occupied Kashmir (POK). The Glacier originates from a pass called Indira Col in the West and runs in southeasterly direction until its snout turns into Nubra River Valley. To its west is the Saltoro range and to its east is Karakoram Range. The major passes along the Saltoro range are Sia La, Bilafond La, Gyong La and Yarma La. A number of towns are located close to the Saltoro range in the POK side and the area is comparatively better developed than on the Indian side. The Glacier is approximately 76 kilometers long with a width varying 2-8 kilometers, is one of the largest glaciers of the world. The average height of the area ranges from 20,000 to 25,000 feet, the terrain is glaciated and requires highly specialised clothing, accommodation, provisions, ammunition and equipment. Proximity wise the Glacier is strategically located between India, POK and China. There are, however, diverse views with regard to its strategic importance.

Neither the Karachi Agreement of 1949 nor the Shimla agreement of 1972 refers to the Siachen Glacier while delimiting the CFL/ Line of Control between the two countries. The northern most point delimited was NJ 9842. The area north of this point was never occupied by the forces of either side till around 1983/84. When it was found that Pakistan was sending mountaineering expeditions through the area and was also preparing to occupy it, Indian troops pre-empted the Pakistani move and occupied the area in 1984. Since then most bloody and expensive battle has ensued in the highest battlefield of the world. The operations in the area are extremely slow, prohibitively expensive and very high in casualties both due to combat and weather. Operations are possible only during the months of summers. Despite a number of meetings between Indian and Pakistani leaders/officials, the situation defies the solution.

Tulbul Navigation Project/Wular Barrage Dispute (Kashmir Valley)

The Indus Water Treaty of 1960 permits four distinct types of uses by India of the waters of the Western Rivers: domestic, irrigation, restricted use for generation of hydro electric power through a run-of-river unit and the non-consumptive use.

At issue is a barrage that is to be constructed at the base of the Wular Lake in Kashmir so as to regulate the flow of the water into river Jhelum to make it navigable between Wular Lake and Baramula during the lean season between late October and mid February. During this lean season the flow of water is less than 2000 cusecs and depth two feet. To make the river navigable a discharge of 4000 cusecs and depth of four feet is the minimum requirement. The proposed Tulbul Navigation Project or Wular Barrage as Pakistan likes to refer to it involves temporary impounding of water of river Jhelum in Wular Lake in order to regulate its flow during the lean season. While India refers to it as non-consumptive use, Pakistan terms it as 'consumption' of water of river Jhelum, whose water has been assigned to Pakistan as per Indus Water Treaty, except for the purposes mentioned above. The issue can be resolved by trade off by surrendering to Pakistan equal quantity of water from the Eastern Rivers. If the two countries cannot resolve this issue bilaterally, the same could be referred to an international tribunal as per the Indus Water Treaty.

Article 371 Specific to Northeastern States

Article 371A Special provision with respect to the State of Nagaland

(1) Notwithstanding anything in this Constitution, -

(a) no Act of Parliament in respect of -

    (i)   religious or social practices of the Nagas,

    (ii) Naga customary law and procedure,

    (iii) administration of civil and criminal justice involving decisions according to Nagacustomary law,

    (iv) ownership and transfer of land and its resources, shall apply to the State of Nagaland unless the Legislative Assembly of Nagaland by a resolution so decides;

(b) the Governor of Nagaland shall have special responsibility with respect to law and order in the State of Nagaland for so long as in his opinion internal disturbances occurring in the Naga Hills-Tuensang Area immediately before the formation of that State continue therein or in any part thereof and in the discharge of his functions in relation thereto the Governor shall, after consulting the Council of Ministers, exercise his individual judgment as to the action to be taken:

Provided that if any question arises whether any matter is or is not a matter as respects which the Governor is under this sub-clause required to act in the exercise of his individual judgment, the decision of the Governor in his discretion shall be final, and the validity of anything done by the Governor shall not be called in question on the ground that he ought or ought not to have acted in the exercise of his individual judgment:

Provided further that if the President on receipt of a report from the Governor or otherwise is satisfied that it is no longer necessary for the Governor to have special responsibility with respect to law and order in the State of Nagaland, he may by order direct that the Governor shall cease to have such responsibility with effect from such date as may be specified in the order;

(c) in making his recommendation with respect to any demand for a grant, the Governor of Nagaland shall ensure that any money provided by the Government of India out of the Consolidated Fund of India for any specific service or purpose is included in the demand for a "grant relating to that service or purpose and not in any other demand;

(d) as from such date as the Governor of Nagaland may by public notification in this behalf specify, there shall be established a regional council for the Tuensang district consisting of thirty-five members and the Governor shall in his discretion make rules providing for -

   (i) the composition of the regional council and the manner in which the members of the regional council shall be chosen:

        Provided that the Deputy Commissioner of the Tuensang district shall be the Chairman ex-officion of the regional council and the Vice-Chairman of the regional council shall be elected by the members there of from amongst themselves;

   (ii) the qualifications for being chosen as, and for being, members of the regional council;

   (iii) the term of office of, and the salaries and allowances, if any, to be paid to members of, the regional council;

(iv) the procedure and conduct of business of the regional council;

(v) the appointment of officers and staff of the regional council and their conditions of services; and

(vi) any other matter in respect of which it is necessary to make rules for the   constitution and proper functioning of the regional council.

(2) Notwithstanding anything in this Constitution, for a period of ten years from the date of the formation of the State of Nagaland or for such further period as the Governor may, on the recommendation of the regional council, by public notification specify in this behalf, -

(a) the administration of the Tuensang district shall be carried on by the Governor;

(b) where any money is provided by the Government of India to the Government of Nagaland to meet the requirements of the State of Nagaland as a whole, the Governor shall in his discretion arrange for an equitable allocation of that money between the Tuensang district and the rest of the State;

(c) no Act of the Legislature of Nagaland shall apply to Tuensang district unless the Governor, on the recommendation of the regional council, by public notification so directs and the Governor in giving such direction with respect to any such Act may direct that the Act shall in its application to the Tuensang district or any part thereof have effect subject to such exceptions or modifications as the Governor may specify on the recommendation of the regional council:

Provided that any direction given under this sub-clause may be given so as to have retrospective effect;

(d) the Governor may make regulations for the peace, progress and good government of the Tuensang district and any regulations so made may repeal or amend with retrospective effect, if necessary, any Act of Parliament or any other law which is for the time being applicable to that district;

(e)

(i) one of the members representing the Tuensang district in the Legislative Assembly of Nagaland shall be appointed Minister for Tuensang affairs by the Governor on the advice of the Chief Minister and the Chief Minister in tendering his advice shall act on the recommendation of the majority of the members as aforesaid; { ICL-Note: Paragraph 2 of the Constitution (Removal of Difficulties) Order, No. X provides (w.e.f. 1-12-1963) that article 371A of the Constitution of India shall have effect as if the following proviso were added to paragraph (i) of sub-clause (e) of clause (2) thereof, namely: "Provided that the Governor may, on the advice of the Chief Minister, appoint any person as Minister for Tuensang affairs to act as such until such time as persons are chosen in accordance with law to fill the seats allocated to the Tuensang district in the Legislative Assembly of Nagaland."}

(ii) the Minister for Tuensang affairs shall deal with, and have direct access to the Governor on, all matters relating to the Tuensang district but he shall keep the Chief Minister informed about the same;

(f) notwithstanding anything in the foregoing provisions of this clause, the final Decision on all matters relating to the Tuensang district shall be made by the Governor in his discretion;

(g) in articles 54 and 55 and clause (4) of article 80, references to the elected members of the Legislative Assembly of a State or to each such member shall include references to the members or members of the Legislative Assembly of Nagaland elected by the regional council established under this article;

(h) in article 170 -

    (i) clause (1) shall, in relation to the Legislative Assembly of Nagaland, have effect as if for the word "sixty", the words "forty-six" had been substituted;

    (ii) in the said clause, the reference to direct election from territorial constituencies in the state shall include election by the members of the regional council established under this article:

    (iii) in clauses (2) and (3), references to territorial constituencies shall mean references to territorial constituencies in the Kohima and Mokokchung districts.

(3) If any difficulty arises in giving effect to any of the foregoing provisions of this article, the President may by order do anything (including any adaptation or modification of any other article) which appears to him to be necessary for the purpose of removing that difficulty:

Provided that no such order shall be made after the expiration of three years from the date of the formation of the State of Nagaland.

Explanation: In this article, the Kohima, Mokokchung and Tuensang districts shall have the same meanings as in the State of Nagaland Act, 1962.

Article 371 B Special provision with respect to the State of Assam

Notwithstanding anything in this Constitution, the President may, by order made with respect to the State of Assam, provide for the constitution and functions of a committee of the Legislative Assembly of the State consisting of members of that Assembly elected from the tribal areas specified in Part I of the table appended to paragraph 20 of the Sixth Schedule and such number of other members of that Assembly as may be specified in the order and for the modifications to be made in the rules of procedure of that Assembly for the constitution and proper functioning of such committee.

Article 371 C Special provision with respect to the State of Manipur

(1) Notwithstanding anything in this Constitution, the President may, by order made with respect to the State of Manipur, provide for the constitution and functions of a committee of the Legislative Assembly of the State consisting of members of that Assembly elected from the Hill Areas of that State, for the modifications to be made in the rules of business of the Government and in the rules of procedure of the Legislative Assembly of the State and for any special responsibility of the Governor in order to secure the proper functioning of such committee.

(2) The Governor shall annually, or whenever so required by the President, make a report to the President regarding the administration of the Hill Areas in the State of Manipur and the executive power of the Union shall extend to the giving of directions to the State as to the administration of the said areas.

Explanation: In this article, the expression "Hill Areas" means such areas as the President may, by order, declare to be Hill Areas.

Article 371G Special provision with respect to the State of Mizoram

Notwithstanding anything in this Constitution, -

(a) no Act of Parliament in respect of -

(i) religious or social practices of the Mizos.

(ii) Mizo customary law and procedure,

(iii) administration of civil and criminal justice involving decisions according to Mizo customary law,

(iv) ownership and transfer of land, shall apply to the State of Mizoram unless the Legislative Assembly of the State of Mizoram by a resolution so decides:

Provided that nothing in this clause shall apply to any Central Act in force in the Union territory of Mizoram immediately before the commencement of the Constitution (Fifty third Amendment) Act, 1986;

(b) the Legislative Assembly of the State of Mizoram shall consist of not less than forty members.

Article 371H Special provision with respect to the State of Arunachal Pradesh

Notwithstanding anything in this Constitution, -

(a) the Governor of Arunachal Pradesh shall have special responsibility with respect to law and order in the state of Arunachal pradesh and in the discharge of his functions in relation thereto, the Governor shall, after consulting the Council of Ministers, exercise his individual judgment as to the action to be taken:

Provided that if any question arises whether any matter is or is not a matter as respects which the Governor is under this clause required to act in the exercise of his individual judgment, the decision of the Governor in his discretion shall be final, and the validity of anything done by the Governor shall not be called in question on the ground that he ought or ought not to have acted in the exercise of his individual judgment:

Provided further that if the President on receipt of a report from the Governor or otherwise is satisfied that it is no longer necessary for the Governor to have special responsibility with respect to law and order in the State of Arunachal Pradesh, he may by order direct that the Governor shall cease to have such responsibility with effect from such date as may be specified in the order;

(b) the Legislative Assembly of the State of Arunachal Pradesh shall consist of not less than thirty members.

Also see the V and VI Schedules to the Indian Constitution

Bibliography

Ann E. Robertson, Terrorism and Global Security

Dr. Marc Sageman, Understanding Terror Networks

Ronald J. Deibert and Janice Gross Stein, Hacking Networks of Terror

Rachel Ehrenfeld, Funding Terrorism: Sources and Methods

Sam Vaknin, Ph.D, Money Laundering in a Changed World, United Press International

South America, International Narcotics Control Strategy Report,

Bureau for International Narcotics and Law Enforcement Affairs

Päivi Lujala, Coca Bush, Opium Poppy, and Cannabis,

Dept. of Economics, Norwegian University of Science and Technology

Central Intelligence Agency, The World Fact Book

Nafeez Mosaddeq Ahmed, American State Terrorism - A Critical Review of the Objectives of US Foreign Policy in the Post World War II Period

Bertil Lintner, Bangladesh, A Cocoon of Terror

Col SK Sharma (Retd), Senior Fellow, CENJOWS, War Against Global Terror

Bruce Bongar, Lisa M. Brown, Larry E. Buetler, James N. Breckenridge, Philip G. Zimbardo; Psychology of Terrorism; OUP

Eric Rosand, Alistair Millar, and Jason Ipe, Center on Global Counterterrorism Cooperation, September 2008, Civil Society and the UN Global Counter-Terrorism Strategy: Opportunities and Challenges

Satish Nambiar, Developing a Cooperative Security Framework for the South Asian Region, South Asia and War on Terrorism, India Research Press

Namrata Goswami, An Assessment of Insurgencies in Assam, Manipur and Nagaland in 2009

Money Laundering, Wikipedia

Lt Gen Chandra Shekhar, PVSM, AVSM (Retd), Tackling Terror and Our Response Mechanism

Vikram Sood, New Face of Terrorism: Analysis of Asymmetrical Threat from Land Air and Sea

Brig VP Malhotra (Retd), Security and Defence Related Treaties of India

Brig VP Malhotra (Retd), Pakistan Threat Unique

Suniti Kumar Ghosh, Naxalbari Before and After

Rahul K Bhonsle, South Asia Political, Security and Terrorism Trends; Vij Books

Bilveer Singh, Talibanisation of South Asia; Vij Books

Siddharth Varadarajan, Nuclear Summit Agenda is to ensure terrorists don't get the bomb; The Hindu, April 12, 2010

Major General Mahmud Ali Durrani (retd), Pakistan Army; Eyeball to Eyeball, Let's Jointly Define Terror; TOI May 6, 2010

Ajit Doval KC*, Islamic Terrorism in South Asia and India's Strategic Response Approach Paper, Rise of Naxalism and its Implications for National Security,

National Security Seminar

VN Singh, Naxalism A Great Menace

Nishant Kumar, Hijacking, a War by Other Means, Renaissance Publishing House Syed Anwar Ali, Quran the Constitution of Islam, Vol 1, Monthly Program

David Gero, Flight of Terror, Aerial Hijack and Sabotage since 1930, PSL

The Rediff Special/B Raman, India's Counter Terrorism Strategy

Index

..

www.ingramcontent.com/pod-product-compliance
Lightning Source LLC
Chambersburg PA
CBHW070809300326
41914CB00078B/1920/J